E S L
Writers

A Guide for Writing Center Tutors

SECOND EDITION

EDITED BY

Shanti Bruce & Ben Rafoth

Boynton/Cook Publishers
HEINEMANN
Portsmouth, NH

Boynton/Cook Publishers, Inc.
361 Hanover Street
Portsmouth, NH 03801–3912
www.boyntoncook.com

Offices and agents throughout the world

Library of Congress Cataloging-in-Publication Data
ESL writers : a guide for writing center tutors / edited by Shanti Bruce & Ben Rafoth.
— 2nd ed.
    p. cm.
  Includes bibliographical references and index.
  ISBN-13: 978-0-86709-594-4
  ISBN-10: 0-86709-594-6
    1. English language—Rhetoric—Study and teaching—Handbooks, manuals, etc.
2. English language—Study and teaching—Foreign speakers—Handbooks, manuals,
etc. 3. Report writing—Study and teaching (Higher)—Handbooks, manuals, etc.
4. Tutors and tutoring—Handbooks, manuals, etc. 5. Writing centers—Handbooks,
manuals, etc.   I. Bruce, Shanti.   II. Rafoth, Bennett A.

PE1404.E83 2009
808'.042'071—dc22   2008048088

Editor: Lisa Luedeke
Production: Vicki Kasabian
Production management: Matrix Productions, Inc.
Cover design: Night and Day Design
Typesetter: Val Levy, Drawing Board Studios
Manufacturing: Steve Bernier

Printed in the United States of America on acid-free paper
13 12 11 10 09 VP   2 3 4 5

We would like to acknowledge the tutors and students
who inspired this project and generously
shared their experiences with us.

Contents

Part 1   Becoming Oriented to Second Language Learners

We tend to see members of our own group as individuals and to see those who are not of our group as all alike. Tutors are in a unique position to get to know ESL students as the unique individuals they are. But first, tutors have to see how language, literacy, and culture interact to create identities for each of us.

Theories of second language acquisition are essential to understanding how people learn a new language. They help us make sense of a complicated process and inform the choices we make when tutoring.

Part 2   The ESL Tutoring Session

Making a plan for what you hope to accomplish in a tutoring session can go a long way. The key is to focus on what is most important and remain flexible.

Knowing how to read the paper an ESL writer brings to the writing center may be the most important part of the session. What are some ways to read an ESL writer's paper, and how does a tutor know which one is right for the session?

When there is a disparity between what native speakers know about their
language and what nonnative speakers seek to learn, it is easy for writing
tutors to exert too much control over a paper. How can tutors find the right
balance between being language informants and taking over nonnative
speakers' projects by "putting words in their mouths"?

When a tutor struggles to understand an ESL writer's text, it is tempting to
leap to conclusions about the meaning an ESL writer intends to convey. This
chapter helps tutors avoid this pitfall.

Understanding the relationship of all the parts of a paper is just as vital in
ESL writing as it is in first language writing. This chapter helps tutors to see
how they can move beyond word- and sentence-level concerns to talking
about the ideas and organization of the entire paper.

Generation 1.5 students tend to have oral fluency and cultural awareness.
These qualities can help them become good writers, so long as their tutors
affirm the qualities as strengths and can apply them to writing assignments.

Just because articles are small words doesn't mean they are easy to learn to
use. In fact, the English article system is highly nuanced, and native English
speakers often have to stop and think before they use *a an* article.

ESL writers often want to know the rule behind every correction they need
to make in their papers. Tutors, meanwhile, often don't know the rule or
can't verbalize it. This chapter helps tutors discover how to deal with aspects
of word- and sentence-level errors that frustrate ESL writers and seem
unexplainable to native speakers.

The tendency to focus on editing instead of higher-order concerns is especially strong in online environments where conversation can be nonexistent. The writing center at one university has found a way to use technology to overcome this challenge.

When tutoring shifts from in-house to online, writers and tutors have to adjust their expectations. In this chapter, we learn from one director's experience with tutoring ESL writers in an online environment.

Avoiding plagiarism is a lesson that most tutors have rehearsed many times. However, some ESL writers come from cultures that do not share fundamental American beliefs about source use, authorship, and citation. This chapter helps tutors understand how American academic rules for documenting sources compare to other cultures' and offers ideas for how to talk with ESL writers about questions and problems of plagiarism.

Promoting writing activities with ESL writers is a good way to help them broaden their experiences beyond the traditional one-on-one tutoring session—and have fun at the same time. This chapter shows how tutors can focus more attention on the act of writing during tutoring sessions and turn their workplaces into creative writing centers for ESL writers.

Part 3   A Broader View

Have you ever wondered what ESL students' experiences with tutors in their own country has been like? What can U.S. tutors learn from their counterparts in other countries? Explore these and other questions with someone who has worked in writing centers in both the United States and abroad.

16 Being a Linguistic Foreigner: Learning from International Tutoring
*Linda S. Bergmann, Gerd Bräuer, Robert Cedillo, Chloe de los
Reyes, Magnus Gustafsson, Carol Peterson Haviland, and Brady
Spangenberg 195*

What if you could be an exchange tutor in an overseas writing center? Meet
tutors who had this opportunity and share their experiences.

17 English for Those Who (Think They) Already Know It
Ben Rafoth   208

Native English-speaking tutors who make an effort to understand English
from a linguistic perspective and bring this understanding to the writing
conference will be better tutors than those who don't.

18 Listening to and Learning from ESL Writers
Shanti Bruce   217

Second language scholars can teach us a lot about assisting ESL students
in the writing center, but if we stop there, we will have gotten only half the
story. There is much to be learned from talking directly with ESL writers
about their personal experiences in writing centers.

Introduction

Since its publication in 2004, *ESL Writers* has had a successful run. It won the International Writing Centers Association Outstanding Scholarship Award for Best Book of 2004, and it received positive reviews in academic journals. More important, tutors liked it. We heard from tutors and directors that the book spent more time on their desks than on their bookshelves. They said it was interesting, meaningful, practical minded, and clearly written.

Thanks to the feedback we received from readers, the second edition of *ESL Writers* is even better. It contains many new and expanded chapters, a new design, and a clearer focus. The new edition does a better job of reflecting the diversity among writers and tutors; today in the United States, writers and tutors may be English as a second language (ESL), bilingual, Generation 1.5, permanent residents, or immigrants. This is important to remember because the diversity of students in colleges and universities across the United States is reflected in today's writing centers. They are visited by students from all walks of life and all corners of the world.

The second edition of *ESL Writers*

- expands the definition of students and tutors with respect to their linguistic backgrounds
- focuses greater attention on the diversity of cultural and literacy identities among students and tutors
- addresses the most common questions we hear from tutors when it comes to helping ESL writers with English grammar.

Chapter 1 is one of five that are new to the second edition. It describes some of the more common linguistic backgrounds of ESL college students and the implications for tutoring in the writing center. Ilona Leki, author of the first well-known book on ESL writing in 1992, *Understanding ESL Writers*, is the author of this chapter.

Another new chapter in the second edition (Chapter 8) focuses on the experiences of a Generation 1.5 student. So-called because they are usually familiar with U.S. culture and schools, these students—and their number is quite large—nonetheless have learning needs different from other English language learners. Jennifer J. Ritter and Trygve Sandvik are the coauthors of this chapter.

Often the smallest words in English—like the articles *a*, *an*, and *the*—seem to cause the most difficulty for ESL writers. In the new Chapter 9, Sharon K. Deckert, an applied linguist, helps put articles in perspective and offers good advice for helping tutors understand the grammar of English articles so that they can better explain these troublesome words to students.

Also new to the second edition is Chapter 11 on online tutoring, written by Lee-Ann Kastman Breuch and Linda Clemens. They describe a successful hybrid model of online tutoring developed in their writing center at the University of Minnesota. New as well is Chapter 16, written collaboratively by a group of tutors and directors who embarked on a student exchange program focused on writing centers. They encourage tutors to study abroad and offer good advice for those who are ready to explore writing centers that operate in very different contexts from their own.

Reasons to Use This Book

ESL Writers is a companion for tutors who work with nonnative English-speaking writers at the college or university level. We believe it is best used as part of a tutor-training program in the context of a campus writing center. We hope readers will reach for it.

To Gain a Better Understanding of Important Concepts and Best Practices

ESL Writers helps introduce readers to key words in the field of second language learning so that tutors can have more intelligent discussions with one another in staff meetings and between sessions. It introduces concepts without jargon but also doesn't try to dumb them down. Each chapter also contains suggestions that reflect the best and most current practices.

To Get Ideas for Dealing with a Specific Challenge

Each chapter in *ESL Writers* is focused on a theme or challenge that most tutors can relate to. When tutors need a starting point or frame of reference for dealing with a challenge they have encountered in a tutoring session, *ESL Writers* is an excellent place to begin thinking about how to overcome this challenge next time it occurs.

To Stimulate Thinking and Discussion

Directors can refer tutors to *ESL Writers* as preparation or follow-up for a staff meeting. Most chapters are advanced enough that even experienced tutors will find them interesting and thought provoking.

To Discover Sources for Further Reading

Graduate students in Composition Studies and related fields will find excellent documentation and current sources. Undergraduates who want to delve into a topic can easily find additional readings.

Organization of the Book

ESL Writers is organized in three parts. Part 1, "Becoming Oriented to Second Language Learners," provides a backdrop to important cultural and cognitive concepts. These chapters help set the stage for the chapters that follow because taken together they show why learning to write in a second language is both a social and cognitive endeavor.

Part 2, "The ESL Tutoring Session," takes tutors straight away into the work they do every day. These chapters address aspects of tutoring that occur with amazing regularity and continue to challenge even the most experienced tutors. Part 2 is the longest section of the book because these chapters face the front lines of tutoring in the writing center—reading, writing, talking, and thinking together. Part 2 balances theory and practice, including frequent citations to the most respected published research in the field and realistic examples that help tutors connect theory and practice. In this section of the book, tutors will find ideas and suggestions for

- beginning the tutoring session
- reading an ESL writer's paper
- avoiding taking over the writer's paper
- helping writers say what they want to say (and not what some readers might *assume* they want to say)
- seeing the paper as a whole (and not as an endless series of error-filled sentences)
- understanding Generation 1.5 students
- dealing with common grammatical problems
- editing line by line
- tutoring online
- addressing cases of possible plagiarism
- promoting creative writing.

Part 3, "A Broader View," takes readers outside the writing center and then back in again. It is a fitting ending for a book whose ideas carry on. It invites readers to consider the following:

- What kinds of experiences with writing do ESL students have in their own countries before coming to the United States?

- What does it feel like to be a "linguistic foreigner"? What can tutors learn by visiting writing centers abroad?
- Is English really so hard to learn?
- What do ESL writers say about their writing center experiences?

There is an urgent need for trained tutors to work with ESL writers, both in the United States and around the world. This book can be an important part of the training process because it has proven effective in writing centers in the United States and abroad. *ESL Writers* speaks directly to tutors, giving readers plenty to think about, try out, and investigate.

1

Before the Conversation

A Sketch of Some Possible Backgrounds, Experiences, and Attitudes Among ESL Students Visiting a Writing Center[*]

Ilona Leki

I didn't learn anything from the [ESL writing] class. I learned from [a tutor] in the WC. We had like a big conversation. . . . We talk about, he's like more getting into content. You gotta make discussion . . . it's like an interview. He's asking like all these questions. You gotta like explain. Later, like he corrects the paper. So . . . it was good, I mean. . . . You had to fight for your ideas on the paper.[1]
—Comments of a student from Poland on his experiences in a writing center

Writing centers may be the ideal learning environment for students whose first or strongest language is not English: one-on-one, context rich, highly focused on a specific current writing need, and offering the possibility of negotiation of meaning (i.e., conversational back-and-forth that is thought to promote second language acquisition). That bilingual and multilingual writers recognize the benefits of writing center support is clear from the increasing numbers of second language (L2) students who take advantage of it.

But it is no secret that writing center tutors may feel less confident of their own ability to respond to the writing of L2 students than they feel in their dealings with domestic students, whose strongest language is English and with whom they likely share more of their cultural, educational, linguistic, and literacy background. Unsure of what they may in fact share with bi- and multilingual visitors to the writing center, tutors may not know enough about these students to avoid viewing them as all of a piece. One goal of this book

---

[*] I am deeply appreciative to Kirsten Benson and Carol Severino for their generous help with this text.

is to help writing center tutors feel more confident in tutoring L2 students, and the purpose of this chapter is to support that goal by "helping tutors see these people not as an undifferentiated group (people who don't speak English) but as individuals who, like all of us, share sets of identities."[2]

Diverse Backgrounds

Like any collection of individuals, multilingual or English as a second language (ESL) students present a wide range of interests, experiences, and characteristics, making it exceedingly difficult, even dangerous, to discuss them as a group or even groups. In fact, the internal variation of this group is so great that perhaps the only characteristic linking them is the fact that they can function, to a greater or lesser degree, in a language other than English. An L2 student may be eighteen or sixty years old, may have lived a life of wealth and privilege or of relative poverty and limitation, may have traveled widely internationally or be experiencing a first venture from a rural village to a foreign country, may have little experience in writing or may be a published author, may come from a country whose population and/or leaders consider the United States an ally or an enemy. L2 students may vary in emotional response to their first language (L1), emotional response to English or to U.S. culture, sense of self as an insider or outsider in the United States, sense of self as novice or accomplished writer or intellect, reception by the target culture, and so on for many more levels of categories. It is also the case that visible minorities among these writers may provoke stereotypical assumptions about them or simply automatic characterization of them as likely to be and to behave in particular ways in line with their "master status" as, say, an Asian (-looking) woman.

Yet at least some of these multilingual university students do share certain traits, and examining some of their interests, experiences, and characteristics may encourage a more nuanced, more differentiated, more complicated and three-dimensional view of them than as simply ESL students, foreigners, or people who don't speak English.

Perhaps my first comment should be to clarify the phrase "people who don't speak English." The multilingual students who seek help at a college or university writing center are doing college in English, a language that they probably did not grow up with. They are reading college-level textbooks, listening to university-level lectures delivered to an intended or envisioned audience of people who did grow up with English, and for the most part writing the same papers and exams as domestic students. They can hardly be regarded as people who don't speak English. But it is sometimes difficult for monolingual English speakers to fully grasp the enormous amount of language a speaker or writer must command to be able to carry out these advanced literacy activities, and it is easy to overreact to grammatical or lexical errors or to an unfamiliar accent.

On the other hand, it is also important to recognize, in regard to the readers of this book, that writing center tutors themselves come in different varieties with respect to their contact with multilinguals and their own language proficiency beyond their first language. Some with less contact may experience greater difficulty with variations from their language expectations than do those familiar with a variety of accents both oral and textual.

Some Characteristics of Multilinguals

To make discussion of this broad population, with its blurry boundaries, manageable, the group needs to be somehow divided. But by what? Gender, home culture, first language, experience with the second language, experience writing in the first or second language, academic discipline ("hard" sciences versus other disciplines), likely need to write in university settings? Any of these categories would yield different discussions with legitimate and potentially interesting and fruitful different emphases. Because it is impossible to talk about all the individual characteristics of any given multilingual person, I have somewhat arbitrarily attempted to break up the larger group of multilinguals that might visit a university writing center into three smaller categories that are likely to share at least some characteristics:

- undergraduate students who graduated from U.S. high schools
- international or visa undergraduate students who expect to return to their home countries after completing their education
- international graduate students or professionals

I describe these categories of people in broad strokes in order to give readers a sense of the range of experiences and reactions/attitudes that may be encountered among individuals within these groups. These characterizations should not be taken to be representative of any individuals, however, or even of the group as a whole, only to provide a sense of the wide and dynamic range of linguistic, psychological, and emotional configurations of certain writing center patrons.

Multilinguals from U.S. High Schools

Many undergraduate ESL students immigrated to the United States from countries where English is not a dominant language, graduated from a U.S. high school, and now find themselves facing a new set of challenges in college. Although the writing of undergraduate multilinguals who attended or graduated from U.S. high schools may exhibit a variety of the kinds of surface-level problems (e.g., grammatical errors) that often take students to writing centers, these students may have become quite proficient in speaking and listening and may sound much like domestic students in their language register (i.e., how formally or informally they speak), vocabulary, and ability to recognize cultural references. They often come to share many of the values of teenage domestic students, including one in which a respect for an interest in education and the life of the intellect for its own sake may, or even must, remain covert. One reason they come to sound and think in this way is that, as some of these immigrant teenagers report, they experience a great deal of pressure to do everything possible as soon as possible to look and act like their domestic peers. This need to conform may even present itself as rejection or avoidance of people (including other newcomer immigrant students) and customs that might serve to link them to their first or previous culture. Immigrant parents of these teens observe with dismay as their Chinese daughter or son, for example, begins to refuse to eat Chinese food or use chopsticks even at home.[3] Sometimes such students do not appreciate a first response to them by tutors or others that positions them as people who come from somewhere else.

On the other hand, in communities with a large immigrant population from a similar background, multilingual high school students who have felt rejection from members of the host culture or who experience pressure to become completely indistinguishable from domestic students and yet know that this may in fact be impossible for them may react by rejecting the host culture and pressing compatriot peers to stay away from domestic people, their culture, their language, and their academic concerns. Furthermore, the literature on immigrant high school students reports multiple examples of these teenagers being isolated from (and sometimes shunned by) their domestic peers as a result of their placement into what has been called the "ESL ghetto" in high school, a stigmatizing, boring, soul-deadening, self-perpetuating space where immigrant students take all their high school classes together all day, mostly nonacademically oriented classes focused on the minutia of worksheets on sentence-level English grammar.[4] Some research indicates little literacy development between eighth grade and first year of tertiary education for certain immigrant students.[5] And, of course, many of these young people are essentially unwilling immigrants in that the decision to leave the home country was probably not theirs but that of their parents.

In terms of their written work, their high school writing teachers may have followed current ideas about the importance of content over errors and encouraged fluency and an emphasis on content over grammatical accuracy. While many would applaud this focus, not all accept the potential results. In one such case, the student arrived in college confident of his good writing skills because of the encouragement that he had received from his high school teachers' feedback on his writing. Unfortunately, he found that his new writing environment in college was not as willing as his high school to accept the errors in his writing, resulting in his not passing out of the ESL track after a term of work there.[6]

Recasting Model Students

In yet other cases reported in the literature, the multilingual high school students have been held up to their domestic peers as model students, sometimes mostly because they were quiet, obedient, and hard working.[7] This characterization could conceivably have created resentment of them on the part of their peers, but it also constructed a positive institutional identity that was then crushed in the students' encounter with college. Suddenly, instead of being viewed as low-demand, and for this reason excellent, high school students, as they entered college they were recast as ESL students, the Other, foreigners, and placed in separate first-year writing classes, despite having spent several years in mainstream classes with domestic peers and considering themselves American. One such student, asked in her ESL writing class in college to compare shopping in the United States to shopping in her home country, was forced to fabricate the fabled home country because she had no real memory of much of anything from her "home country"; the only home country she knew was the United States.[8]

In terms of their writing, because their oral and informal language may be quite well developed and, if so, will have been the key vehicle of their integration into high school life, they may have some difficulty in shifting to the more formal, academic styles demanded of them in college and may have less familiarity with and a smaller range of registers and genres than many domestic students. Furthermore, in the context-poor medium of writing, the many extralinguistic cues (e.g., body language, facial expressions) that these students use to communicate their meanings orally are less available to them. At the same time, in writing the demand is greater for absolute accuracy in regard to, for example, articles or prepositions (see Chapter 9 for more on helping ESL students with articles), features of language that can often be fudged in oral communication without much confusion or loss of meaning; or the confusion or loss of meaning can be eliminated through immediate negotiation that is not really available in writing. The missed article that a listener may not have even noticed in speech may become confusing in writing or at the least flag the writing as "nonnative." As will be discussed in other chapters in this book, appeals to intuition about how a phrase should sound may not be effective for writers who have not needed to develop those intuitions.

Literacy Skills of Generation 1.5 Students

Most of this description appears to have little to do with the central concern of a writing center, developing students' literacy skills, but in fact these emotional and cultural pressures, the perhaps fragile new identities that these students are forming, and the need to construct a comfortable public image of themselves, perhaps especially vis-à-vis their domestic peers, all influence how much students like this are able and/or willing to benefit from their work in a writing center. They might have learned in high school more or less the same things about writing that domestic students did, although the texts of these Generation 1.5 students may exhibit sentence level features that deviate from the expected. But they may also carry the additional burden of an unclear and sometimes unhappy relationship to either or both the home culture/language and the target culture/language/people. At a time of life when identity formation and peer approval is paramount, these students may have experienced intense social isolation and may not be secure in who they are in an even more profound and conflicted way than is the usual case for this age group.

In terms of their visits to the writing center, these immigrant students are likely to have the oral fluency and back channeling proficiency (i.e., responding to statements with "uh huh" or "I get it" in ways that seem natural) of their domestic peers, making their linguistic and paralinguistic behaviors (e.g., body language, clothing) seem familiar. They are likely to face many of the same struggles as domestic students: understanding and addressing their assignments fully, leading into quotes, paraphrasing without plagiarizing, formulating and following through on an argument, analyzing rather than summarizing, and overly idiomatic or oral register phrasing. Because they share so much with their domestic peers, writing center tutors may find these students easier to work with than international or visa students.

However, these multilingual students may face additional difficulties that their domestic peers do not. For example, they may cling to writing strategies they learned in high school, even if they don't seem to be working,[9] partly because the strategies worked well enough in high school to get them to college and partly because they have limited other options to draw on. They may also be surprisingly slow to shift the structure of the English they use in the direction of target norms (i.e., the usual and natural language of native speakers). The reason for this difficulty in restructuring their version of English is at least in part psycholinguistic: The language they use has filled their communicative needs, and they may not really perceive (or be able to remember) the difference between what they produce and the target forms or correct language expected of them in writing. This slowness to respond to corrective feedback combined with their verbal fluency combined almost certainly with having missed full and deep development of academic knowledge in high school because they couldn't quite completely understand the content of their history, science, or social science classes may have the devastating and unfair consequence of making some of these students seem intellectually behind where they should be. (For more on tutoring this kind of student, see Chapter 8.)

International/Visa Students

International students, or foreign students, as they were once referred to, travel from countries around the world to study in the United States (or another country) with the official permission of the government in the form of a student visa. In many ways, undergraduate visa or international students have an easier lot in college than do immigrant high school graduates and may be the ones most likely to benefit most quickly from writing center interactions. Most of the time, students who have completed high school in a non-English-speaking country and go to study in an English-speaking country do not report feeling threats to their identities of the same kinds or with the same intensity as U.S. high school multilingual students report. They may miss their homes and families intensely, but usually, unlike the U.S. high school graduates, they themselves have chosen and are proud and excited to be studying abroad. Their relationship with their first languages seems less complicated; interviews with international students show them to be quick to claim allegiance to those languages and proud of their ability to flexibly access and manipulate their first languages smoothly and easily, a facility that they may not feel in their second language either orally or in text form.[10]

Despite their lack of the familiarity with slang or popular culture that U.S. high school graduates usually develop, international students nevertheless are often very successful academically (purportedly more so than their U.S. high school graduate counterparts), carry the reputation among disciplinary professors of having an impressive work ethic, and may display an overt interest in the life of the mind, sometimes viewing themselves as the intellectual elite of their countries. Although this may seem counterintuitive, it appears that the longer L2 students experience high school in their first languages, the better they do in college in their second languages.[11] The academic knowledge they build in their high schools at home helps compensate for potential lack of L2 proficiency. Furthermore, for the most part, by the time they go abroad to study, they have already formed the foundations of stable identities and are eager for new cross-cultural experiences with domestic students, contacts that are sometimes more difficult to establish than might be expected. In other words, international students may be more eager to penetrate domestic student friendship networks than domestic students are willing to incorporate them into their already established groups of friends.

Effects of a Reading Emphasis

The writing of international students is likely to show the effects of formal study of English in language classes in the home country and of an emphasis on reading. In other words, many are quite at home with traditional grammar terminology (including terms and grammatical categories that monolingual English speakers may not feel fully in control of themselves, like present perfect verbs or adverbial clauses). Tutors who are familiar with grammar terminology may be able to take advantage of this shared language in their explanations or discussion of such students' work. The emphasis on reading often translates into initial greater facility with reading than with speaking, writing, or understanding oral language. But that facility usually does not come close to matching the reading fluency of domestic students, at least not at first; international students take longer to process texts and may need to reread several times in order to understand what domestic students can grasp in a single read. A highly successful Japanese undergraduate student in social work, for example, reported having to read articles in her field as many as five times to feel that she really understood them, and material from the popular press, which was quite easy and relaxing for her domestic peers to read, was especially difficult for her because of the informal vocabulary and unfamiliar macrostructure, or organization, of the journalistic texts.[12] On the other hand, international students may be particularly adept at learning through memorization and may use this approach to try to develop more extensive academic vocabularies. They are also likely to have developed a strong sense of how to study well. At the same time, international students are likely to be fully, even painfully, aware of how much effort it takes to succeed in an English-speaking environment where the bar is set by students who have been using English in academic settings all their lives; they may translate this awareness into what often seems to university personnel as amazing devotion to study and willingness to work as hard as necessary to succeed academically.

But this devotion to study varies. Students from exam cultures, where students' futures are dependent on a series of academic exams, may in fact be perceived as unduly focused on doing well on exams. A great deal of what they can expect in terms of material rewards in their future lives in their home countries may hinge on passing important exams, and the orientation toward succeeding at them may be carried over to completing a degree in the United States. On the other hand, some international students regard their enrollment in a United States university primarily as an opportunity to experience a foreign culture. What they are directed to learn in classes and how well they do in their courses are less important to them than being able to travel in the host country, for example, and these students may not at all demonstrate the single-mindedness of purpose that keeps the others at the library on weekend nights.

Learning an Overly Structured Writing Style

Although the formal teaching of writing at the tertiary level is pervasive in the United States, this is not necessarily the case worldwide. Nevertheless, in many countries that send students to the United States to study, more attention than ever before has been focused on writing, both in the first language and in English. (See, for example, the intense discussions on the role of writing instruction and writing centers in universities in Europe in the publications and presentations of the European Association of Teachers of Academic Writing and the recently instituted writing exams as part of college entrance and exit exams in Korea, China, and Japan.)[13] Still, some international students (especially those from countries like Taiwan, China, and Japan, where so-called

English essay writing style is widely taught)[14] become impatient with what they regard as the overly structured and scripted style of writing they learned to produce in English classes at home or in the United States.[15] They describe English essays as extremely lockstep: introduction of two to three sentences ending with a thesis statement, body paragraph(s) of two to three points (depending on how many words the writing prompt requires) or reasons for position taken, and concluding paragraph repeating the main idea.[16] These students, and others from Europe where English writing is less of a focus, may perceive writing in their first language as not structured (though of course it is, if differently) and feel that any structure imposed on what they experience as the free flow of their thoughts, opinions, and feelings is distorting and unnecessarily constraining, even when the results of that free flow reads like disorganization to a domestic reader. The free-flow style of expression combined with lack of English-writing experience, vocabulary, and fluency may cause these students to have a hard time making their point clearly to a U.S. academic reader.

Despite the impatience that some students feel with what they see as rigid writing prescriptions in English, for a variety of reasons, they may be reluctant to exhibit negative responses to L2 writing, L2 academic culture, or the United States generally. Students like Luc from Viet Nam may feel that it is inappropriate to criticize the school or culture that hosts them, that they don't know enough about the host environment to criticize it publicly, or simply that it is impolite to criticize.[17] As a result, teachers and writing center tutors may develop the erroneous impression that these students do what they are told without objection, complaint, or criticism, but they are of course not privy to the private (negative) observations that these students most definitely do make about their host environment. At the other side of the spectrum, the academic cultures of some international students from Europe and the Middle East encourage vociferous debate and a highly critical stance as a mark of intellectuality. These students may come off as excessively aggressive and resistant to, for example, suggestions for altering work they might bring to the writing center. Yet, again, what might be perceived as passivity or aggressiveness may simply represent unexpected interactional styles that can be worked around.[18]

Those students whose home cultures emphasize essay writing for exams are also likely to be most concerned about grammatical accuracy in their texts because this accuracy is often sought in the exams. Depending on the professors they encounter in the United States and how accustomed these professors are to having international students in their classes (which in turn may depend to some degree on where in the country the institution is located and the particular discipline involved), concern for grammatical correctness may be fired up or dampened. If the students realize that their professors are relaxed about grammatical perfection and do not penalize L2 students for errors, the students respond by focusing less on those features of their writing. If they experience the opposite, they ratchet up their own fretting over accuracy, often to the detriment of the substance of their writing.[19]

One area where writing center tutors may be able to make good inroads is in promoting audience awareness. Partly because previous writing instruction in their school systems may have neglected audience concerns and partly because international/visa students may have so often experienced writing primarily as writing for exams, some international students do not automatically consider audience issues, viewing the only possible audience as an evaluator of some kind, with the purpose of writing being only to display proficiency in English. These writers may be especially receptive to an emphasis on audience awareness and may benefit dramatically from pointers on developing sensitivity to their academic audience. Furthermore, international students may be quite unfamiliar with a host of writing conventions in English academic writing such as finding and integrating source material (at all, let alone effectively). Interventions in these areas are likely to have a substantial impact on these students' writing quality, particularly because, of the three groups (perhaps artificially) described in this chapter, international undergraduates may be the most eager to learn the broadest range of language and writing skills.

International Graduate Students

Unlike most undergraduate students, international graduate students' advanced disciplinary knowledge may far exceed their ability to express that knowledge in writing in their second language, as they are often intensely aware.[20] Because these graduate students have a high degree of disciplinary knowledge and must typically write within norms particular to given disciplines, writing center tutors with more generalized training may feel less well positioned to offer writing help. Depending on the type of writing center available, graduate students may also be less likely to turn up at writing centers than undergraduates because graduate students report expecting to rely on the advisors and project directors they work with to help shape their writing.[21] But there is evidence that L2 graduate students crave more feedback on their written work than their professors and/or advisors are able or willing to give.[22] Their professors may in fact be unaware of this greater desire for writing support and, looking to make life easier on the L2 students, may require fewer revisions of papers than they do from domestic students, thereby depriving these writers of the opportunity to engage in a cycle of drafts and revisions.[23]

High Stakes

Furthermore, the level of writing skill required of graduate students is typically greater than that demanded of undergraduates and yet in many instances, L2 graduate students are expected to develop these skills with the aid of only the most basic and generalized L2 writing instruction, not focused on their disciplinary literacy needs but rather on generic essay writing typical of, for example, undergraduate essay exams or certain types of first-year writing courses. Thus, as a result of such less than ideal circumstances, these students may find themselves in the anomalous situation of completing course work in their disciplines but without much opportunity for multiple drafting and with less feedback on their writing than they would have liked and yet then being expected to plunge directly into such high-stakes writing as theses, dissertations, and even articles for publication.[24]

International graduate students may also exhibit less L2 proficiency (particularly oral proficiency) than international undergraduates and experience greater difficulty developing it. For some graduate students, their last formal instruction in English may have taken place several years before they decided (or were sent) to study in the United States; they may have lost some of the proficiency they once commanded. In addition, usually being older than typical undergraduates, they may be slower at or have somewhat more psycholinguistic difficulty with developing greater L2 proficiency than younger L2 users. Also, many undergraduates can assume that they have four years to function in their second language in completing their undergraduate degrees; some graduate students are sent abroad with the expectation of staying a considerably shorter length of time. Furthermore, in terms of sociolinguistic development, graduate students are more likely to bring their families abroad with them, in which case they do not experience as great a need as undergraduates might to turn to domestic peers to fill their social and emotional needs. This lesser need combined with the heavy work schedules of graduate students, including lab and research duties, often makes it difficult for them to find time for the very kind of socializing that would advance their familiarity with informal language and with L2 cultural norms. As a whole, they are probably more instrumentally, or pragmatically, oriented than their undergraduate counterparts and perhaps somewhat less motivated by the cultural experience of living abroad.[25] It is also likely that more is at stake for these international graduate students than for L2 undergraduates. Although some come abroad with their families, it is also not unusual for these students to leave families (i.e., not their parents but their children and spouses) behind, sometimes for years. In addition, they may be giving up important jobs to pursue degrees abroad.

When Roles Reverse

As might be expected, however, there is a fairly wide range of disciplinary experience represented in the L2 graduate student population, from beginning master's students to students who may already have completed course work in their majors. Some still see themselves essentially as students and need to learn the types of literacy practices typical to their disciplines. Others, however, not only come with experience writing in their disciplines in their first language but also read a great deal professionally and often in English. They are likely to be quite sophisticated about such features of disciplinary writing as deploying the textual means of positioning themselves appropriately in their writing in relation to their professional audiences.[26] In fact, international graduate students and professionals writing in their second language often write better in English in their technical areas than they do in their first language either because, functioning professionally only in their second language, they develop their professional vocabulary and genre familiarity in the second language rather than in the first language or because the same technical terms or concerns do not exist in their first languages.

Many international graduate students arrive in graduate school in the United States as already highly respected and established professionals in their home countries, with thriving careers as published authors, researchers, professors or other high-ranking academics, or successful business managers. Studying in graduate school in a second language may entail a considerable loss of social, professional, and even familial status.[27] Although these adults do not usually have the identity formation issues that teenage immigrant students may have, leaving positions of authority and prestige to study abroad in a language they may not fully control may be experienced as humiliating. Identity building is likely not at stake but gaining acknowledgment and recognition of professional status may be.[28] Roles may feel uncomfortably reversed to the L2 graduate student who is a university professor in Argentina and who finds herself working with a tutor at the writing center who could be that professor's undergraduate student at home. The constraints that restricted language proficiency puts on L2 graduate students' abilities to present themselves as they are used to being seen through interactions in their first languages can cause embarrassment and frustration.

Appropriate Words and Sign Posts

Whether or not a given writing center is positioned to do this, L2 graduate students may hope for help in such areas as communicating with their advisors (e.g., even knowing—or knowing how to find out—just how much they can impose on an advisor's time and office hours), getting feedback from their advisors on their writing, determining how much they can/should rely on peers for help, writing for an audience who may not know the jargon of their field, formulating an argument instead of just writing to inform (as in merely reporting the results of an experiment instead of making the significance of the experiment clear), knowing and using the appropriate words and phrases to establish the right amount of hedging or forwarding of claims, and of course, using appropriate idiomatic phrasing, tenses, articles, and prepositions.

Although these L2 graduate students are likely to have developed a sensitivity to basic macrostructures in the writing in their disciplines, they often express the need for disciplinary signposting phrases such as "In light of the previous" or "Taken together." Some collect these (and longer stretches of language) from publications they read and reuse them[29] to such an extent that

L2 writing researchers have suggested that a different standard for "plagiarism" needs to be used in the sciences (where most of these students work) and in the humanities.[30]

It is also not unusual for advisors of these graduate students to approve of the science, the thinking, and the content exhibited in their writing but be exasperated by language issues they do not want to have to deal with. Because the students get less of this kind and other mentoring than they crave, they may turn to the writing center (if they know about its services) for help but are likely to feel that the only help the writing center can give is language help,[31] which may in fact be the case. Although they may have excellent technical reading skills and technical vocabularies, they may lack the kinds of semi- or subtechnical phrasings or vocabulary items such as "parameter, discrete, comprise, hypothesis, preliminary, corroborate, projected, issue" that might be required for their writing to make sense and read smoothly.[32] Yet, focused as they often are on the demanding writing required of them, they may be the least interested of the three groups in learning general language or writing.

Conclusion

To varying degrees, it is important to humans that others know who they are. The essential means that humans have of making themselves known to others is through language. When an individual does not fully control language, this person may be unable to make himself or herself seen by others as the individual would wish to be seen. There is also a tendency among humans to see their own social and cultural group as highly nuanced and differentiated but to be less able to fully grasp that all social and cultural groups are equally nuanced and differentiated. It is in the hope of helping those who work with multilingual students in writing centers to better see these people as nuanced and differentiated that this certainly overly simplistic attempt has been made to point out a few features of some of the subgroups encompassed under the rubric of "ESL student." But the most effective way for writing center tutors to experience these nuances firsthand is to take advantage of the visits of these multilingual, multicultural individuals to the writing center and show interest in their home language, country, or culture by engaging them in the kind of small talk that usually accompanies tutoring sessions, and so get to know them one by one.

Notes

1. Leki (2007).
2. Shanti Bruce, personal communication, August 11, 2007.
3. Leki (2007).
4. Valdes (2001).
5. Blanton (2005); Hartman and Tarone (1999); Tarone et al. (1993); Valdes and Sanders (1998).

6. Frodensen and Starna (1999).

7. Harklau (2000).

8. Harklau (2000).

9. Hamp-Lyons (1997).

10. Leki (2008); Silva (1992); Silva et al. (2003).

11. Bosher and Rowenkamp (1992); Cummins (2001); Muchinsky and Tangren (1999).

12. Leki (2007).

13. The European Association of Teachers of Academic Writing can be reached through their website, www.eataw.org, or their list server, EATAW-CONF@LISTSERV.HUM.KU.DK.

14. You (2004).

15. Hyland (1998).

16. Hamp-Lyons and Zhang (2001); Leki (2008).

17. Johns (1991).

18. And, as with any student, they may simply not have enough writing or language proficiency to know how to implement or even entirely understand revision suggestions.

19. Leki (2007).

20. Hirvela and Belcher (2001); Ivanic and Camps (2001); Schneider and Fujishima (1995); Silva (1992).

21. Leki (2006).

22. Dong (1998); Leki (2006).

23. Dong (1998).

24. Leki (2006).

25. This discussion of L2 graduate students focuses on graduate students in all disciplinary fields except TESOL (i.e., those who come to study English and education in order to become English teachers.) The many graduate students who are English teachers and professors in their home countries, or plan to be, are typically much more concerned about general language and cultural issues than their counterparts in other disciplines.

26. Hirvela and Belcher (2001); Tardy (2005).

27. Fox (1994); Hirvela and Belcher (2001).

28. Hirvela and Belcher (2001).

29. Pecorari (2003).

30. Flowerdew and Li (2007).

31. Radecki and Swales (1988).

32. Pearson, 387.

Works Cited

Blanton, Linda Lonon. 2005. "Student, Interrupted: A Tale of Two Would-Be Writers." *Journal of Second Language Writing* 14: 105–21.

Bosher, Susan, and J. Rowenkamp. 1992. "Language Proficiency and Academic Success: The Refugee/Immigrant in Higher Education" (Eric Document ED 353 914).

Cummins, Jim. 2001. *Negotiating Identities: Education for Empowerment in a Diverse Society*. Los Angeles: California Association for Bilingual Education.

Dong, Yuen. 1998. "From Writing in Their Native Language to Writing in English: What ESL Students Bring to Our Writing Classrooms." *College ESL* 8: 87–105.

Flowerdew, John, and Yongyan Li. 2007. "Language Re-use Among Chinese Apprentice Scientists Writing for Publication." *Applied Linguistics* 28: 440–65.

Fox, Helen. 1994. *Listening to the World: Cultural Issues in Academic Writing*. Urbana, IL: National Council of Teachers of English.

Frodesen, Jan, and Norinne Starna. 1999. "Distinguishing Incipient and Functional Bilingual Writers: Assessment and Instructional Insights Gained Through Second-Language Writer Profiles." In *Generation 1.5 Meets College Composition*, edited by Linda Harklau, Kay Losey, and Meryl Siegal, 61–79. Mahwah, NJ: Lawrence Erlbaum.

Hamp-Lyons, Liz. 1997. "Exploring Bias in Essay Tests." In *Writing in Multicultural Settings*, edited by Carol Severino, Juan Guerra, and Johnnella Butler, 51–66. New York: Modern Language Association.

Hamp-Lyons, Liz, and Wen-xia Bonnie Zhang. 2001. "World Englishes: Issues in and from Academic Writing Assessment." In *Research Perspectives on English for Academic Purposes*, edited by John Flowerdew and Matthew Peacock, 101–16. New York: Cambridge University Press.

Harklau, Linda. 2000. "From the 'Good Kids' to the 'Worst': Representations of English Language Learners Across Educational Settings." *TESOL Quarterly* 34: 35–67.

Hartman, Beth, and Elaine Tarone. 1999. "Preparation for College Writing: Teachers Talk About Writing Instruction for Southeast Asian Students in Secondary School." In *Generation 1.5 Meets College Composition*, edited by Linda Harklau, Kay Losey, and Meryl Siegal, 99–118. Mahwah, NJ: Lawrence Erlbaum.

Hirvela, Alan, and Diane Belcher. 2001. "Coming Back to Voice: The Multiple Voices and Identities of Mature Multilingual Writers." *Journal of Second Language Writing* 10: 83–106.

Hyland, Fiona. 1998. "The Impact of Teacher-Written Feedback on Individual Writers." *Journal of Second Language Writing* 7: 255–86.

Ivanic, Roz, and David Camps. 2001. "I Am How I Sound: Voice as Self-Representation in L2 Writing." *Journal of Second Language Writing* 10: 3–33.

Johns, Ann. 1991. "Interpreting an English Competency Examination: The Frustration of an ESL Science Student." *Written Communication* 8: 379–401.

Leki, Ilona. 2006. "'You Cannot Ignore': Graduate L2 Students' Experience of and Responses to Written Feedback Practices." In *Feedback in Second Language Writing: Contexts and Issues*, edited by Ken Hyland and Fiona Hyland, 266–85. New York: Cambridge University Press.

————. 2007. *Undergraduates in a Second Language: Challenges and Complexities of Academic Literacy Development*. Mahwah, NJ: Lawrence Erlbaum.

————. 2008. "Genre Interfaces: Investigating Prior and Evolving Genre Knowledge of Second Language Writers." Paper presented at the Writing Research Across Borders conference, February, Santa Barbara, California.

Muchinsky, Dennis, and Nancy Tangren. 1999. "Immigrant Student Performance in an Academic Intensive English Program." In *Generation 1.5 Meets College Composition*, edited by Linda Harklau, Kay Losey, and Meryl Siegal, 211–34. Mahwah, NJ: Lawrence Erlbaum.

Pearson, Sheryl. 1983. "The Challenge of Mai Chung: Teaching Technical Writing to the Foreign-Born Professional in Industry." *TESOL Quarterly* 17: 383–99.

Pecorari, Diane. 2003. "Good and Original: Plagiarism and Patch Writing in Academic Second-Language Writing." *Journal of Second Language Writing* 12: 317–45.

Radecki, Patricia, and John Swales. 1988. "ESL Students' Reaction to Written Comments on Their Written Work." *System* 16: 355–65.

Schneider, Melanie, and Naomi Fujishima. 1995. "When Practice Doesn't Make Perfect. The Case of an ESL Graduate Student." In *Academic Writing in a Second Language: Essays on Research and Pedagogy*, edited by Diana Belcher and George Braine, 3–22. Norwood, NJ: Ablex.

Silva, Tony. 1992. "L1 vs. L2 Writing: ESL Graduate Students' Perceptions." *TESL Canada Journal* 10: 27–47.

Silva, Tony, Melinda Reichelt, Yoshiki Chikuma, Natalie Duval-Couetil, Ruo-Ping Mo, Gloria Velez-Rendon, and Sandra Wood. 2003. "Second Language Writing Up Close and Personal: Some Success Stories." In

Exploring the Dynamics of Second Language Writing, edited by Barbara Kroll, 93–114. New York: Cambridge University Press.

Tardy, Christine. 2005. "'It's Like a Story': Rhetorical Knowledge Development in Advanced Academic Literacy." *Journal of English for Academic Purposes* 4: 325–38.

Tarone, Elaine, Bruce Downing, Andrew Cohen, Susan Gillette, Robin Murie, and Beverly Dailey. 1993. "The Writing of Southeast Asian-American Students in Secondary School and University." *Journal of Second Language Writing* 2: 149–72.

Valdes, Guadalupe. 2001. *Learning and Not Learning English: Latino Students in American Schools*. New York: Teachers College Press.

Valdes, Guadalupe, and P. A. Sanders. 1998. "Latino ESL Students and the Development of Writing Abilities." In *Evaluating Writing*, edited by Charles R. Cooper and Lee Odell, 249–78. Urbana, IL: National Council of Teachers of English.

You, Xiaoye. 2004. "'The Choice Made from No Choice': English Writing Instruction in a Chinese University." *Journal of Second Language Writing* 13: 97–110.

2

Theoretical Perspectives on Learning a Second Language

Theresa Jiinling Tseng

While trying to help English as a second language (ESL) students in your writing center, you may have wondered: Why do ESL writers seem to have trouble getting the correct word order? Why do ESL writers need help choosing the right word? Why do they continue to make the same errors time after time? Is there anything teachers or tutors can do to make learning English any easier for ESL students? These are also some of the same questions that drive research in the field known as second language acquisition (SLA), a part of the discipline of applied linguistics. Although second language scholars have not settled the answers to these questions, their theories have provided important background knowledge to help explain the challenges of learning a second language.

I have organized this chapter around four of the major theories of SLA. They will bring you closer to understanding how those students who write in English as their second (or third or fourth) language process a new language, English, in their minds. The theories can be briefly described as follows:[1]

1. Behaviorist: We learn by drill and practice.
2. Innatist: We are hardwired to learn a language.
3. Cognitivist: Learning involves noticing, practicing, and eventually making the skill automatic.
4. Interactionist: Learning takes place mainly through interaction with a more proficient speaker.

This chapter introduces you to these theories and illustrates how they can apply to ESL writers in the context of a tutorial. It is my hope that this knowledge will make you not only a more informed tutor but also one who is more curious about, engaged in, and empathetic to the challenges that ESL writers face.

Behaviorist—You Learn by Drill and Practice

Anyone who has ever had to recite multiplication tables or memorize lines for a play knows that repetition can be a helpful strategy for learning new material. When this repetition becomes so automatic that you no longer have to think about it, you have formed a habit. This habit formation is one way to account for second language (L2) learning. In this view, language learning involves

- receiving input (exposure to the new language)
- imitating and practicing it repeatedly (drill)
- getting encouragement (positive reinforcement) for doing it correctly
- eventually, forming associations between words and objects or events.

For example, to use the expression "Bless you" correctly, an L2 learner goes through

1. receiving input (someone teaches her, "Say 'Bless you' when you see someone sneezing" or she sees a person say "Bless you" to someone sneezing)

2. practicing "Bless you" whenever she sees someone sneezing

3. receiving "Thank you" in response, and

4. after many practices, eventually establishing the habit of saying "Bless you" when someone sneezes.

In language teaching, practices such as sentence drills and memorization of sentence patterns are often used to form and strengthen the habit of using the new language correctly. Tutors and other native speakers often use similar drill-and-practice exercises in foreign language classes of their own to establish the new language habits, and errors are corrected immediately so that bad habits will not be developed.

Applying the behaviorist view to SLA, we assume that the language habits of L2 learners' first language (L1) influence their learning of the second language. This assumption is called the *contrastive analysis hypothesis* (CAH), and it states that learners have an easier time learning a second language when it is structurally similar to their first language, and that they have a more difficult time when the two are substantially different.[2] Here is a conversation between a tutor, Joe, and an L2 learner, Maria, about an error caused by the influence of Maria's L1, which is Spanish:

Joe: Maria, why did you write "I received a pair of *shoes news* for my birthday"?

Maria: Look (*pointing to her shoes*), they are *news*.

Joe: Oh, you mean they are your *new shoes*.

Maria: Why can't I say *shoes news*? In Spanish, we say, "zapatos nuevos" (shoes news).

Joe: In English, we put the description (the adjective) before the thing (the noun) we describe. So, *new* goes before *shoes*. And, we don't make the adjective plural even though the noun might be plural.

The error in this example is known as a *transfer error* because Maria followed two Spanish grammar rules that do not transfer to writing in English: (1) Nouns go before adjectives in word order, and (2) adjectives must match nouns in singularity/plurality. Tutors could help Maria by pointing out the error to her. At this point, you may wonder why it is necessary to point out the error instead of letting her discover it herself. Errors caused by the interference from the learner's first language are difficult, and sometimes impossible, for her to figure out without help. In the example, Maria felt that she was correct because she followed Spanish grammar rules. Without explicit correction, Maria's meaning gets distorted because *news* is not the plural form of *new,* as Maria had imagined. When tutors notice that the errors that are caused by the L2 learner's mother tongue remain unchanged after the learner's self-editing, tutors should not hesitate to point them out because the L2 learner often appreciates tutors who correct transfer errors that she could not detect by herself. However, unless tutors know their student's native language, they will not be able to recognize specific transfer errors. Some knowledge of the student's first language may help.

Like most theories, the CAH does not tell the whole story of L2 learning. For example, it cannot identify all of the errors that students need to correct. It also predicts many errors that do not occur, and it cannot account for learners who avoid using structures with which they are not familiar. In sum, it may be that the CAH gives us a snapshot of part of the theoretical landscape rather than the entire view.

Innatist—You Are Hardwired to Learn a Language

Another way to account for an L2 learner's language development is related to an idea about L1 learning proposed by the well-known linguist Noam Chomsky: Children come with a blueprint of their native language to the world. [3] Thus, all young children are hardwired to learn a language. Some linguists believe that this innate ability is not available for L2 learners past puberty, but others say that it may still be available because adult L2 learners create many sentences that they have never heard before. Some linguists believe that L2 learners' language learning ability must be different from the L1 learners' because L2 learners have already learned one language.

Chomsky drew an important distinction in his theory of language learning—the distinction between *competence* and *performance*. *Competence* refers to one's intuitive knowledge about the system of his native language, and *performance* refers to the use of that language. A native speaker's competence develops naturally (hence, *innate*), and he can rely on it to judge whether the performance in speech or writing is grammatical (as a native speaker would say it). A nonnative speaker's competence of the target second language (the language that she is trying to learn), on the other hand, does not develop completely naturally. Many L2 learners do not grow up with or acquire their second language through immersion but take classes to learn it. As a result, the competence of this type of L2 learners often takes the form not of intuition but of knowledge of the grammar rules that they have learned. They rely on these rules to judge whether or not something is grammatical. Here's an example that illustrates how a tutor, Tina, and an advanced L2 learner, Ling, judge grammaticality as Ling was reading her writing aloud:

Ling: (*Reading aloud*) . . . so my teacher gave me an advice.

Tina: An advice? That doesn't sound right.

Ling: Why not? My writing teacher told me that I need to remember using an article before a noun. The word *advice* begins with a vowel, so I used *an* before *advice*.

Tina: But we don't say "an advice."

Ling: What about "some advices"? Can I use the plural form?

Tina: Hmm, we don't say "some advices" either. We say, "some advice."

Ling: Why? Why can't we use the plural form?

The article system (*a/an/the*) in English often presents problems for learners whose L1, such as Chinese or Japanese, does not have articles. The usage of articles may often depend on the native English speaker's intuition to decide when to use one and which one to use.[4] This intuition for the English article system is what Ling, a Chinese speaker, does not have. Because her teacher had reminded her to use articles in writing, Ling carefully added *an* before *advice* but was told that it did not sound right. Then her attempt to change *an advice* to *some advices* still resulted in an error. In fact, Ling's problem is yet another example that shows Ling's lack of native English speakers' intuition that helps them distinguish between count and noncount nouns in English. To Ling, *advice* is countable, yet in English grammar, *advice* is considered to be a noncount noun. Tina, the native English-speaking tutor, could tell by intuition that it was not grammatical because it did not sound right. In addition, the example also shows that Ling depended heavily on her knowledge of grammar rules to reason through the usage. The point here is that grammar rules cannot possibly tell the learner everything that she needs to know in order to produce error-free sentences because there are some aspects of language production that depend upon L1 intuition.

In fact, there are many instances that cannot be explained by learning the rules in grammar books. For example, we say that people eat *rice* (always in singular form) versus *beans* (always in plural form); people are *in* the car but *on* the bus, and people *watch* TV but *see* a movie. When a tutor is asked why the choice is this but not that, he will usually reply, "It just is" (see Chapter 17). For idiomatic expressions and usages that cannot be explained by grammar rules but only by the native English-speaking (NES) tutor's intuition, the best way to help the learner is simply to tell her, "This is what a native speaker would use intuitively."

Applying Chomsky's distinction between *competence* and *performance*, Stephen Pit Corder relates *error* to failure in *competence* (wrong knowledge or lack of knowledge) and *mistakes* to failure in *performance* (e.g., typos or slips of the tongue).[5] A tutor cannot always tell whether the deviant sentences she sees are errors or mistakes; nonetheless, if she notices that the same problem appears repeatedly even after the L2 learner has proofread her writing, then there is a good chance that the learner's knowledge of the usage is incorrect. In other words, it may be an error or competence problem. In addition to L1 transfer errors (involving, e.g., prepositions, article usages, and word order), errors caused by L2 learners' insufficient or incorrect knowledge are also the ones that learners cannot detect by themselves. This is true no matter how many times they read their writing aloud. If the learners are motivated to learn, tutors should not hesitate to point out those errors explicitly.

The innatist view on language acquisition provided a springboard for Stephen Krashen, one of the most influential applied linguists, to develop his *monitor model*. Because young children's acquisition of their first language is a feat that adult L2 learners cannot help but admire, Krashen proposed to re-create the naturalist language acquisition experience of young children for L2 learners.[6] For tutors interested in how people learn a second language, the monitor model is a useful guide.

Krashen's monitor model of SLA consists of five key ideas:

1. acquisition/learning hypothesis
2. monitor hypothesis
3. natural order hypothesis
4. comprehensible input hypothesis
5. affective filter hypothesis

What follows is an explanation of each of the above key ideas.

The Acquisition/Learning Hypothesis

According to Krashen, *acquiring* a language is different from *learning* one. *Acquisition* refers to the process of picking up a language the way young children do—subconsciously. The best way for the L2 learner to become competent in another language is by acquisition, or exposure to the L2 input (such as reading a book in the second language) at a level that the learner understands, while the learner's attention is on meaning but not on grammar. *Learning*, on the other hand, is consciously studying the language (the grammar rules). In Krashen's view, learned competence does not become acquired competence, so he denies a role for conscious learning in language acquisition.[7] Also, Krashen indicates that acquisition, but not learning, is responsible for fluency. This is so because formal learning makes the learners conscious of grammar rules. Consequently, the learners tend to inspect or monitor their grammar, and hence reduce the fluency, in their speech or writing.

Krashen's *learning/acquisition hypothesis* can explain the differences in writing difficulties between immigrant and international ESL students. For example, an immigrant student of mine wrote *firstable* instead of *first of all* to state his first point. He understood the meaning and he knew how to use the expression, yet the form was incorrect. Apparently, this student had acquired or picked up the use of the expression, but he had not acquired the form. Joy Reid points out that immigrant students often acquire with their ears many English expressions from the environment without formally learning about them.[8] Immigrant students may be relatively fluent in speaking, but they may have limited understanding of the structures of the English language. Similar to L1 students' errors, many immigrant ESL students' errors are caused by the differences between speaking and writing. For this reason, oral fluency does not always go hand-in-hand with grammatical accuracy, and oral proficiency is not necessarily related to writing proficiency. Though immigrant students may have more intuitive sense than international students of what sounds right, they may need to explicitly learn some grammar rules when their acquisition-by-ear has misled them. (See Chapters 4 and 18.)

Many international students, by contrast, have learned English by studying vocabulary and grammar rules. They often understand and can explain grammar, yet they lack the experience of hearing and using English in daily life. Their word choice and sentence structures are often unconventional. "I don't know how to express my meaning in English" is often their complaint. The point is that international students lack native English speakers' intuitions about what sounds right. They need corrections that are pointed out explicitly for the problems that they cannot fall back on their own intuitions to fix. As Ben Rafoth (Chapter 17) points out, this is a good reason for tutors to study the structure of English grammar.

It is worth noting that Krashen does not deny the value of grammar teaching for high school and college students, but he does not assume that the rules students *learned* will become *acquired*.[9] As an L2 learner, I have studied grammar in a non-English-speaking environment, and I have lived in an English-speaking environment for quite a few years. Consequently, my competence probably comes from both explicit learning and implicit acquisition. Although Krashen believes learning does not turn into acquisition, I believe the explicit grammar knowledge that I gained earlier has facilitated my aquisition of English later. I don't always have to rely on others' paraphrasing to make input comprehensible. Sometimes I am able to understand the input by analyzing its structure. For instance, once when I heard a phrase, "to zero in on," my first reaction was that I had hardly ever used two prepositions (*in* and *on*) together. Next, I figured that "to zero in on" must be an idiomatic expression and that the *on* indicates the direction. After I analyzed the structure and figured out the meaning from the context, the use of two prepositions started making sense to me, and I was able to pick up the use of this idiomatic expression without much trouble. Pienemann indicates that the learning of linguistic structures before the learner is ready to pick up the structures can still be beneficial because the learner might be able to store these structures in her mind and recall them for active use when she has arrived at a stage where they can be processed.[10] In my case, learning, although not the same as acquisition, at least *facilitates* acquisition.

The Monitor Hypothesis: The Spotlight

Monitoring is like examining each word or structure in the grammar spotlight. Krashen argues that an L2 learner's monitor operates when time allows, when correctness matters, and when the learner knows the rules. It is easier to employ your monitor in writing than in spontaneous conversation because writing allows more time to focus on form. Therefore, when L2 writers focus on meaning, it is likely that their monitors are not fully operating; consequently, they often forget about inflections (e.g., -s or -ed endings) when they talk or write in a hurry or even when they are too relaxed, not paying enough attention to the inflections. In other words—and this is an important point for tutors to remember—it appears to be difficult to have fluency and accuracy at the same time. Because monitoring is like editing, an appropriate amount of monitoring is necessary to achieve accuracy. However, overmonitoring may cause writer's block, which is something many ESL students have experienced in the process of writing when they worry too much about grammatical accuracy.

The Natural Order Hypothesis: Similar Order in L1 and L2 Acquisition

Krashen's *natural order hypothesis* states that both L1 and L2 learners follow a similar order in acquiring certain morphemes (grammatical structures such as *-ing*, *-s*, or articles) and make similar mistakes in the developmental processes. For example, at a stage of their language development, some young children and adult L2 learners may overgeneralize (overuse) the past tense *-ed* and use *goed* for the past tense of *go*. Tutors need to be patient with morpheme errors such as missing the third personal singular (*-s*) and plural noun (*-s*) because they often add no meaning to communication and hence are very difficult for L2 writers to acquire.

The Comprehensible Input Hypothesis: Understanding Leads to Acquisition

The *comprehensible input hypothesis* predicts that for L2 learners to move from one stage to the next, they need to be exposed to L2 input (the new language) that is a little bit beyond their current level but easy enough to understand. The context sometimes helps the learner understand the new language.

For example, an L2 learner may understand the word *chilly* when someone is shivering and saying, "It's chilly today." Input can also become comprehensible to the learner when native speakers use so-called *foreigner talk,* which is characterized by a slower rate of speech, repetition, or paraphrasing. When tutoring, tutors may want to paraphrase certain difficult words or make use of gestures or contextual clues to increase comprehensibility.

The Affective Filter Hypothesis: Low Anxiety Is Conducive to Acquisition

The *affective filter* refers to the emotional state of the learner. To put it simply, when the L2 learner's anxiety, or filter level, is high, then it is difficult for her to acquire the new language. On the other hand, when the learner is motivated and confident—the filter level is low—she acquires the new language more easily. An encouraging and relaxing atmosphere may lower the learner's affective filter, creating conditions conducive to language learning. Thus, recognizing the L2 writer's strengths and complimenting her on them is one way a tutor can make the student feel confident in her writing ability.

So far, we have examined two views of how people learn a second language—behaviorist and innatist. We will now turn to another view: the cognitivist view.

Cognitivist—Noticing Is Important

SLA scholars have also been influenced by cognitive psychology in explaining how people learn a second language. From this perspective, language learning is similar to learning other skills, and it involves these steps:

noticing → practicing → making the skill automatic

Noticing is an indispensable first step.[11] Learning an odd spelling of a word usually begins with noticing it when it appears in print, for example. To help the learner notice a word or phrase, a tutor may highlight it by pointing to it, saying it with a rising intonation or underlining it. The learner may attempt to correct his own error when he notices the tutor's highlighting. If not, the tutor may give more help, such as grammatical commentary, to enhance noticing.

When learning a second language, learners move from *controlled processing* (paying attention) to *repeated activation* (practicing) to *automatization* (being available whenever called on). To attain fluency, the learner needs to make sure that many component, or supporting, skills are automatized.[12] Like a driver who does not need to consciously recall all the component skills, such as when to turn the wheel or use the accelerator, a language learner can be fluent only when she does not need to think about component skills such as subject–verb agreement and word order before she speaks.

During the learning process, the learner's new language system may be restructured due to the increased knowledge. When this occurs, the learner may make impressive progress at some times and backslide at other times. For example, a student who has used the word *came* correctly for several months may backslide to write *comed* after learning how to use the past tense *-ed* form before finally returning to the correct use of *came* with a new understanding. When this happens, backsliding is actually a sign of the learner's language development. It may be the reason why a student begins making mistakes that he does not usually make.

When a controlled sequence becomes automatized, it is difficult to modify. This helps explain the concept of *fossilization*, a condition when learners stop making any visible progress or when their L2 errors persist, no matter how many classes they attend.[13] Based on McLaughlin's model, fossilization occurs when the learner's language becomes automatized before it is nativelike.[14] To prevent fossilization, some researchers say that error correction and grammar instruction are necessary,[15] but other researchers question the value of error correction because findings on its effectiveness have been inconsistent.[16]

Tutors may wonder if error correction really works because L2 writers often seem to repeat the same errors even after correction. As an L2 learner, I feel it is important to remember that the process of moving from noticing to repeated activation to automatization takes time. The cognitive process is often hidden, and the effect is not immediate. For instance, I used to write "to emphasize on . . . ," without any awareness of the wrong usage until a professor crossed out the *on* in my writing. This explicit error correction enhanced my *noticing* of the correct usage. A few days later as I was editing a paper, I noticed that I had written "to emphasize on . . . ." Later, as I was writing an email, I noticed that I was typing "emphasize on" once more, and I deleted the *on* immediately. Though I had been corrected once, I repeated the same error twice. However, I was aware of the error after I made it the second time. My self-correction happened sooner after I made the same mistake each time. Based on the recent cognitive-psychological views of language learning, I would say that I started restructuring my interlanguage (developing language), but my production of the correct form had not yet become automatized. Through repeated activation—that is, repeatedly using the word and self-correcting the error—the correct form gradually became stabilized. Now, every time I use the word *emphasize*, I feel as if there were a spotlight shining on it, and I always use it correctly.

Looking back, I am sure I had seen or heard the word *emphasize* used correctly countless times in context, but I did not pick up the correct form. Why? The answer may be that *focus*, one of its synonyms, is followed by *on*. It was not until my professor corrected the error did I realize that there was a gap between my usage and the target form. It took me quite a while to produce the correct form automatically. If you have ever watched a duck swimming, you will notice that the duck does not move fast. Sometimes it even looks as though it were not moving at all. What you cannot see, however, are the duck's webbed feet paddling under the surface of the water. Likewise, what is happening in the L2 learner's mind is like the duck's webbed feet paddling in the water. It is not noticeable, but with time and practice the learner does make progress, and errors are less likely to become fossilized.

As you have probably observed already, one theory can never sufficiently explain the complexity involved in learning a second language. Each of the behaviorist, innatist, and cognitivist theories adds something that the others do not to our understanding of L2 learning. Yet there is one more important theory that forms a piece of the puzzle of L2 learning—the interactionist theory, to which we now turn.

Interactionist—It Helps to Talk with an Expert

Interactionist theorists state that acquiring a second language takes place mainly through interaction.[17] Although using easier vocabulary and grammatical forms in place of more sophisticated ones can improve comprehensibility, learners may miss out on opportunities to learn more advanced forms. But with interactional or conversational modification between learners and more proficient speakers—like tutors—the more advanced forms become easier to understand, and the learners' attention is drawn to them.[18]

Interestingly, when the L2 learner notices that the new language does not make sense to her or when her writing confuses a tutor, she might come to the realization that she needs to make some changes in the way she understands or uses the new language.[19] Tutors can facilitate this by using interactional tactics such as checking comprehension, requesting clarification, confirming meaning, self-repeating, and paraphrasing.[20] Here is an example of interactional modification between Hui, an ESL writer, and Dan, a tutor, as Hui is reading her draft:

Hui: (*Reading aloud*) To pass the college entrance exam, I had to study hardly.

Dan: You mean the college entrance exam was very easy? [clarification]

Hui: No, no. I read my book *hardly*. I studied ten hours every day. [clarification]

Dan: Are you saying you *studied a lot* in order to pass the college entrance exam? [elaboration, clarification/confirmation]

Hui: Yes, I studied very much. [modification]

Dan: Oh, OK, I see what you mean. [confirmation]

   You had to *study hard* in order to pass the college entrance exam. You see, *hardly* means "almost never." [clarification]

Hui: Then, I studied *hard* to pass the exam. [modification]

Essentially, interactional modifications give learners opportunities to pay attention to potentially troublesome parts of their L2 production. Through clarification and modification of the message, L2 learners have a chance to not only hear the words or grammatical structures that they wish to know but also notice the features in their new language that need to be corrected or modified.

Another perspective on the role of interaction in SLA is Lev Vygotsky's social cultural theory of cognitive development.[21] Vygotsky's work may be familiar to tutors who are education majors. Vygotsky's theory usually refers to the ways children learn, but it has been applied to adults' second language acquisition.[22] In this view, L2 learning takes place while the learner interacts with an expert (a tutor or teacher). Such interaction is helpful when it is appropriate to the learner's current and potential level of development, or what Vygotsky called the learner's *zone of proximal development* (ZPD).[23] To determine a student's ZPD, the tutor can talk with the student and find out precisely what he is able to do without help and what he can accomplish with assistance. The example below shows how a tutor, Michelle, applies the concept of ZPD in assisting an ESL student, Reiko, who brought a draft of her research paper to the writing center:

Michelle: Tell me what you found out in your research. [detecting what the learner can say without help]

Reiko: I found out that the earth is getting hot every year.

Michelle: The earth is getting . . . ? [detecting if the learner can do self-correction]

Reiko: The earth is getting warmer every year. [successful self-correction]

Michelle: And scientists call that . . . ? [detecting what the learner can say without help]

Reiko: Greenroom effect.

Michelle: Green*room* effect? [detecting if the learner can do self-correction]

Reiko: Yes. [confirmation]

Michelle: You mean the green*house* effect. [providing help when the learner was not able to do self-correction]

Reiko: Yes, yes, the green*house* effect. [reformulation]

In the example, Michelle figured out what Reiko was able to do with and without assistance. Michelle provided help, a word choice correction, for Reiko because word choice problems are often difficult for L2 writers to self-correct. As a result, Reiko improved her English when she talked with Michelle. This is also a good example of how the talk that occurs in tutoring sessions can be just as important as the writing.

Conclusion

This chapter has summarized four of the major theories on how L2 learners process second languages in their minds as they learn. It is clear that understanding how ESL learners learn English is not a simple matter. The four major theories may help answer some puzzling questions as raised in the beginning of this chapter.

The behaviorist view of L2 learning explains that L2 learners' unconventional word order and word choice may be attributed to their L1 influence or lack of experience in hearing and using English in their daily lives. Different languages imply different habits. Therefore, prepositions, articles, and idiomatic expressions are particularly difficult areas for learners whose L1 is very different from English.

Based on the theories proposed by innatists, we learn that L2 learners, especially international students, do not have the native English speaker's intuition for what sounds right or wrong in English. Therefore, when L2 learners do not know the grammar rules or their hypotheses of how English works are false, they will not be able to detect their errors no matter how many times they read their writing aloud, which is also a reason why their errors persist.

Some L2 learners' errors seem resistant to correction. From the perspective of cognitivists, it is possible that (1) the wrong usages have become fossilized or (2) if not, the cognitive change (in restructuring the interlanguage) is taking place but is unobservable, or the effect has not yet appeared. Furthermore, backsliding, insufficient monitoring, and stress also bear on the persistence of errors. Tutors should remember that L2 learning never proceeds in a linear, smooth manner. Learners may backslide and use a wrong form due to their overuse of a new grammar rule. According to the monitor model, L2 learners may also forget to follow certain grammar rules when they are not fully monitoring or when they are under stress.

To make English learning easier for L2 writers, tutors might aim for the following in their interaction with the L2 writers:

- Recognize learners' strengths.
- Provide a friendly and encouraging ambiance in the writing center.
- Draw learners' attention to the target structure they need to learn.
- Have conversations with learners to figure out what they can do with or without assistance.
- Provide appropriate help at the right time.

In this chapter, I have shared with you some major theories of SLA and illustrated them with some of my personal experiences and those of other L2 learners. After all, you have probably learned an important lesson: Learning a second language is hard work, and it takes a long time.

With an understanding of the theories and challenges that L2 learners face, you may become more empathetic and better prepared to tutor L2 writers.

Recommendation: The discipline of SLA is fast growing and fascinating. Interested readers may find more information about SLA in publications by, for example, Rod Ellis, Rosamond Mitchell and Florence Myles, and Patsy Lightbown and Nina Spada.

Notes

1. Rod Ellis (1994) indicates that a thorough approach to second language acquisition (SLA) covers (1) the black box (learner language processing mechanisms in the mind), (2) individual learner factors (e.g., age, sex, motivation), and (3) environmental factors (e.g., social settings). All three aspects interact. Some aspects are more controversial than others. For example, not all researchers agree that individual learner factors have a direct impact on language processing. Due to space limits, this chapter discusses only some major theories of the first of these approaches, the black box. To explain learner language processing mechanisms, I follow Patsy Lightbown and Nina Spada's categorization of theoretical approaches to explaining second language learning. See Lightbown and Spada (1999, 35–45).

2. The CAH is usually attributed to Robert Lado's work in 1957. See Lado, 2.

3. Chomsky, 32.

4. Buell.

5. Corder, 167.

6. Krashen, 26–27.

7. Krashen, personal communication, March 17, 2002.

8. Reid, 3–17.

9. Krashen, personal communication, March 17, 2002.

10. Pienemann, 72.

11. Schmidt, 129–158.

12. McLaughlin, 133–34.

13. Michael Long (2003) believes that *stabilization* is a more appropriate term for what has commonly been called as *fossilization* in interlanguage development.

14. Mitchell and Myles, 86.

15. Higgs and Clifford, 57–80.

16. Truscott (1996).

17. Long and Robinson (1998).

18. Long and Robinson, 22.

19. Gass, Mackey, and Pica, 301.

20. Michael Long indicates that native speakers constantly modify their language when they talk with nonnative speakers. See Long (1983).
21. Vygotsky (1987), 21.
22. See, for example, Ohta, 54.
23. Vygotsky (1978), 84–91.

Works Cited

Buell, M. 2002. "I Know It's Wrong, but I Can't Show Why: Addressing Articles in Writing." In Panel: *Alternative Discourses, Alternative Languages: Taking Language Issues Seriously*. CCCC, Chicago, Illinois, March 22, 2002.

Chomsky, N. 1965. *Aspects of the Theory of Syntax*. Cambridge, MA: MIT Press.

Corder, S. P. 1967. "The Significance of Learners' Errors." *International Review of Applied Linguistics* 4: 161–70.

Ellis, R. 1994. *The Study of Second Language Acquisition*. Oxford: Oxford University Press.

Gass, S. M., A. Mackey, and T. Pica. 1998. "The Role of Input and Interaction in Second Language Acquisition." *The Modern Language Journal* 82(3): 299–305.

Higgs, T., and R. Clifford. 1982. "The Push Toward Communication." In *Curriculum, Competence, and the Foreign Language Teacher*, edited by Theodore V. Higgs, 57–80. Skokie, IL: National Textbook Company.

Krashen, S. 1983. *The Natural Approach*. Hayward, CA: Alemany Press.

Lado, R. 1957. *Linguistics Across Cultures: Applied Linguistics for Language Teachers*. Ann Arbor: University of Michigan Press.

Lightbown, P., and N. Spada. 1999. *How Languages Are Learned*. Oxford: Oxford University Press.

Long, M. H. 1983. "Native Speaker/Non-Native Speaker Conversation and the Negotiation of Comprehensible Input." *Applied Linguistics* 4: 126–41.

———. 2003. "Stabilization and Fossilization in Interlanguage Development." In *The Handbook of Second Language Acquisition*, edited by C. Doughty and M. H. Long, 487–535. Oxford: Blackwell.

Long, M. H., and P. Robinson. 1998. "Focus on Form: Theory, Research, and Practice." In *Focus on Form in Classroom Second Language Acquisition*, edited by C. Doughty and J. Williams, 15–41. Cambridge: Cambridge University Press.

McLaughlin, B. 1987. *Theories of Second Language Learning*. London: Edward Arnold.

Mitchell, R., and F. Myles. 1998. *Second Language Learning Theories*. New York: Oxford University Press.

Ohta, A. S. 2000. "Rethinking Interaction in SLA: Developmentally Appropriate Assistance in the Zone of Proximal Development and the Acquisition of L2 Grammar." In *Sociocultural Theory and Second Language Learning*, edited by James P. Lantolf, 51–78. Oxford: Oxford University Press.

Pienemann, M. 1989. "Is Language Teachable? Psycholinguistic Experiments and Hypotheses." *Applied Linguistics* 1: 52–79.

Reid, J. 1998. "'Eye' Learners and 'Ear' Learners: Identifying the Language Needs of International Students and U.S. Resident Writers." In *Grammar in the Composition Classroom*, edited by J. Reid and P. Byrd, 3–17. Boston: Heinle and Heinle.

Schmidt, R. 1990. "The Role of Consciousness in Second Language Learning." *Applied Linguistics* 11: 129–58.

Truscott, J. 1996. "The Case Against Grammar Correction in L2 Writing Classes." *Language Learning* 46(2): 327–69.

Vygotsky, L. S. 1978. *Mind in Society*. Cambridge, MA: Harvard University Press.

—————. 1987. *The Collected Works of L. S. Vygotsky. Volume 1. Thinking and Speaking*. New York: Plenum Press.

3

Breaking Ice and Setting Goals
Tips for Getting Started

Shanti Bruce

When most students enter one-to-one tutoring situations for the first time, they expect tutors to manage introductions and dictate the way their sessions will go. While tutees often behave like guests and need to be introduced to the writing center and the conferencing process on their first visit, on subsequent visits they may continue to take their cues from tutors. Even when students become familiar with the conferencing process, they may be shy about starting or wait for the tutor to begin out of respect. For all of these reasons, tutors who know how to take the first step, to bring the writer into the conference by offering a friendly greeting and finding a comfortable place to meet, will put students at ease by showing them that they are a welcome part of this peer tutoring duo. This is true for U.S. students and even more so for international ones.

Getting started is often the hardest part of any task or assignment, and it is especially so for English as a second language (ESL) students. The reasons for this are varied, but for many students they include feeling intimidated, fearing being judged, worrying about taking risks, or being unfamiliar with the assignment. These reasons account for many of the students who put off going to the writing center. Aside from procrastination, some students are just not convinced that a visit to the writing center will be worthwhile. Some may also feel that a tutoring conference will be uncomfortable and even scary. They may be afraid to take that first step of walking into the writing center—an unfamiliar place where it is hard to blend into the background and remain anonymous. Just by walking in the door, students are admitting to themselves and everyone there that they need help.

Sami, an ESL student from Saudi Arabia, is a prime example of this conundrum: He needs the help the writing center offers, but he is uncomfortable admitting it. (I discuss my meeting with Sami in Chapter 18.) He revealed that asking for help is actually a cultural taboo for many Arab male students. He explained how the writing center made him uneasy because it was a public place where other students could see that he needed help. For Sami, working with someone privately was the only answer because he feared the shame of being perceived as weak by others.

In general, international students have had little experience with writing centers. For them, the concept of shared responsibility for writing is often alien. In Chapter 15, Gerd Bräuer says that most ESL students have no idea what a writing center is or how it functions, and because of that, many of them end up avoiding writing centers altogether.

Aware of the uncertainty many ESL students feel about coming to the writing center, tutors have a special obligation to help reduce this anxiety. But how do they do this? One way is to take a few minutes at the beginning of each session to make a plan: to set goals for the conference and discuss ways to accomplish those goals. It is important to note that planning, prioritizing, goal setting, and sticking to a schedule are all markedly Western in nature. The U.S. writing center has in many ways become a microcosm of U.S. society, an artifact of the culture, where values such as education for everyone, punctuality, taking turns, and staying on schedule are enacted every day.

Making a plan is not just helpful for the student, but it can make the tutor's job easier as well. It creates a shared responsibility for how the session will unfold, and it reduces uncertainty about what to do next. When the tutor and student make the plan together, the responsibility for the session is shared, and the tutor doesn't have to worry that she is entirely liable for its outcome. "The student's contributions in these opening minutes," Thomas Newkirk explains, "need to be used to give the conference a mutually agreeable and mutually understood direction."[1] By collaboratively setting goals and creating a visual representation of them at the beginning of a session, the expectations for the conference will be clear and shared.

Tika, an ESL student from Indonesia, shared her first writing center experience with me. In her account, she expresses many of the common fears students have about entering a writing conference, and her statement reminds us of how important it is to make an effort to put students at ease when they visit the writing center.

> I was ready to go there, but I hesitated because there was an afraid feeling inside me. I was so nervous, tense, uneasy—it was a mixed feeling. But then, I would like to experience this new thing because universities in Indonesia don't have this service.
>
> When I was approaching the door, I could hear my heart beating so fast. I didn't know what to expect, and there were so many questions in my mind: "What should I tell them when they ask me about my writing? Can I understand when they speak?" I found that most Americans speak very fast like a Concorde jet! That makes me more nervous. "Are they patient people? Would they understand when I speak?" I tend to beat around the bush rather

than get to the point. That is definitely a cultural matter! "What if they find that my writing was really bad, would they laugh at it or get angry at me?" In my country, it's embarrassing to make mistakes.

Having lots of questions made me uneasy.

When the tutor called my name, I was just like, "This is it. Whatever will be will be!" I was trying to comfort myself.

The tutor greeted me and complimented my jacket. We had a very short conversation. Was it an ice-breaker? After that, I found myself totally involved with the conference—no worries anymore.

Tika candidly recounted her feelings as she approached her first tutoring session. While some students want to avoid the writing center, many native English-speaking (NES) students and ESL students are similar to Tika in that they look forward to getting help at the writing center but are unsure of how things will go. Days of stress and apprehension were eased as the tutor casually greeted Tika and began a conversation by offering a positive comment, in this case a compliment on an article of clothing. Showing interest in the student can ease a tense situation and make her feel welcome.

Once introductions have been made and pleasantries exchanged, it is time to focus on the work of the tutoring session. To do that, you need to make a plan. Many tutors skip this step, thinking they can just plunge right in because tutoring sessions have become so routine for them, because they think they know what is best, or because they think it will save time to skip that first step. Tutors may also fear the rigidity of outlining the way the session will go. But this is a mistake. Making a plan will give the conference direction while allowing the tutor to bond with the tutee right from the beginning by deciding and sharing a common goal. Also, organization does not preclude flexibility, and it actually saves time.

Make a Plan

Why Is This Important?

If you don't take the time to get organized and set goals, you might not use your time together effectively. "It might seem a little odd to make a plan for how you will spend the next thirty minutes together," says William Macauley, Jr., "But there's a worse problem: looking back at the past half hour and realizing you went practically nowhere with your tutoring session because you never really thought about where you wanted to end up."[2]

Because not all cultures prefer the Westernized manner of getting right down to business, an explanation of the time allotted for the session may help the student see the need for an organized plan. Students usually come to the writing center with specific requests in mind, and it is best to give them a chance to discuss what they perceive are their most pressing needs at the beginning. That way, you will both be sure to consider them when planning the session.

NES and ESL students regularly come to the writing center wanting tutors to check their papers for grammar errors. While many of these students are unfamiliar with writing terminology and simply do not know how to ask for help with anything else, we can't always dismiss this request in favor of what we may consider the higher-order concerns to be.[3] For many ESL students, grammar may in fact be a higher-order concern. For example, almost all Asian students have problems with personal pronouns and articles, and Chinese students in particular have difficulty with verb tenses and verb endings because these are not features of their native languages. Offering suggestions for alternatives to focusing on grammar is beneficial, but we also need to trust our students and be willing to explore grammar concerns with them. (See Chapter 7 for a discussion of grammar vs. higher-order concerns.

When asking for help with grammar, NES and ESL students tend to mean different things. NES students typically want assistance with editing and correctness, whereas ESL students, who are often very knowledgeable about the language and its grammar rules, generally want to make sure they are saying things the way NES students would. Many ESL students have difficulty with collocations and receive comments from professors indicating that their phrasing "just isn't right." When these variations confuse their intended meanings, these seemingly lower-order concerns actually rise to utmost importance.[4] However, along with Ben Rafoth in Chapter 12, I caution tutors not to attempt to fix every phrase just because it sounds different. Sometimes, these variations can be refreshing, if not poignant, and leaving them intact goes a long way toward preserving the student's voice. For example, Jung-jun, an ESL student from Korea, explained to me what it felt like when she found out that her writing center tutor was going to be a person who was also in one of her classes. She said she felt bad because they were in the same class, and she needed help and he didn't. When she realized that, she said, "I feel . . . I shrink." Her phrasing was at once unusual and moving. (I discuss my meeting with Jung-jun in Chapter 18.)

If you do decide together that looking at grammar is the goal, or one of the goals of the session, keep in mind that even checking grammar requires a plan. If you skip this step and plunge right in thinking you can just tackle errors as they come, you will quickly get bogged down. Some of the paper may get edited, but it is unlikely that students will leave with any new understanding of grammar rules or editing techniques they can do on their own. Taking the time to read a bit of the paper and decide which errors are most important and persistent is a more organized and productive approach. Cynthia Linville offers strategies for helping ESL students become proficient self-editors in Chapter 10. But remember, editing an entire paper in one session is typically not a writing center's mission and more often than not will produce a better piece of writing instead of a better writer.[5] Some ESL students can become consumed by wanting to get their papers *fixed* and lose sight of the big picture; in other words, a tutoring session isn't just about one particular paper; it's about learning expectations for writing in English and learning how to prioritize issues.

Tutors can help ESL students understand how to navigate the English language and the cultural and educational expectations that go along with it. It may be necessary to explain that setting goals for the session will benefit their writing in the long run. But believing that a plan is good is one thing, making the plan is another.

How Do I Do This?

To make an effective plan, first ask the writer a few questions about her work and her expectations for the session. Using the writer's responses, set the goals for the session collaboratively, sketch a map or list that will illustrate those goals, and finally, be ready to change the plan as the need arises.

Find Out What the Student Knows About the Center

One of the first questions to ask is whether the student is familiar with the writing center. If not, take the time to explain the peer tutor format, the goal-setting process, and any other techniques that could be used, such as reading the draft aloud (see Chapter 4) or serving as a scribe while clarifying meanings (see Chapter 7). Explaining how the writing center and the tutoring conference typically operate can go a long way toward easing a student's anxiety. In Chapter 15, Gerd Bräuer discusses the rarity of writing centers abroad and how new the concept is for most ESL writers.

Ask About the Student's Piece of Writing

Regarded as one of the masters of the tutoring conference, Donald Murray suggests asking "questions which draw helpful comments out of the student writer" such as

- "What did you learn from this piece of writing?"
- "What do you intend to do in the next draft?"
- "What do you like best in the piece of writing?"
- "What questions do you have of me?"[6]

ESL students may never have been asked questions like these about a piece of writing, so be patient if the answers don't come easily. Asking open-ended questions will help you learn more about the writer as well as the assignment and the draft so far. Maintaining a dialogue will also reinforce the writer's responsibility in the conference.

If Necessary, Ask More Direct Questions

If you have not gotten enough specific information, you may need to ask more direct questions. Paula Gillespie and Neal Lerner offer three basic questions that will get right to the point:

- "What was the assignment?"
- "What is your central point or main argument?"
- "What concerns you, or what do you want me to pay careful attention to?"[7]

The first question will familiarize you with the student's task, and the second will give you insight into how the student has approached the task. The second question skillfully avoids using the term *thesis*, which could be troubling for some students. The last question brings us to the next step in the process: setting the goals for the session. Let the writer know that his input is important. Remember, the best kind of plan is the one that tutor and tutee devise together. However, tutors should be prepared for ESL students who are uncomfortable or unwilling to take an active role because they see the tutor as the authority. These students may insist on repeatedly asking a tutor what she thinks and might leave the tutoring session feeling it was a waste of time if the tutor refuses to do or say anything directive. In these cases, the tutor can take the lead, and with multiple visits, these students will likely become accustomed to actively participating in writing center tutorials. (See Chapter 7 for a discussion of the difference between being *direct* and being *directive*.)

Set Goals Together

If the student only wants an editing session and you feel that she would benefit from spending time on global items, you could acknowledge the student's request and add a request of your own. Your ideas are valuable to the student and to the success of the session. You could say, "Okay, we will address one or two grammar issues, but if I see any unclear meanings, we will take a look at them as well." Collaboration fosters a dialogue that will help develop trust between tutor and tutee while preserving the student's ownership of the piece and responsibility in the session. "When the map is negotiated," says Macauley, the session is planned "without either dominating."[8]

The number of goals for each session will vary. There is no set formula for determining how many items you will have time to address. With practice, you will become more accurate at gauging the amount of time certain goals take. If global writing concerns are on the agenda, tackling one or two goals will probably be all you can expect to cover. If issues of mechanics are to be the focus, you may have time to cover two, three, or even four goals. Sometimes it is okay to overplan because it will remind the student of items that still need attention after the conference ends.

Make the Plan Visible

Once you have both become stakeholders in the conference by agreeing on a set of goals, it is time to make the plan visible. Methods such as listing, clustering, and formal and informal outlining are familiar to ESL students, but there are also ways to be creative in visually representing the goals for the session. Creative representations aid visual learners, and for ESL students, where language fails, visuals can fill in. Sociolinguistics professor Nancy Hayward shared an anecdote with me about a graduate ESL student who was having trouble grasping the concept of an overarching idea. She said she finally turned the student's paper over and drew a picture of an umbrella. She wrote the broad idea across the umbrella and then filled in all of the different components that made up the idea underneath. She said the student caught on immediately.[9]

Visual representations of plans for tutoring sessions can take many forms. Play with different ideas and see which ones work for you and the students you meet. Keep in mind that it may not be possible to fill in the specific grammar, punctuation, or formatting goals for the session until you read some of the student's paper. The student may be unaware of these issues and therefore unable to tell you about them at the beginning of the session.

Once you have an idea of what type of visual aid will work best for the goals you have established, even if it is just a list, sketch an outline of it on a piece of paper so that it remains visible throughout the conference. Explain the sketch to the student and how it represents the goals for the conference. Involve him in the process by inviting him to help fill in the sketch with the goals.

Points to Remember

- *Let the plan guide you but remember to remain flexible.* While making a plan is important, writing and conferencing are, without a doubt, unpredictable processes. "A tutoring session," Donald McAndrew and Thomas Reigstad explain, "shows emergent adaptation as the session is negotiated and defined through the conversation of tutor and writer."[10] Refer to your map, but don't be afraid to revise it: Add to it, scratch out items, arrow in new items, circle or highlight items that emerge as the most important, and star items that you probably won't get to cover so that the student will remember to address these issues on her own. (In Chapter 18, Zahara and Jane discuss taking notes so that they can remember to address issues on their own after a conference.)

- *It will be easy to assess what you have accomplished during the conference by referring to the map as the session concludes.* You can go over it together and check off the items you have completed, or if you checked them off along the way, you can enjoy reviewing how much you covered during the session. Even if you only got to a couple of items, it will be pleasing to know that one or two of the goals you set were covered completely. Of course, it is important to note that the pleasure of checking off items on the to-do list is Western in nature. "We are a doing society rather than a being society," Hayward asserts, "We are judged and we judge people on their accomplishments."[11]

- *If you haven't done so already, explain to the student that the value of the map extends far beyond this single tutoring session.* It will serve as a guide when he revises the paper on his own, and it could give him ideas for outlining and goal setting for his next assignment. It will help tutors as well when it comes to filling out faculty reports or writing center logs on student conferences. Going over the map at the end of the session will provide a visual representation of what has been accomplished and will bring closure to the conference while providing the student with direction for the revisions he will now make on his own.

Most important, remember that when you tutor ESL students you are dealing with much more than main ideas and verb endings. You are helping to further introduce a student to U.S. cultural and educational expectations.

Notes

1. Newkirk, 313.
2. Macauley, 1.
3. McAndrew and Reigstad, 42.
4. McAndrew and Reigstad, 56.
5. North, 438.
6. Murray, 68.
7. Gillespie and Lerner, 29–30.
8. Macauley, 3.
9. Hayward, personal communication, December 11, 2003.
10. McAndrew and Reigstad, 28.
11. Hayward, personal communication, December 11, 2003.

Works Cited

Gillespie, Paula, and Neal Lerner. 2008. *The Longman Guide to Peer Tutoring*. New York: Pearson.

Macauley, William J., Jr. 2005. "Setting the Agenda for the Next Thirty Minutes." In *A Tutor's Guide: Helping Writers One to One*. 2nd ed. Edited by Ben Rafoth, 1–8. Portsmouth, NH: Boynton/Cook.

McAndrew, Donald A., and Thomas J. Reigstad. 2001. *Tutoring Writing: A Practical Guide for Conferences*. Portsmouth, NH: Boynton/Cook.

Murray, Donald M. 2000. "The Listening Eye: Reflections on the Writing Conference." In *The Writing Teacher's Sourcebook*. 4th ed. Edited by Edward P. J. Corbett, Nancy Myers, and Gary Tate, 66–71. New York: Oxford University Press.

Newkirk, Thomas. 2008. "The First Five Minutes: Setting the Agenda in a Writing Conference." In *The Longman Guide to Writing Center Theory and Practice*, edited by Robert W. Barnett and Jacob S. Blumner, 302–15. New York: Pearson.

North, Stephen. 1984. "The Idea of a Writing Center." *College English* 46: 433–46.

4

Reading an ESL Writer's Text

Paul Kei Matsuda and Michelle Cox

In this chapter, we discuss the part of a writing center conference that is at the center of the conferencing process—the reading of the writer's draft. Although the process of reading may be the least visible part of the conference, it is one of the most important because it is during this process that tutors begin to formulate their initial responses to the text. In many cases, reading texts written by English as a second language (ESL) writers—whether they be resident or international students—is not radically different from reading those written by native English-speaking (NES) writers; tutors can use many of the same principles and strategies they use in reading NES texts. Yet, because ESL writers often come from different linguistic, cultural, and educational backgrounds, some aspects of ESL writers' texts may stand out, especially to the eyes of native English speakers who do not have extensive background in working with ESL writers.

Some of the initial reactions to ESL writers' texts may be quite positive. Inexperienced readers of ESL texts may be fascinated by details about the ESL writer's native language, culture, country, or stories of how they or their family came to the United States. Some may be intrigued by the extensive use of metaphors and figurative language in some ESL writers' texts. Others may be amazed by how much the writers have accomplished with a language they did not grow up with. Yet others may note the richness of ESL writer's texts that come from their hybridity and alternativeness.[1] Unfortunately, not all encounters with ESL texts produce such generous responses. Readers with little or no experience in working with ESL writers may be drawn to surface-level errors and differences that they see as problematic.

Readers may find differences between NES and ESL writers' texts at various levels—from word formation to sentence structure to organization. The texts may contain many errors, such as missing articles, "wrong" prepositions and verb endings, and unusual sentence structures that "just don't sound right." The word choices may seem odd, or the use of idiomatic phrases may seem inappropriate. The organization of the text may not resemble what NES readers might expect. The thesis statement may be missing or located in places where the reader does not expect to find it, such as near the end of the paper. In a persuasive writing assignment, the writer's stance may not be clear. For a research paper assignment, the writer may have written a paper filled with allusive references without citing the sources. While these generalized statements may sound familiar to those who are used to working with inexperienced NES writers, the specific ways in which these differences appear in ESL writers' texts often differ from those written by NES writers.

Because of these and other differences, ESL writing is sometimes seen as "deficient," especially when it is evaluated in comparison with texts produced by NES writers. In "Toward an Understanding of the Distinct Nature of L2 Writing," Tony Silva synthesized research studies comparing ESL and NES writers and writing. The picture of ESL writers and their texts that emerged from the synthesis was overwhelmingly negative: Second language (L2) writing is "simpler and less effective (in the eyes of L1 [first language] readers) than L1 writing"; composing in an L2 is "more constrained, more difficult, and less effective"; "L2 writers' texts are less fluent (fewer words), less accurate (more errors), and less effective (lower holistic scores)."[2] As Silva points out, however, it may be unreasonable to use the same criteria to evaluate ESL texts and NES texts. Based on the findings of his review, Silva suggests the need to ask questions such as: "When does different become incorrect or inappropriate? and What is good enough?"[3]

It is important to realize that differences are not necessarily signs of deficiency. In fact, some of the differences may reflect the writer's advanced knowledge of conventions in other languages or in specific English discourse communities including disciplines with which the tutor may not be familiar. Yet, readers may find the differences distracting when, for example, the text contains certain kinds of errors or too many errors, or when the text is organized in ways that do not match a reader's understanding of the particular genre or other conventions. In some cases, tutors may be drawn to those differences so strongly that they feel lost or frustrated; they may even feel unqualified to work with ESL writers. The initial fear that some tutors have in working with ESL writers is not insurmountable. Becoming familiar with some of the characteristics of ESL texts and their sources can help tutors work with ESL writers with more confidence, read beyond the differences, and recognize the strengths of those texts more easily.

Understanding ESL Writers' Texts

ESL writers and their texts vary widely from individual to individual and from situation to situation, and overgeneralization should be avoided. Still, it is useful to understand some of the general characteristics of many ESL writers and their texts as well as various sources of influence. One of the important factors is the ESL writer's L2 proficiency. Many ESL writers are still in the process of developing the intuitive understanding of the English language—its structure and use—and for that reason, they may not be able to produce grammatical sentences as easily as NES writers can. As pointed out in the Conference on College Composition and Communication (CCCC) Statement on Second-Language Writing and Writers, "the acquisition of a second language and second-language literacy is a time-consuming process that will continue through students' academic careers and beyond. . . . Furthermore, most second-language writers are still in the process of acquiring syntactic and lexical competence—a process that will take a lifetime."[4] Because ESL writers often have not internalized some of the rules of grammar, they are often not able to identify errors on their own by, for example, reading the text aloud, a common writing center practice that works well with many NES writers.

Although language proficiency affects the overall quality of ESL texts, the relationship between language proficiency and writing proficiency is not simple; the ability to speak English does not necessarily correspond directly with the quality of texts they produce.[5] Even ESL writers who do not seem to be able to communicate their thoughts in spoken English may be able to write prose that puts many NES writers to shame. This is the case with some international students who have learned English mostly through the medium of writing. Other students are more fluent in spoken English—they may be familiar with a wide variety of colloquial and idiomatic expressions—but they may still produce texts that do not seem to reflect the high level of their spoken fluency. This is typical of so-called Generation 1.5 writers—ESL students who have lived in an English-dominant society for a number of years and acquired English primarily through spoken interactions. Needless to say, these are extreme cases; most ESL writers fall somewhere in-between.[6]

ESL writers' texts are also shaped in part by their prior experiences with literacy. Although some ESL writers may have received extensive instruction in writing, others have been schooled in educational systems that did not focus on composition. Some ESL writers are highly experienced—even published—writers in other languages; others have not received instruction in writing beyond the sentence level. Some ESL writers may even be native speakers of a language that does not have a written form. Research on contrastive rhetoric suggests that writers' linguistic, cultural, and educational backgrounds may influence texts in various ways as "the nature and functions of discourse, audience, and persuasive appeals often differ across linguistic, cultural and educational contexts."[7]

It is important to remember that these generalizations do not apply to all ESL students and that not all differences can be attributed to differences in ESL writers' native language or cultural background. The lack of organization in some ESL texts, as Bernard Mohan and Winnie Au-Yeung Lo have pointed out, may be a result of the overemphasis on grammar in some educational systems.[8] International students, who learn English as a foreign language while in their native country, may have been taught how to compose English sentences but not necessarily entire compositions. As Carol Severino points out in "The 'Doodles' in Context," "organization is often the last feature to be taught and learned in both first- and second-language writing, if it is taught at all."[9] Experience with composing grammatical sentences, however, does not lead directly to the ability to compose full compositions.

Ways of Reading Difference

In "The Sociopolitical Implications of Response to Second Language and Second Dialect Writing," Carol Severino draws on Min-Zhan Lu's framework in describing three stances that readers can take when responding to ESL texts: *assimilationist*, *accommodationist*, and *separatist*. When readers take an assimilationist stance, their goal is to help the ESL writer "write linear, thesis-statement and topic-sentence-driven, error-free, and idiomatic English as soon as possible,"[10] encouraging the writer and her text to assimilate into the dominant culture. The assimilationist, then, reads differences as deficiencies— errors to be corrected.

Readers who take an accommodationist stance may also try to teach the NES norm, but their goal is different from that of the assimilationist. The accommodationist reader's goal is to help the writer learn new discourse patterns without completely losing the old so that the writer can maintain both his L1 and L2 linguistic and cultural identities. The accommodationist, then, reads differences as, well, differences, explaining to the writer how some differences may be seen as deficiencies by some readers; it is up to the writer "how much like a native speaker" she wants to sound.[11]

When readers take a separatist stance, their goal is further away from the assimilationist goal of teaching ESL writers to write like NES writers. The separatist reader's goal is to support the writer in maintaining separate linguistic and cultural identities and to advocate for NES readers to read ESL texts "generously" with more appreciation for multicultural writing. The separatist, then, reads to overlook and therefore preserve difference.

The stances come down to ways of reading difference and whether tutors should read to "correct" difference, explain difference, or overlook difference. Severino provides three scenarios showing how she, when conferencing in the writing center, shifted between stances in relation to the writers' goals and situations. When working with Takaro, a resident ESL student, Severino took an accommodationist approach, focusing first on what Takaro was communicating through the writing, explaining how rhetorical choices are related to situation and audience. When working with Michael, a speaker of a nondominant variety of English, Severino took a separatist approach during the first few sessions—focusing on what Michael was communicating, and encouraging confidence in writing—and then moved toward an accommodationist approach later, to help Michael see how various audiences would read his writing.

In each case, Severino steered clear of the assimilationist stance. She had felt tempted to take this stance after first reading Michael's writing because she felt "stunned" by the number of errors in the text. However, she resisted the urge in order to remain consistent with the writing center pedagogy. Instead, she "responded to his piece as an act of communication, which it was, rather than as a demonstration of how well Michael knew and/or could apply the rules."[12]

Inexperienced readers of ESL texts tend to lean toward the assimilationist approach out of their desire to help ESL writers. In doing so, however, they inadvertently read difference as deficiency. As readers makes the effort to move away from the deficiency model, however, they become more open to understanding their own responses to ESL writing and to learning from the writer. Today, many second language writing specialists advocate for a broader definition of what counts as "good writing," urging NES readers to see "accented English" as part of that spectrum. In *Understanding ESL Writers*, Ilona Leki writes,

> ESL students can become very fluent writers of English, but they may never become indistinguishable from a native speaker, and it is unclear why they should. A current movement among ESL writing teachers is to argue that, beyond a certain level of proficiency in English writing, it is not the students' texts that need to change; rather it is the native-speaking readers and evaluators (particularly in educational institutions) that need to learn to read more broadly, with a more cosmopolitan and less parochial eye.[13]

According to Leki, the assimilationist goal of making ESL writing indistinguishable from NES writing is unrealistic. In many cases, the assimilationist stance is also undesirable because it leads to the imposition of the norms of dominant U.S. academic discourse as well as various cultural values that come with it.

Resisting the Assimilationist Stance

Those who take the assimilationist stance do not usually have malicious intent. As Severino suggests, people who take the assimilationist stance often do so in order to "smoothly blend or melt [the ESL writer and their text] into the desired discourse communities and avoid social stigma by controlling any features that[,] in the eyes of audiences with power and influence[,] might mark a writer as inadequately educated or lower class."[14] In other words, the assimilationist stance may be an attempt to protect the ESL writer from other readers—especially those readers who have institutional authority over ESL writers. Tutors may feel the same responsibility and may try to represent what they consider to be the possible response from the intended audience of the ESL writer's text: the professor.

Sometimes ESL writers come into the writing center because they were told by their professors to visit the writing center to get their drafts "cleaned up" or to work on their "grammar." From these experiences with professors' reactions to ESL writing, tutors may believe that professors tend to be assimilationists. While there are professors who do approach ESL students with assimilationist intentions, several error gravity studies—studies that review which errors tend to attract more attention by specific groups of readers—show that many professors are more tolerant of differences in ESL writing, or at least of certain types of differences, than of those in NES writing.

Terry Santos, for example, showed that professors were able to overlook local errors—errors that do not directly affect meaning—such as articles, prepositions, spelling, comma splices, or pronoun agreement.[15] Studies of error gravity generally show that professors tend to react more negatively to global errors—errors that affect the comprehension of meaning—such as the wrong word choice, word order, and verb tenses.[16]

One of the implications of error gravity studies is that tutors may want to focus more of their attention on global errors rather than on local errors when reading ESL texts. It may not be possible to define global and local errors in terms of particular grammatical features because whether and how a particular error affects meaning depends on the context. Instead, tutors can prioritize their responses by paying attention to their own initial reactions to particular errors that seem to interfere with their understanding of the meaning of the text. As discussed in the next section, this approach applies to not only grammatical errors but also other aspects of writing.

Reading Strategies

Though each writing center session demands different approaches, there is a general process of reading ESL writing that can be useful. It is generally a good idea to start with a quick reading of the ESL writer's text, focusing on what the writer is trying to communicate and how the paper is organized. A common practice among tutors is to ask writers to read their draft aloud during the conference, rather than the tutor read the draft silently. This strategy is often effective for NES writers who can use their intuitive sense of the grammar and the flow of English to assess their own writing. This strategy may not work well for some ESL writers who have not developed that intuitive sense of the English language. For many ESL writers, reading their paper out loud may shift their attention to the pronunciation of the English language—an aspect of language proficiency separate from writing in English.

It may be more helpful for the ESL writer to hear the tutor read the paper out loud—to note when the reader stumbles, pauses, fills in missing articles and modifiers, or reads smoothly. The interpretation of meaning that takes place in the process of reading aloud "rhetorically with feeling and meaning" may also help the tutor identify where the writer's intended meaning is not clear to the tutor.[17] Yet, on the first reading, especially if the number of errors prevents the tutor from reading aloud without stumbling too often, it may be more effective for the tutor to read silently, focusing on sorting through meaning.

Sometimes less experienced readers of ESL texts get so overwhelmed by the sheer number of errors that they have to give up on the draft and stop reading somewhere in the middle of the paper. However, if a paper isn't read to the end, the reader may miss out on information that could clarify the meaning or organization of the paper. The point of the paper may not become clear until the end if the text is organized inductively. Questions that arise in the tutor's mind while reading the beginning of the paper may be answered toward the end. Reading a piece of ESL writing in full allows the reader to come to an understanding of how the paper is organized on its own terms. Reading to the end of a piece of ESL writing is only beneficial if the reader can suspend judgment while reading—reading past variations in sentence structure, waiting to see how the writer will pull the paper together, maintaining an open mind when the writer's opinions and beliefs vary substantially from the tutor's.

Another feature of some ESL writing that may be disorienting is the lack of metadiscourse or signposts—the transitional words and sentences that move readers between ideas and the structures that mark the organization of a text. Even though a text may not have an organization that is immediately recognizable, there may be an organization at work. The trick is to identify and piece together the logic that is not immediately apparent to the reader by formulating questions with the assumption that there is logic in it—by giving the writer the benefit of the doubt.

After reading the whole text for the gist, it is often a good idea to reread the text, this time placing brief marks—such as checkmarks or asterisks—near features or details that seem surprising or those that jar the reading process: the unexpected. It is the unexpected in ESL writing that can make reading ESL writing challenging because it demands tutors become more aware of their tacit expectations for style, rhetorical choices, genre conventions, and relationships to audience. But it is also the unexpected that can teach tutors the most about their own responses to writing. Teachers often call the unexpected occurrences that happen in the classroom "teachable moments"—moments where significant learning could occur. It may be helpful to think of the unexpected in ESL writing with the same positive twist.

To capitalize on the unexpected, the tutor needs to be aware of his or her own responses as a reader. For instance, if a particular passage seems disorienting, the reader can take advantage of this situation by focusing on where he or she started feeling lost and why. What in the text caused the reader to wander? What is it about the reader's own expectations that contributed to the feeling of disorientation? The reader should also focus on areas where he or she feels "stuck"—unable to generate meaning from the text—and use this experience as an opportunity to consider what would be needed to move forward in the reading process. Does the reader need to ask the writer a question? Does the reader need to mark the area and then move on with reading, in the hope that another section of the paper will help the reader negotiate the challenging section?

Some of the unexpected features of ESL writing may be rich cultural details or unique perspectives that students bring with them. Making note of those details or perspectives that are particularly interesting or insightful to the tutor is useful in encouraging the ESL writer. Sometimes, however, readers of

ESL texts can get distracted by their own curiosity about certain details such as descriptions of unfamiliar places, cultures, and ways of thinking. Although these details do make ESL writing compelling to read, they can also lead the tutor away from the writer's goals and more toward their own goals, which could include asking the writer about their cultures or experiences, leading the reader to become more a tourist than a tutor.

Listening to ESL Writers

People always pay attention to *how* I say things, and never listen to *what* I say.

—An undergraduate ESL student

In this chapter, we have suggested that, while ESL writers' texts may have features that are distinct from NES writers' texts due to many sources of influence, it is possible to read beyond the differences if tutors can suspend judgments, focus on meaning, and be aware of their own preferences and biases. Ultimately, reading is an act of communication—the act of listening to what the writer has to say. When we listen—truly listen—we treat ESL writers with the respect they deserve, regarding them as peers rather than as uninformed learners of the English language and the U.S. culture. It is only in such an atmosphere of mutual respect that the collaborative pedagogy of the writing center can turn differences into opportunities for growth both for the reader and the writer.

Notes

1. Matsuda (2002), 194–96.
2. Silva, 668.
3. Silva, 670.
4. CCCC Committee on Second Language Writing, 669–70.
5. Cumming, 81–141.
6. Matsuda (2008); Matsuda and Matsuda (2009).
7. CCCC Committee, 670.
8. Mohan and Lo (1985).
9. Severino (1993a), 47.
10. Severino (1993b), 187.
11. Severino (1993b), 189.
12. Severino (1993b), 194.
13. Leki, 132–33.
14. Severino (1993b), 187.
15. Santos, 81.
16. Santos, 81; Vann, Meyer, and Lorenz, 432.
17. Severino (1993b), 190.

Works Cited

CCCC Committee on Second Language Writing. 2001. "CCCC Statement on Second-Language Writing and Writers." *College Composition and Communication* 52(4): 669–74.

Cumming, Alister. 1989. "Writing Expertise and Language Proficiency." *Language Learning* 39(1): 81–141.

Leki, Ilona. 1992. *Understanding ESL Writers: A Guide for Teachers*. Portsmouth, NH: Heinemann.

Matsuda, Paul Kei. 2002. "Alternative Discourses: A Synthesis." In *ALT DIS: Alternative Discourses and the Academy*, edited by Christopher Schroeder, Helen Fox, and Patricia Bizzell, 191–96. Portsmouth, NH: Boynton/Cook Heinemann.

———. 2008. "Myth 8. International and U.S. Resident ESL Writers Cannot Be Taught in the Same Class." In *Writing Myths: Applying Second Language Research to Classroom Teaching*, edited by Joy M. Reid. Ann Arbor: University of Michigan Press.

Matsuda, Paul Kei, and Aya Matsuda. 2009. "The Erasure of Resident ESL Writers." In *Generation 1.5 in College Composition: Teaching Academic Writing to U.S.-Educated Learners of ESL*, edited by Mark Roberge, Meryl Siegal, and Linda Harklau, 50–64. Oxford, UK: Routledge.

Mohan, Bernard, and Winnie Au-Yeung Lo. 1985. "Academic Writing and Chinese Students: Transfer and Developmental Factors." *TESOL Quarterly* 19(3): 515–34.

Santos, Terry. 1988. "Professors' Reactions to the Academic Writing of Nonnative-Speaking Students." *TESOL Quarterly* 22(1): 69–90.

Severino, Carol. 1993a. "The 'Doodles' in Context: Qualifying Claims About Contrastive Rhetoric." *The Writing Center Journal* 14(1): 44–62.

———. 1993b. "The Sociopolitical Implications of Response to Second Language and Second Dialect Writing." *Journal of Second Language Writing* 2(3): 187–201.

Silva, Tony. 1993. "Toward an Understanding of the Distinct Nature of L2 Writing: The ESL Research and Its Implications." *TESOL Quarterly* 27(4): 657–77.

Vann, Roberta, Daisy Meyer, and Frederick Lorenz. 1984. "Error Gravity: A Study of Faculty Opinion of ESL Errors." *TESOL Quarterly* 18(3): 427–40.

5

Avoiding Appropriation

Carol Severino

When I was studying Intermediate Italian in a study-abroad program in Italy, I wrote for our last assignment a brief essay "Un Viaggio a Venezia" about a trip to Venice I had taken some weeks before. In my simple syntax and vocabulary, I explained the theme of my mini-travel essay: Despite the fact that we travelers—four students, another professor, and I—had conflicting interests and itineraries, we managed to negotiate and compromise so that each person could do or see one thing she wanted to. We managed to shop for jewelry, masks, and shoes; feed the pigeons on St. Mark's Square; eat pizza by the Grand Canal; and watch the parade of boats in celebration of the Feast of the Redeemer. I was proud of my composition because I felt I had successfully communicated a complex travel experience in a foreign language I had studied for less than a year.

The day after I returned to the United States, I received a friendly email from my Italian teacher saying he had read and enjoyed my essay and had made just "a few corrections." When I opened the attachment and read my essay, I realized that not only had he taken the time to type directly in my handwritten essay, but he had in fact typed in a different essay—a more accurate and sophisticated one with vocabulary and verb tenses I did not know how to use yet. It was still more or less my experience in Venice, but now more in my teacher's language and my teacher's voice. For example, my original opening sentence had read, in translation:

> Trips to foreign cities are always a challenge, but when there are many travelers, the challenges become greater.

The revised sentence now read:

> Trips in foreign lands are always challenging, but when the travelers are many, the challenges multiply.

At the time I didn't know how to say either "challenging" or "multiply." I had also written, rather clumsily, "Before the trip I had read my guidebook with a map," but the new version read, "I had read my tourist guide and took a look at the topographical map." Almost every sentence was changed and elevated to a higher register. I wondered if my original wordings were grammatically incorrect or just not as native- and mature-sounding as these new, improved ones. Perhaps my well-meaning, hard-working Italian teacher thought that it was inappropriate for a middle-aged American professor to sound like a grade-schooler. Realizing that his embarrassment for me might have motivated his editing, I felt ashamed of myself and the quantity and quality of his changes. Humbling second language (L2) writing experiences such as this one (I have had many others) have enabled me to identify with the feelings of ESL writers who may also have overzealous teachers and tutors.

Reformulation and Appropriation

Helpful and generous as he was, my Italian teacher had revised my writing so it no longer sounded like me or reflected the state of my L2 learning at the time. Ironically, I liked my original simple and nonidiomatic style; my hybrid Italian American voice expressed who I was and what I knew. On the other hand, I continue to learn from his edits; whenever I reread my transformed essay, I reinforce the authentic native expressions that real Italians use. The intent of my teacher's "few corrections," after all, was not to humble or discourage me but to teach me the authentic Italian I needed to replace my interlanguage "Inglesiano."

Such language learning is the main justification for the teaching strategy called *reformulation* that my teacher used. Reformulation is recommended as an optional tutoring strategy for English as a second language (ESL) students. Reformulation is a tool for L2 learning in general because it is said to cause learners to "notice" differences between their version and the native speaker's version of a passage and to learn from realizing the discrepancies.[1] Reformulation in this context means correcting and revising L2 writing, making it not only more grammatical but also more idiomatic and native-sounding. In effect, reformulating involves "native-speaker-izing" L2 writing—changing the wording so that the writing sounds more like first language (L1) writing. To be accurate in our discussion, though, we should posit a continuum of L2 and L1 writing instead of thinking in terms of two opposites: L1 versus L2 writing. When we think of L1 and L2 writing as points on a continuum, reformulation means reducing the number of L2 features and increasing the number of native language features. Thus, the number of reformulations can range from slight to extensive.

For example, here is a sentence that Satomi, an ESL writer working in our writing center, wrote in her personal essay about calligraphy for her rhetoric class:

It is said that in Japan to write own names well is to represent how intelligent people are.

Many options exist for revising Satomi's sentence—from correcting the only actual grammar error (*one's* own name vs. *own names*) to reformulating and "naturalizing" the sentence with gerunds and eliminating the copula *is* and infinitive *to represent*:

> It is said in Japan that writing one's name well represents how intelligent people are.

A second further reformulation would be to use the more idiomatic expression "a sign of" that might be in Satomi's passive but not active working vocabulary:

> It is said in Japan that writing one's name well is a sign of intelligence.

Yet a third, more extreme option would be to eliminate the passive voice expression "It is said":

> The Japanese say that writing one's name well is a sign of intelligence.

Which reformulations would we say preserve Satomi's voice? Which distort or remove Satomi's voice? To what extent would such a judgment about the resulting voice depend on Satomi's input into the decisions of whether and how much to reformulate?

On some occasions, such as with my Italian essay or perhaps with the third option for Satomi's sentence, when writing has been reformulated, we might evaluate the changed product as having been *appropriated*, or taken away from the student writer by the teacher, tutor, or editor. Appropriation usually involves the writer feeling, as I did when reading my Italian professor's corrections, a loss of voice, ownership, authorship, or emotional and intellectual connection to the writing and how it was composed. Such an event—when control of a text is removed from an author who then feels alienated from it—might be considered an "act of appropriation" although undoubtedly one can still learn language and about language use from the experience. On other occasions, however, when language has been reformulated in whole or in part by a teacher, tutor, or editor, for example, with the consent and participation of the student, we might conclude that the student's writing has not been appropriated. What are the situational factors that influence the evaluation of an act of reformation as appropriation or not? In this chapter, after giving a brief overview of the history of appropriation, I identify and discuss some of these situational factors with the help of tutors from the University of Iowa Writing Center, all of whom work intensively with ESL students.

Some Background on Appropriation

In Composition Studies, issues of appropriation first arose in relation to native speakers of English (L1 writers) and the topics and content of their papers. As Lil Brannon and Cy Knoblauch have pointed out, teachers often wrest the direction of their students' writing from them so that they will write about what interests the teachers instead of what interests the students. Then students are confused or demoralized by having to puzzle out their teachers' expectations and write to fulfill them instead of writing from their own impetus and intentions. Teachers appropriate or take over the texts of their students when they respond to their students' papers with their own ideal texts in mind instead of negotiating with the students about what the students' intentions are and how best to fulfill them.[2] Not only are students' texts removed from them by teachers, but more important, also their control over these texts. Issues of appropriation, therefore, are usually issues of control over composing and revising. Who has more control of the text—the writer or the teacher or tutor? We can probably say that the more control the tutor, teacher, or editor has over the writer's text, the greater is the likelihood of appropriation.

Control is also related to authority. Teachers take control of students' texts because they do not accord their students or their texts the authority they grant to canonical authors and their texts, according to Brannon and Knoblauch.[3] Rather than struggle to get meaning from opaque student texts as they would do with a William Faulkner or Dylan Thomas work, they assume control over those texts and over the writers themselves. Brannon and Knoblauch and others, such as Nancy Sommers[4] and Richard Straub,[5] have recommended that teachers relinquish some of their authority and control over the students' texts and return it to their students, thus empowering them. They recommend that teachers act as respondents, informing students of the effects of their intentions and words on them as readers. Most tutoring guides, such as those by Toni-Lee Capossela[6] and Paula Gillespie and Neal Lerner,[7] also recommend that tutors not interfere with their students' control of their texts. They advocate the tutor roles of collaborator, facilitator, coach, and consultant rather than more teacherly, controlling, and directive roles of informant, editor, and evaluator.

Appropriation and Foreign and Second Language Writers

Well-meaning teachers and tutors can exert too much control over the topics, content, and development of their ESL students' papers, although the motivation for their assuming control may be different than it is with native speakers. The motivation to control may stem from disparity in cultural knowledge; either the tutor or student may have more cultural expertise, depending on the topic of the assignment. Sometimes the assignment situation seems to demand the tutor's directiveness. In our roles as cultural informants advocated by Judith Powers[8] and surrogate academic audience advocated by Joy Reid,[9] we tutors often know more about the assigned U.S. culture-bound topics of students' papers than our ESL students do, especially if they are international students who have lived for only a short time in the United States but must still write convincingly about U.S. culture, history, or controversies. Unless students can interpret and stretch their assignments to compare, for example, birth control and reproduction in China with those practices in the United States, they may have no other choice but to use the tutor's background information or stance on these U.S. controversies. Sometimes it is only with the historical context and position provided by the tutor that the student can make sense of the material that he has gathered from researching the controversy. This kind of assignment-induced appropriation often cannot be avoided without more widespread changes; writing programs would have to allow ESL students a choice of controversies and/or provide courses with international or multicultural curricula such as those recommended by Paul Kei Matsuda and Tony Silva.[10]

Ironically, a kind of reverse cultural appropriation can also occur when the topics for writing are from the student's own culture. In composition and ESL classes and in writing centers such as ours in which ESL students do personal writing, well-meaning teachers and tutors often urge ESL students to write about (too) familiar topics, such as the Moon Festival or Chinese New Year, even when, as Ilona Leki points out, those topics might be considered stale, providing little opportunity to discover new ideas and personal meaning.[11] Call it the equivalent of "What I Did on My Summer Vacation."

Most commonly, the issue of appropriating L2 writing in general arises not in relation to control of topic or content but to control of language. Here the disparity is in linguistic knowledge, not cultural knowledge; the linguistic repertoire of a tutor who is a native speaker of the language is far greater than that of her students. My Italian teacher was much more likely to exert control over my Italian phrasing than he was to ask or require me to write on a trip to Florence or on an American holiday such as the Fourth of July. As a result of his elevating my style in the direction of his ideal text, some of my voice was sacrificed for increased vocabulary or, more precisely, passive vocabulary because I cannot guarantee I will use those new expressions correctly when I try them in different contexts in the future.

The Trade-Off Between Voice and Authentic Language

When I wrote my travel essay, I had been satisfied with sounding like an American English speaker and intermediate Italian learner in this foreign language situation; later, I felt that some of the language had been appropriated by my teacher and some of my voice had been lost. I had become accustomed to reading my personal writing in L1 or L2 in a possibly self-indulgent manner—as if I were looking in a mirror. Thus, as I read my work, I expected to see and hear myself, not someone else.

Yet my situation as a foreign language learner and writer is unquestionably different from an L2 situation with an L2 learner and writer. I was simply writing mini-travel essays, not studying in a degree program, taking rigorous humanities and social and natural sciences in Italian, and competing with Italian native speakers writing research papers, exams, and dissertations. The stakes are much higher for L2 learners, who are learning the target language of the country in which they are being educated, than they are for foreign language

learners, who are usually residing in their own country learning the language
of another. At stake for L2 learners are grades, scholarships, graduate school,
publication, employment, income, quality of life and attendant status, prestige,
confidence, and self-esteem. With such pressures and challenges, more ESL
writers may be more willing to trade some of their voice for accuracy, idiomaticity, and increased language learning. If I as a tutor had made the equivalent
changes in the essay of an ESL student in the writing center, would she also
feel as if I had appropriated it? Probably not—if she had expressed the desire to
sound as native as possible, if she had participated in making the changes, and
if I had done my best to explain why particular expressions were ungrammatical or unidiomatic. Several things contributed to my sense of appropriation: I
had been satisfied with sounding nonnative, I did not understand the reasons
for my teacher's changes, and I had not participated or been offered any control in making them.

Avoiding Appropriation

We can identify from these discussions the situational factors that can contribute to avoiding appropriation in tutoring ESL students in the writing center.
When and how are we more likely to avoid appropriation? Paralleling the discussion of the continuum of L2 and L1 writing features, appropriation should
also be discussed in terms of probabilities and of gradations on a continuum
of tutor and writer control and directiveness, as Straub recommends,[12] and not
in terms of absolutes. It is not always clear—to a tutor or even to an outside
observer such as a researcher—when appropriation has taken place, except
possibly when a writer thinks and feels at a gut level that it has. If the notion
of "appropriation" is applied in a judgmental fashion every time a tutor suggests changing an expression on an ESL student's paper and replacing it with
a more idiomatic one—a labeling that Reid calls a "myth of appropriation,"[13]
it will cause unnecessary tutor anxiety, paralysis, and guilt, and the term will
ultimately lose its meaning. The myth of appropriation also denies the student
agency. According to Christine Tardy's broader, alternate view, appropriation
is not only negative and unidirectional but also can be positive and dialogic
when the student writer has agency to make decisions as well as the teacher. Tardy maintains that student writers in control can also appropriate from
peers, teachers, and texts while maintaining ownership of their texts.[14] (See
also Canagarajah and Prior as cited by Tardy for other alternative, positive
models of appropriation.)[15]

To avoid the negative, unidirectional appropriation of a student's work,
tutors should strive to do the following:

1. *Address expressed needs.* We are more likely to avoid appropriation
   when students, especially more advanced students and English learners,
   tell us that they want their writing to sound as much like that of native

English speakers as possible. We can endlessly debate whether ESL writers *should* feel they should sound like native speakers rather than themselves, but the fact is many do, especially advanced undergraduates and graduates, faculty, and visiting scholars; the feedback and pressure they receive from their professors, their supervisors, their dissertation advisors, and their journal editors convinces them that they need to feel this way.

According to Kathy Lyons, formerly a tutor at University of Iowa and now program coordinator for the nonprofit organization Iowa Shares,

> When you factor in what's at stake for these more advanced students (opportunities for publication, the need to write a defendable thesis, jobs), it seems wrongheaded to resist their desire to gain mastery over American writing styles. . . . In resisting the request of an ESL student to help with learning the "American way" or simply the "standard English" way of expressing something, we might be doing a great disservice, though with the best of intentions. We should be prepared to do what's in the student's best interest and to allow her to learn what she feels is important to her own professional and/or educational advancement if that is what she is asking us to do.[16]

However, shouldn't we work to convince the gatekeepers in graduate and professional schools and in academic departments and on editorial boards that L2 writers will probably always write with an accent? We should support the efforts the field of L2 writing has made, such as the Conference on College Composition and Communication's resolution to educate teachers about the length of the L2 writing acquisition process,[17] and how, according to Virginia Collier, it takes at least seven years to acquire an academic vocabulary.[18] (See Chapter 4 for more about this.) Yet until the effects of globalization are more strongly felt and teachers and other gatekeepers are sufficiently educated and become more tolerant of accents and nonnative features in writing, some ESL students will ask to be taught how a native English speaker would say what they suspect they are saying awkwardly. Such requests might put pressure on a hands-off tutor into taking what I have called a more assimilationist stance so that the student's writing will blend better into the linguistic mainstream of American academic English.[19]

Yiyun Li, a Chinese English bilingual who formerly tutored at the University of Iowa and is now a creative writer teaching at Mills College, generally agrees with Lyons when it comes to responding to students' expressed needs. Her perspective as an ESL writer who has both tutored and been tutored is especially valuable:

> As an ESL student myself, I understand that students really hope to learn the most correct English from our tutors. I remember in our writing center class last year, we talked about whether we should want our

students to write like Americans. The concern was that they would lose their uniqueness. But a lot of times, this uniqueness is just what makes them uncomfortable about their own writings. For myself, I usually ask my readers to point out all things that sound unusual for a native speaker. Some of them I know I have put in intentionally to give the writing a little foreign-ness, but with others, I just don't know *the right ways*, and I always feel happy to learn how to say them right.[20]

Bilingual ex-tutor Carmen Mota, a professor at Venezuela's University of the Andes, feels the same way about her English academic writing:

> In spite of my intentions to reduce [my writing center students'] anxiety by stressing their potentials as writers, I started to feel the same pressure when writing my own dissertation. I always wanted to be reassured that my ideas were clearly expressed. For this reason, I usually asked a native speaker to read over my various drafts and point to those ideas that did not sound right.[21]

Bilingual tutor Jia Zhu from China feels similar pressures in her academic writing:

> Many of my professors have emphasized that they never use a double standard to evaluate our academic work just because we are international students. I take it as acceptance and trust of our academic ability from our professors as well as a responsibility for us to write our papers as clearly as we can. This may partially explain why we always want our writing to sound as much like that of native English speakers as possible. To sound foreign is not a problem for me, but when it creates confusions and mis-understandings of what I really want to express, that's where I need to have my papers checked by an English speaker to make sure I have used conventional English before getting them submitted or published.[22]

Writer-tutors like Li, Mota, and Zhu would want tutors to point out in-stances of inadvertent or intentional poetry in their writing so they can decide whether they want to leave them in their texts or reformulate them. Such writers want control over when they are sounding foreign or even, ironically, when they are sounding inappropriately colloquial—for example, when they are using the word *stuff* incorrectly or overusing it to try to sound like native English speakers. If their writing contains foreign features, they want to know it is because of a conscious decision on their part, not an accident or a result of not knowing an expression or idiom. In this case, the ESL writer paradoxically has control over the tutoring situation even when it seems that the tutor has more control over the writer's language. What might seem like appropriation to an outsider unfamiliar with the expressed needs of the writer is actually a balanced tutorial interaction.

If tutors are not sure how unique or how much like native English speakers their students want to sound, they should ask them rather than guess. They should have a frank discussion of the pros and cons of leaning toward either pole. Such metadiscourse—communicating about how to communicate—is probably the most significant way to avoid appropriation. For confusing passages, tutors can generate with the student's help two or three options that vary in idiomaticity, style, or register and have the student choose among them as in the previous options for revising Satomi's sentence.

2. *Ask writers to participate in reformulation decisions.* We are more likely to avoid appropriation if students actively participate in the reformulation and revision process and, more important, in the metadiscourse about the process. According to the Interaction Hypothesis, such participation is said to increase the chance that language learning takes place, as Jennifer Ritter points out.[23] Even if ESL students request a reformulation of their paper, when a tutor revises *for* them rather than *with* them, it is possible that that tutor crosses the line, as Molly Wingate says,[24] into appropriating the students' texts. Ex-tutor LuAnn Dvorak, now teaching at UCLA, tells students who pressure her to change all incorrect or nonidiomatic features that they will not learn if she fixes everything for them; there is just too much new language in new contexts, she explains, for them to process in too little time and with too little participation on their part.[25]

One common way for the student to participate is to read her own paper aloud and stop or put a check mark when she thinks a passage does not communicate well because it is ungrammatical, unnatural, or both. The tutor might stop her when he does not understand a passage to ask her if she can explain it. Another way for the student to participate more is for tutors to participate less, thus balancing the interaction. To establish this balance, we need to monitor the ways in which we are participating. Megan Knight, another University of Iowa writing center tutor and rhetoric teacher, tries to limit herself to asking ESL students questions and mirroring what they have said.[26]

3. *Avoid misrepresenting the student's language level on the page.* We are more likely to avoid appropriation if our recommended changes and the resulting reformulation do not project a level of language proficiency and sophistication that is inaccurate. Intermediate ESL students should not come across as advanced on a paper after a few trips to the writing center. Ethical issues are involved in misrepresenting the student's language level to outside audiences of teachers and other gatekeepers. Such misrepresentation is unfair not only to these audiences but also to the students themselves. What if I submitted my teacher's revision of "Un Viaggio a Venezia" to an Italian program and was admitted on the basis of my supposed ability to manipulate the language but then could not understand

my courses and professors? When readers of reformulated essays compare them to the students' in-class writing and speaking, they may feel betrayed by both the students and the writing center (see Chapter 13). Bilingual tutor Olga Kulikova, an ESL teacher from Russia, sees other dangers in appropriation and misrepresentation—misleading readers into thinking that writers are more culturally assimilated into the host society than they actually are, in this case, making teachers expect "American" or "United Statesian" cultural behaviors:

> Absence of a foreign accent in writing can make professors or gatekeepers expect absence of a foreign accent in communicating; people who write properly should behave "properly." I do not want to seem more authentic than I am. It is not easy to learn to observe cultural rules, and I think it is much easier to excuse a grammar mistake than an unexpected cultural one.[27]

4. *Accord the ESL writer authority.* We are more likely to avoid appropriation if we accord ESL students authority as fluent, proficient speakers of and writers in their own native languages and advanced speakers and writers in English who may know more about the rules of English syntax, grammar, and usage than we do. When we compare their proficiency in English with ours in our L2, we can gain an appreciation and admiration for their amazing achievements. By respecting their authority as bilingual speakers and writers, as knowledgeable students of their disciplines, and as cultural informants about their own native languages and cultures, we are less likely to assume control of their texts and impose our ideal ones.

5. *Work on higher-order concerns before lower-order concerns.* We are more likely to avoid appropriating language and voice if we adhere to the principle of higher-order concerns versus lower-order concerns recommended by Donald McAndrew and Thomas Reigstad.[28] The assignment, focus, argument, development, and organization are usually more important than expression unless some language clarifications and corrections are needed simply to understand whether the student has followed the assignment and to understand her points. In the case of language completely obscuring argument, the level of language would be considered a higher-order and global concern. Otherwise, there is no point in working carefully and slowly to reformulate language that should not or probably will not appear in the next draft because the student needs to refocus or revise her entire argument.

6. *Select particular passages to work on.* We are more likely to avoid appropriation if we prioritize and select passages from a student's writing to revise. Because there may not be time in one tutoring session and because it could be cognitively overwhelming for both tutor and student to reformulate all nonnative constructions, a few should be chosen, particularly

- global problems that interfere with meaning, as Muriel Harris and Tony Silva recommend[29] (see also Chapters 6 and 7)
- nonidiomatic passages about which the student expresses concern
- features that are ungrammatical rather than just nonidiomatic.

7. *Use speaking-into-writing strategies.* We are more likely to avoid appropriation if we use speaking-into-writing techniques that use the student's direct spoken language. This helps capture and preserve his voice. Marilyn Abildskov, a former University of Iowa tutor and now a creative writing professor at St. Mary's College, says that "Tell me more" is the best question tutors can ask to elicit both participation and content for writing and to reflect the writer's voice.[30] Tell-me-more questions about expression cause the student to clarify her intended meaning and often result in language that is clearer and more idiomatic than what is on the page. Working from reading aloud and from speaking in order to rephrase written passages is what ex-tutor John Winzenburg, now a music professor at Agnes Scott College, calls the "outside-in approach." In contrast, "the inside-out approach," he says, is when the ESL writer is concentrating on how she thinks she should write rather than on what she is trying to say.[31] By having the student verbalize and converse to find and revise written language, ex-tutor Jennifer Ryan, now teaching at Buffalo State College, says she ensures that the voice on the page is not an English voice or, for example, a Chinese voice but the student's voice.[32]

8. *Explain the recommended changes.* We are more likely to avoid appropriation if we offer brief explanations for why the student's passage is faulty and why our recommended changes are better, rather than just writing or typing them on the page. If the feature is based on a rule and the tutor can explain the rule, then this provides an opportunity for learning and carries over to the next writing rather than just repairing that one expression. For example, I would tell Satomi that the words "own _____" are preceded by a possessive adjective: *my own car, one's own name.* Why this word or expression and not that? Why should we say two chemicals "competed" with another to bond with a third chemical rather than "contended" with one another? Look up both words in the dictionary together to learn the connotations and contexts. Why this verb form and not another? Why a gerund rather than an infinitive in the second reformulation of Satomi's sentence? The changed construction has fewer words, is more economical and streamlined, and is easier to process, even though the infinitive in the original sentence was not ungrammatical. If a tutor doesn't know the explanation, then rather than invent one, it is best to look it up together in a grammar book or ask the tutors sitting next to you. We don't have to have an explanation for every change we suggest; indeed, students may not want or need them, and there may not be enough

time for them, but "this is the way we say it in English" should not be our explanation for every change or replacement.

9. *Try to assess language learning.*   We are more likely to avoid appropriation if the student learns new language or more about using language from the interaction and reformulation. It is difficult to determine whether learning has taken place because writing centers do not test and they often don't see the same students regularly enough to monitor their learning. Yet, tutors who find themselves correcting and explaining the same features week after week should be aware that the student is possibly not participating enough in the exchange or the explanations are not communicated well (see Chapter 2).

10. *Consider the type of writing.*   We are more likely to avoid appropriation if we gauge the purpose, genre, and type of writing we are working on with the student. Informal writing, narratives, and reader responses may benefit more from nonidiomaticity and features of the student's unique voice; formal essays, abstracts, proposals, and dissertations may benefit less. For example, if Satomi writes in a personal essay that her hometown is "abundant of green," we might let it go and not comment about it at all. Or we might compliment her on her poetic phrasing but at the same time mention that native English speakers might say "abundantly green" or "very green." But if Satomi writes "abundant of green" to describe a land mass in a formal geography paper, we would more likely point out the lack of idiomaticity and offer the previous options. These decisions— whether to point out such instances and whether and how to change them, even in personal writing—should be negotiated with the student.

A Ten-Step Program?

To avoid appropriation, must all ten conditions be met and all the strategies implemented within a tutoring session? Some of these conditions and strategies are undoubtedly more significant than others. The first three are especially important. Responding to the writer's expressed needs and feelings (condition 1), ensuring the writer's participation (condition 2), and not misrepresenting the writer's second language proficiency level (condition 3) are probably the more important criteria and advice for avoiding appropriation, although not necessarily in that order. Most important, periodic metacommunication and perception checking about whether and how to reformulate will work to help tutors avoid taking control over ESL students' texts and voices. According to bilingual ex-tutor Kai Lin Wu, now a professor at Tunghai University in Taiwan, tutors must establish a balance between their own direction and control and the student's, which depends on the student's second language level and experience:

> Establishing a balanced relationship between the student writer and the tutor-reader is one way to avoid appropriation. Students' texts are where ESL

writers and tutors negotiate meanings. Some ESL writers, especially those with little or no L2 writing instruction, need more directive feedback from tutors because they are probably still seeking a voice to express themselves in a new academic setting. When tutors grant to ESL students the authority of writers, they would also need to take on the responsibility of responsive readers.[33]

Just as the travelers in my Italian essay negotiated and compromised but still met their needs and goals, so should tutors and ESL writers.

Notes

1. Cohen (1985); Swain and Lapkin (2002); Qi and Lapkin (2001).
2. Brannon and Knoblauch (1998).
3. Brannon and Knoblauch, 213.
4. Sommers (1982).
5. Straub (1996).
6. Caposella (1998).
7. Gillespie and Lerner (2003).
8. Powers, (1993).
9. Reid, 273–92.
10. Matsuda and Silva (1999).
11. Leki (1992).
12. Straub, 225.
13. Reid, 290.
14. Tardy (2006).
15. Canagarajah (2002); Prior (1998).
16. Kathy Lyons, personal communication.
17. CCCC Statement on Second Language Writers.
18. Colljer (1987).
19. Severino, 190.
20. Yiyun Li, personal communication.
21. Carmen Mota, personal communication.
22. Jia Zhu, personal communication.
23. Ritter, 104.
24. Wingate, 9.
25. LuAnn Dvorak, personal communication.
26. Megan Knight, personal communication.
27. Olga Kulikova, personal communication.
28. McAndrew and Reigstad, 42.
29. Harris and Silva (1993).

30. Marilyn Abildskov, personal communication.
31. John Winzenburg, personal communication.
32. Jennifer Ryan, personal communication.
33. Kai Lin Wu, personal communication.

Works Cited

Brannon, Lil, and Cy Knoblauch. 1998. "On Students' Rights to Their Own Texts: A Model of Teacher Response." In *Harcourt Brace Guide to Peer Tutoring*, edited by Toni-Lee Capossela, 213–22. Fort Worth, TX: Harcourt Brace.

Canagarajah, Suresh. 2002. *Critical Academic Writing and Multilingual Students*. Ann Arbor, MI: Multilingual Matters.

Capossela, Toni-Lee. 1998. *The Harcourt Brace Guide to Peer Tutoring*. Fort Worth, TX: Harcourt Brace.

CCCC Statement on Second Language Writers. Retrieved on September 8, 2007, from www.ncte.org/positions/lang2.shtml.

Cohen, Andrew. 1985. "Reformulation: Another Way to Get Feedback." *Writing Lab Newsletter* 10(2): 6–10.

Collier, Virginia. 1987. "Age and Rate of Acquisition of Second Language for Academic Purposes." *TESOL Quarterly* 21(4): 617–41.

Gillespie, Paula, and Neal Lerner. 2003. *The Allyn and Bacon Guide to Peer Tutoring*. 2nd ed. Boston: Allyn and Bacon.

Harris, Muriel, and Tony Silva. 1993. "Tutoring ESL Students: Issues and Options." *College Composition and Communication* 44(4): 525–37.

Leki, Ilona. 1992. *Understanding ESL Writers*. Portsmouth, NH: Boynton/Cook.

Matsuda, Paul Kei, and Tony Silva. 1999. "Cross-Cultural Composition: Mediated Integration of U.S. and International Students." *Composition Studies* 27(1): 15–30.

McAndrew, Donald A., and Thomas J. Reigstad. 2001. *Tutoring Writing: A Practical Guide for Conferences*. Portsmouth, NH: Boynton/Cook.

Powers, Judith. 1993. "Rethinking Writing Center Conferencing Strategies for the ESL Writer." *Writing Center Journal* 13(2): 39–47.

Prior, Paul. 1998. *Writing/Disciplinarity: A Sociohistoric Account of Literate Activity in the Academy*. Mahwah, NJ: Lawrence Erlbaum.

Qi, Donald S., and Sharon Lapkin. 2001. "Exploring the Role of Noticing in a Three-Stage Second Language Writing Task." *Journal of Second Language Writing* 10: 277–303.

Reid, Joy. 1994. "Responding to ESL Students' Texts: The Myths of Appropriation." *TESOL Quarterly* 28(2): 273–92.

Ritter, Jennifer. 2002. "Recent Developments in Assisting ESL Writers." In
A Tutor's Guide: Helping Writers One to One, edited by Ben Rafoth,
102–10. Portsmouth, NH: Boynton/Cook.

Severino, Carol. 1998. "The Political Implications of Response to Second
Language Writing." In *Adult ESL: Politics, Pedagogy and Participation in Classroom and Community Programs*, edited by Trudy Smoke,
185–208. Mahwah, NJ: Lawrence Erlbaum.

Sommers, Nancy. 1982. "Responding to Student Writing." *College Composition and Communication* 33(2): 148–56.

Straub, Richard. 1996. "The Concept of Control in Teacher Response: Defining the Varieties of 'Directive' and 'Facilitative' Commentary." *College
Composition and Communication* 47(2): 223–51.

Swain, Merrill, and Sharon Lapkin. 2002. "Talking it Through: Two French
Immersion Learners' Response to Reformulation. *International Journal
of Educational Research* 37: 285–304.

Tardy, Christine. 2006. "Appropriation, Ownership, and Agency. Negotiating
Teacher Feedback in Academic Settings." In *Feedback in Second Lan-
guage Writing: Contexts and Issues*, edited by Ken Hyland and Fiona
Hyland, 60–78. New York: Cambridge University Press.

Wingate, Molly. 2002. "What Line? I Didn't See Any Line." *A Tutor's
Guide: Helping Writers One to One*, edited by Ben Rafoth, 9–16. Portsmouth, NH: Boynton/Cook.

6

"Earth Aches by Midnight"

Helping ESL Writers Clarify Their Intended Meaning*

Amy Jo Minett

In 1993 I joined the Peace Corps and went to Hungary to teach English. And just as the commercials promise, it was a time of adventure: I stomped grapes during a harvest festival, got lost in a Transylvanian blizzard, and fell off bicycles on muddy village roads. But as I look back, most vivid to me now is how I struggled to learn the language, to express myself, and to make my meaning clear. It was—and is—a challenge shared every day by learners of other languages all around the world.

A story to illustrate this challenge was told to us by our Hungarian teachers. One newly arrived volunteer sat down to eat with her homestay family: They didn't speak English, nor she Hungarian, yet. Wanting to be gracious, she tried to ask what the main course—a delicious meat dish—was. Once she got her question across (through pointing, upturned palms, and a wondering tone), her homestay father smiled with delight. He lacked the vocabulary but knew the sound the animal made. "Ruff ruff," he replied proudly. The volunteer dropped her fork. "Ruff ruff?" she asked, a little fearful. "Ruff ruff!" repeated the father, and the rest of the family chimed in. "Ruff ruff!" The volunteer hesitated, then picked up her fork and went bravely on to eat her supper. Only later did it turn out that in Hungarian, the pig says, "Ruff ruff!"

In this story, the volunteer leaped to what seemed a logical conclusion (same sound, even if, in Hungary, a different animal makes it). Similarly, when we struggle to understand an ESL writer's text, it is tempting to leap to conclusions about the meaning the writer wants to convey. This chapter helps avoid

* For his many research insights and invaluable guidance with this chapter, I am indebted to Dr. Dan Tannacito of Indiana University of Pennsylvania. Thanks also to Diane Harley at Madison Area Technical College.

66

this pitfall, first, by helping you, the tutor, understand *why* you might not understand. You might ask the following questions:

- Has the writer tangled the syntax as in this typical example: "But most of people feel not natural that making small talk with strangers in my country?"
- Or has the writer used sudden, strange words? One of my students once wrote, in a lovely if confusing instance, "I do not want to know the earth ache."
- Or did the writer compose whole paragraphs of seemingly unconnected ideas or save the thesis statement until the very end?

Baffling though such texts sometimes are, in this chapter you'll also find strategies that you can use to help English as a second language (ESL) writers clarify just what it is they want to say (and it's hard enough in a first language, right?).

First, though, let's explore *why* you may not understand an ESL writer's intended meaning, keeping in mind as we explore that expectations of clarity are context and culture specific and always reflect a particular set of values: in this case, the values of academic English. Then we'll look at how you can help clarify meaning at four levels: essay, paragraph, sentence, and word.

Clarifying the Essay's Main Idea

In 1966 Robert Kaplan published an article that although controversial has nevertheless dramatically influenced how we understand ESL writers' texts. In it, Kaplan says that logic is not universal but culture specific and it may be reflected in the patterns we use to organize texts in our first languages.[1] He arrives at this conclusion after studying hundreds of ESL student essays and identifying different types of development. For instance, English essays are typically expected to be linear (stating claims explicitly and then supporting those claims with evidence), but essays written by Asian students may be much less direct and even withhold the thesis statement until the very end. In my experience, too, Russian, Polish, and Hungarian writers frequently delay stating their main points—believing it creates more suspense for the reader—which is how they learned to write. The problem, however, is that if you are accustomed to reading texts developed according to the conventional rhetorical patterns and preferences of academic English, the effects of *other* ways of structuring essays (be it Spanish, Russian, or Chinese) can cloud your understanding of an ESL writer's meaning.

Here's one rather startling example from the Budapest center in which I tutored. Magda, a Polish writer of a history paper, almost seemed sympathetic toward the Nazis in the Holocaust, right up until the last paragraph, when she finally spun around and lamented the tragedy (in which members of her own family had died). When the somewhat anxious tutor asked why she had waited until the very end to make her position clear, Magda told her, "Because that's how I'd write it in Polish. It sounds best this way. Readers in Polish would *know* what I was trying to say!" The tutor, on the other hand, accustomed to a different pattern of essay development, was confused by the writer's rhetorical choice of saving her thesis until the very end. Another reader may not even have finished reading, which would have been unfortunate, because the reader would have missed the writer's main point.

If you feel that cultural differences in text organization may be affecting your understanding of an ESL writer's intended meaning, you might spend some time talking directly with the writer about *contrastive rhetoric*. In Magda's case, the tutor asked her how arguments were typically organized in Polish, and then they explored together how essays are usually structured in English. In this way, Magda came to understand how cultural differences and preferences might shape a particular reader's understanding of the intended meaning—in this example, a U.S. reader with U.S. expectations of essay structure—and she understood what changes she needed to make to meet those expectations. Her conclusion, with some tinkering, became her introduction, which made her intended meaning quite clear (and poignantly so). Equally important, as Ilona Leki says, open discussion of contrastive rhetoric can produce in ESL writers "instant enlightenment about their writing in English, as students suddenly become conscious of the implicit assumptions behind the way they construct written ideas and behind the way English does."[2] Helen Fox, too, believes in talking directly with ESL writers about cultural differences in "communication styles" so that they can better understand the audience for whom they're writing, especially professors in U.S. universities who may expect writing to be "so explicit and precise that they can follow the argument without any effort at all."[3] Perhaps most important, such discussion also helps make clear how English conventions and audience expectations are, as Kaplan said, no better or worse than other conventions—a point that can't be emphasized enough.[4] They're just different. Finally, the writers' stories will be fascinating and may further put writers at ease as they become aware of what backgrounds and traditions they bring to the writing conference and why they're not always understood.[5]

Clarifying Paragraphs

Not only essay structure but also paragraph development may differ in other cultures and can blur our understanding of an ESL writer's meaning. Paragraphs might, for instance, seem flip-flopped to us if ESL writers state the main point of the paragraph in the last sentence (as opposed to the first). John Hinds concludes that—whereas English writing is typically reader friendly in its directness and clarity—Japanese writing, in contrast, is *writer* friendly, and it's mainly the reader's job to determine the writer's intention.[6] He describes how Japanese authors like "to give dark hints and to leave them behind nuances" and how Japanese readers "anticipate with pleasure the opportunities that such writing offers them to savor this kind of 'mystification' of language."[7] Maho

Isono, a Japanese student at Oregon State University, provides one example of such "mystification":

> In Japanese writing there are so many pronouns. And there are so many pronouns but this is the reader's job to understand what this "he" is and what this "she" is and what "this" refers to. I tend to do that in American writing, in English essays, and everyone asks me who this "he" is and who this "she" is . . . I don't understand, but for me, guess what, this is your job to understand it.[8]

Another source of "mystification" may come from the different use of connectors like *however* or *in contrast*. In English we are taught to use these connectors to guide the reader explicitly through our logic, whereas in Japanese and other languages, these "landmarks" may be absent or at least more subtle, thereby demanding the reader be more active and work harder to understand the writer's meaning.[9] For someone who expects the reader-friendly conventions of academic English, understanding the meaning in such texts may feel like driving in a strange city without street signs or a road map. We want the writer to tell us exactly where to go. We want coherence and cohesion.

Topical Structure Analysis

One strategy that you can use to help ESL writers whose paragraphs aren't coherent (and whose meaning is therefore unclear) is called *topical structure analysis*.[10] With it, writers can look at both global coherence (what the whole text is about) and local cohesion (how sentences "build meaning" by connecting to each other and to the text as a whole).[11]

In its simplest form, topical structure analysis works like this. Start by asking ESL writers to find sentence topics (what the sentence is about) in individual sentences. I might offer a sentence of my own such as "<u>Writing poetry</u> feels like meditation to me." Writers should underline "writing poetry" as the topic.

Next, ask them to find and underline the sentence topics in whole paragraphs and then discuss the relationship between the topics and the paragraph and the paragraph and the whole essay. In so doing, writers should discover (1) different ways that sentence topics build meaning and (2) that the reader's ability to understand the meaning depends in part on how the topics in the paragraph progress.[12] Here are examples I've used to help writers understand:

1. Parallel progression:

   > <u>Writing</u> is often a struggle. <u>It</u> can also be a joy. <u>Writing poetry</u>, for example, feels like meditation to me."

   Here the writer can see that the meaning of the underlined topics (*writing, it, writing poetry*) is the same. The main idea of the paragraph (*writing*) remains clear to the reader (though too much progression of this type may lead to monotony).

2.   Sequential progression:

> My room is undoubtedly the messiest in the house. Books and papers are
> scattered everywhere. My clothes lie about in sad piles. Anyone entering
> does so at their own risk. My brother, for instance, last week tripped on a
> bean-bag chair and broke his foot."

In this example, the topics are all different (*my room, books and papers, my clothes, anyone entering, my brother*) though the meaning usually comes from the previous sentence. Clearly, too much development of this type can disorient the reader, a point that ESL writers quickly come to understand when they see how, as in this example, the writer goes off on one dizzying tangent after another and sentence topics continually shift and change.[13]

3.   Extended parallel progression:

> My room is undoubtedly the messiest in the house. Books and papers
> are scattered everywhere. My clothes lie about in sad piles. My room is
> a disaster.

Here we find the last sentence returning neatly to the first topic (*my room, books and papers, my clothes, my room*). In this way, the main idea is developed in detail but then restated again directly, which helps the reader understand the main focus of the passage. The paragraph is clear and coherent.

Once ESL writers get the hang of finding and analyzing progressions in sentence topics, you can ask them to "test" how coherent their own writing is by diagramming *their* underlined sentence topics, like this:

Parallel Progression

1. Writing
2. It
3. Writing poetry

Sequential Progression

1. My room
     2. Books and papers
          3. My clothes
               4. Anyone entering
                    5. My brother

Extended Parallel Progression

1. My room
     2. Books and papers
          3. My clothes
4. My room

With the topics diagrammed this way, ESL writers can better see the relationships and coherence (or lack thereof) between sentences, paragraphs, and the main idea of the paper.[14] They can then revise so that the topics of their sentences build the intended meaning consistently and coherently throughout the paragraph. As a final check of coherence, Ann Johns recommends students write a one-sentence summary of paragraphs, which becomes more difficult if coherence is lacking and the sentence topics are constantly changing.[15]

This might also be a good time for you and the writer to discuss cohesion, or how sentences build meaning by connecting to each other. For this purpose, I always keep a handy list of common connectors (like *however*, *nevertheless*, *in addition*) over my desk to yank down and share with ESL writers who might need to make explicit the logical links that may be missing between sentences. Many college writing texts include such lists, Eli Hinkel notes, and ESL students especially need to understand what they mean, when and how to use them, and how vital they are when writing for college classes in the United States.[16] It's one more way that you, the tutor, can help ESL writers clarify their intended meanings.

Clarifying Sentences

Focus on Form

So far, we've seen how cultural differences and preferences in essay and paragraph organization might obscure an ESL writer's intended meaning. Sometimes, however, single sentences are difficult to understand. To help the writer in this case, you might try a strategy from second language research called *focus on form.* [17]

Interestingly, focus on form works best during a writing conference in which you and the writer still mainly concentrate on higher-order concerns. Don McAndrew and Tom Reigstad spell out these concerns as being "central to the meaning and communication of the piece" like "matters of thesis and focus, development, structure and voice."[18] However, during such a conference, if you just *occasionally* direct the writer's attention to problems with language that obscure meaning, you can help the writer more clearly express herself, provided she is developmentally ready—that is, provided the writer has enough background knowledge about the meaning and use of the language form (see Chapters 2 and 5). For instance, can the writer use negatives correctly? Is the word choice accurate? Are verb tenses in control? In most cases, we can probably safely assume that ESL college writers are developmentally ready. Furthermore, if you as tutor help ESL writers notice their existing language issues, then you are actually engaging their developmentally sharpened language-processing mechanisms, which help the writer break into the new language system like spies cracking a code.[19] In short, you are helping writers extract the form, which they can then map to meaning and function.[20]

Here's an example (to clarify my own meaning). If a writer has made a mistake and you don't understand the text, try repeating the unclear sentence back to the writer, perhaps in the form of a question, but with the mistake corrected. If the writer has written "I study by midnight," you could ask, "You study *until* midnight? Or *around* midnight? *At* midnight?" This might be enough to help the writer notice the problem with the preposition and how the meaning changes with each choice (unless he is too tired, having been up all night). Or, if we return to the example provided at the beginning of this chapter, "I do not want to know the earth ache," you might ask, "Earth ache? Hmmm. . . . Well, *ache* means hurt. Does the earth hurt in some way? Are you writing about environmental problems?" If the writer shakes her head, you might volunteer more suggestions. "Do you not want to experience an earache? Or do you mean an earthquake, like what they have in California and Japan?" (The answer, by the way, was earthquake, which the writer most definitely did not want to experience.)

This technique is simple and useful, but we shouldn't forget that writers will benefit most from only the *occasional* focus on form and on just one or two problems at a time.[21] For the most part, higher-order concerns probably should remain just that—a higher priority.

This is probably also a good time to bring up the issue of "taking over" a writer's text, which, as a trained writing center tutor, you might be worried about (see Chapter 5). After all, we want the writer's work to remain just that—the *writer's* work—and volunteering words might seem like too much help. With ESL writers, however, we might need to rethink our approach to the conference. Joy Reid believes we have responsibilities as "cultural informant[s]" to our students.[22] I would add that we may also have—to some extent, at least—responsibilities to them as language resources. When we offer the writer a number of choices related to meaning (earth hurts? earache? earthquake?), it's still the writer's choice in the end to decide which word (and which meaning) he wants to convey. We might even see this as one way meaning is negotiated between tutor and writer, and second language research suggests quite strongly that negotiated meaning (1) facilitates learning and (2) leads to better writing (and therefore probably a clearer expression of meaning).[23]

Should We Help, How Much, and When?

If we take the view that you, the tutor, and the ESL writer will together negotiate the intended meaning as a part of clarifying what the writer wants to say, then it's also important to know how much help to give and when. Some researchers suggest that as a tutor (and therefore probably a more capable user of English), you can best help ESL writers work at their potential level of ability by offering help only so long as it's needed and then withdrawing your help as soon as writers "show signs of self-control" and the ability to go it alone.[24] So, if Vlado, a Bulgarian writer, comes to me, here's what I might do to help him express his meaning more clearly.

First, I'd ask Vlado to read his paper silently and, on his own, underline and correct the errors he can find. When he says he's ready, I would sit beside him, and together we would discuss the corrected errors, which might go like this:

"Yes, good, that's right: you are *bored* by television, not *boring*. I'm rarely *interested* in TV myself because there aren't many *interesting* programs."

If he missed an error that obscures meaning, I might point to the sentence and look puzzled or ask him, "Hmmm . . . is there anything wrong *here*?" If Vlado still cannot see the problem, I would offer more direct help by pointing this time to the phrase or word and asking again: "What—about—here?" If Vlado is still unsure, I would target the problem directly: "Look at the verb tense here. 'I had been lived in Sofia for one year.' Now, I know you don't live in Sofia now because we're in Budapest. What's wrong with the verb tense?" If necessary, I will give the correct answer and explain the grammar rule, or we'll look it up together, but I will first offer help in ever more explicit and guided forms. Vlado will need my help only so long as he doesn't notice the error, or notices it but can't correct, or corrects just with specific pointing. Over time, however, he should rely less and less on my guidance until finally he has consistent control over the problem structure, be it verb tense, word form, or something else.[25]

Interactional Cues

In the previous example, you may have noticed how my puzzled look communicated to Vlado that there was some kind of problem with the sentence. I might also have frowned, grinned, stroked my chin, or widened my eyes. What you didn't see were Vlado's facial expressions and the other signals he gave me that showed when he was struggling with something and when he was about to solve a problem by himself. Amy Snyder Ohta calls these *interactional cues*, and she presents quite convincing research that shows that, as a tutor, you can help the writer the most when you pick up on and respond to these often very subtle signals, for that's when the writer is most developmentally ready to listen, and learn.[26] In other words, you can read these cues to know when it's time to help clarify writers' intended meanings and when they are probably on the verge of clarifying it for themselves. Here are some things you should listen for before jumping in:

- *Rising or falling tones of voice.* "The verb tense is past . . . present? I had lived . . . I have had . . . lived?" When the voice goes up at the end in question form, the writer is ready for help. If the voice doesn't go up at the end, the writer is still thinking, so don't jump in yet. Wait for more signals.

- *Restarts of sentences.* "The author, the author pre . . . per . . . , the author persites, presits, *persists*!" Restarts indicate that the writer is still working out the problem, so wait.

- *Rates of speech.* If the writer is speaking quickly, she is probably still figuring out the best solution. When the rate slows down, you should get ready to offer help.[27]

These are just a few examples. As a tutor, you too can learn to interpret the writer's many differing cues, especially if you meet with the same writer regularly. And one last point here: It's also important to remember that ESL writers frequently need more wait time after questions or when they are working out problems for themselves, so don't be afraid of longer silences. One way or another—by sigh or tone—the writer will let you know when he is ready for your intervention.

Clarifying Words

Lastly, a few words about words. Hinkel discusses an important survey in which U.S. college faculty describe ESL papers as too often "vague and confusing," precisely because the writer may lack the necessary vocabulary to clarify their intended meaning.[28] You can, therefore, also help ESL writers by talking about certain words that can help clarify meanings dramatically. Hinkel describes the following as top priorities for ESL writers:

- qualifying hedges like *apparently, probably, ostensibly, seems, perhaps, most likely*
- modal verbs like *may, might, should, could, can*[29]

In both cases, using these words can impact meaning considerably. Just listen to the difference in meaning between these two sentences:

Raising tuition will lower student enrollment.

Raising tuition will likely lower student enrollment. (We can't be sure it will, can we?)

You should also be prepared to talk with ESL writers about the use of vague nouns like *society, people, world,* or the vaguest of all perhaps, *truth*. My Hungarian students loved to use the English phrases "to tell the truth" and "to be honest," which they had learned and were (justifiably) proud of. Given the preferences and expectations of most college writing in the United States, however, these phrases can be problematic. Helping ESL writers build their academic vocabularies this way can not only help clarify their intended meaning but also relieve some of the anxiety and frustration they feel when they get their papers back all marked up in red ink.

This chapter has explored why you may not always understand an ESL writer's meaning, and it has offered the following strategies that you can use to help writers clarify just what it is they want to say.

- You can explore with writers how they learned to write and what's probably expected at U.S. universities.

- You can help them analyze how coherent their paragraphs are.
- You can guide them through rough sentences and help them choose clearer words.

Through my work tutoring ESL writers, I've learned that in Egypt babies are welcomed into the world by a party on the seventh day. In Taiwan the number four is unlucky (it rhymes with the word for *death*). What challenging work, I say. And how rewarding.

Notes

1. Kaplan, 12.
2. Leki, 138.
3. Fox, 114.
4. Kaplan, 12.
5. For more on contrastive rhetoric, see Panetta (2001) or Connor (1996). For a critical view of contrastive rhetoric, see Kubota and Lehner (2004).
6. Hinds, 65.
7. Suzuki, quoted in Hinds, 66.
8. *Writing Across Borders* (2005).
9. Hinds, 67.
10. This idea comes from Connor and Farmer, 126–39. Connor and Farmer draw on the work of Finnish linguist Liisa Lautamatti.
11. Connor and Farmer, 127.
12. Connor and Farmer, 128–33.
13. Connor and Farmer, 130.
14. Connor and Farmer, 130.
15. Johns, 256.
16. Hinkel, 144.
17. Long in Doughty, 259–84.
18. McAndrew and Reigstad, 42.
19. Doughty, 276.
20. Doughty, 265.
21. Doughty, 290.
22. Reid, 218.
23. See, for instance, Goldstein and Conrad (1990).
24. Aljaafreh and Lantolf, 466–68.
25. Modeled after Aljaafreh and Lantolf, 469–71.
26. Ohta, 52.

27. Ohta, 62–77.

28. Hinkel, 52.

29. Hinkel, 247–50.

Works Cited

Aljaafreh, Ali, and James P. Lantolf. 1994. "Negative Feedback as Regulation and Second Language Learning in the Zone of Proximal Development." *The Modern Language Journal* 78(4): 465–83.

Connor, Ulla. 1996. *Contrastive Rhetoric: Cross-cultural Aspects of Second-Language Writing*. Cambridge: Cambridge University Press.

Connor, Ulla, and Mary Farmer. 1990. "The Teaching of Topical Structure Analysis as a Revision Strategy for ESL Writers." In *Second Language Writing: Research Insights for the Classroom*, edited by B. Kroll, 126–39. New York: Cambridge University Press.

Doughty, Catherine. 2003. "Instructed SLA: Constraints, Compensations, and Enhancements." In *The Handbook of Second Language Acquisition*, edited by C. Doughty and M. Long, 256–310. Oxford: Blackwell.

Fox, Helen. 1994. *Listening to the World: Cultural Issues in Academic Writing*. Urbana, IL: National Council of Teachers of English.

Goldstein, Lynn M., and Susan M. Conrad. 1990. "Student Input and Negotiation of Meaning in ESL Writing Conferences." *TESOL Quarterly* 24(3): 443–60.

Hinds, John. 2001. "Reader Versus Writer Responsibility: A New Typology." In *Landmark Essays on ESL Writing*, edited by T. Silva and P. K. Matsuda, 63–73. Mahwah, NJ: Lawrence Erlbaum.

Hinkel, Eli. 2002. *Second Language Writers' Text*. Mahwah, NJ: Lawrence Erlbaum.

Johns, Ann M. 1986. "Coherence and Academic Writing: Some Definitions and Suggestions for Teaching." *TESOL Quarterly* 20(2): 247–65.

Kaplan, Robert B. 2001. "Cultural Thought Patterns in Intercultural Education." In *Landmark Essays on ESL Writing*, edited by T. Silva and P. K. Matsuda, 11–26. Mahwah, NJ: Lawrence Erlbaum.

Kubota, Ryuko, and Al Lehner. 2004. "Toward Critical Contrastive Rhetoric." *Journal of Second Language Writing* 13(1): 7-27.

Leki, Ilona. 1991. "Twenty-Five Years of Contrastive Rhetoric: Text Analysis and Writing Pedagogies." *TESOL Quarterly* 25(1): 123–43.

McAndrew, Donald A., and Thomas J. Reigstad. 2001. *Tutoring Writing: A Practical Guide for Conferences*. Portsmouth, NH: Boynton/Cook.

Ohta, Amy Snyder. 2000. "Rethinking Interaction in SLA: Developmentally Appropriate Assistance in the Zone of Proximal Development and the Acquisition of L2 Grammar." In *Sociocultural Theory and Second Language Learning*, edited by J. P. Lantolf, 51–78. Oxford: Oxford University Press.

Panetta, Clayann Gilliam. 2001. *Contrastive Rhetoric Revisited and Redefined*. Mahwah, NJ: Lawrence Erlbaum.

Reid, Joy. 2001. "The Myths of Appropriation." In *Landmark Essays on ESL Writing*, edited by T. Silva and P. K. Matsuda, 209–24. Mahwah, NJ: Lawrence Erlbaum.

Writing Across Borders. 2005. Dir. Wayne Robertson. DVD. Oregon State University Writing Intensive Curriculum Program and Center for Writing and Learning.

7

Looking at the Whole Text

Jennifer E. Staben and Kathryn Dempsey Nordhaus

"What should I do? I feel torn," a new peer tutor writes in her weekly journal. The emotion she feels comes from the tension of conflicting demands. On the one hand, many voices are telling her to avoid an initial focus on grammar in her tutoring sessions. Her textbook, *The Longman Guide to Peer Tutoring*, recommends working on higher-order concerns like focus, development, and organization before addressing a student's editing concerns; there's even a table that contrasts her role of tutor with the role she's not supposed to play— that of editor.[1] This philosophy has been echoed in many of the articles she has read for her tutor development course and in the discussions she has had in class with her fellow tutors. Yet, week after week, second language writers sit down beside her, pull out their drafts, and voice their grammar concerns: "Can you check my grammar?" "I'm worried about my grammar." "My English is terrible. Can you help me with it?"

Because writing centers strive to be student-centered, writing conferences with English as a second language (ESL) students often make tutors feel that they are faced with an impossible choice: Comply with the ESL students' invitations to focus on grammar and other surface errors or ignore the ESL students' requests and focus on the whole text. Opting for the former often leaves tutors feeling like traitors to the cause: They have helped contribute to the perpetuation of the image of a writing center as a "skills center, a fix-it shop."[2] Opting for the latter, however, sometimes leaves tutors feeling more like *intruders* than *collaborators*, especially when the writers they're working with actively or even passively resist this more holistic focus.

What's a tutor to do? Though there are no easy solutions to the tension this apparent dichotomy produces, the dichotomy itself is false: Tutoring objectives are rarely as simple as *either* grammar *or* the whole text. Yet even in situations when the student and the text pull you toward focusing solely on grammar, we believe there are reasons to resist. ESL students, like their native English-speaking (NES) counterparts, have much to gain from looking at the whole text.

Some Background

Muriel Harris and Tony Silva succinctly explain why new writing center tutors are tempted to approach conferences with ESL writers differently than they approach conferences with NES writers: "To the untrained tutor's eye what is most immediately noticeable is that a draft written by an ESL student looks so different."[3] In short, the surface errors, when combined with ESL students' hesitancy, accent, and uncertainty, can make language issues appear more urgent than they really are—to tutors and students alike. In response to this perceived urgency, tutors tend to become language police, focusing on issues like sentence structure and word choice.

Sentence-level assistance can be helpful to ESL students. However, it robs both ESL students and their tutors of an opportunity to learn so much more. As Kenneth Bruffee writes in "Peer Tutoring and the 'Conversation of Mankind,'"

> We create knowledge or justify belief collaboratively by cancelling each other's biases and presuppositions; by negotiating collectively toward new paradigms of perception, thought, feeling, and expression; and by joining larger, more experienced communities of knowledgeable peers through assenting to those communities' interests, values, language, and paradigms of perception and thought.[4]

The community to which both peer tutor and ESL student are being introduced is a community of academic writers whose language, conventions, and expectations are new and foreign. It is, in short, a foreign culture—and it's a culture that often is underestimated in terms of its significance and scope.

Most writing tasks in U.S. colleges and universities are based on cultural conceptions about clear writing and effective argumentation—ideas that may not be shared by ESL writers and may indeed run counter to the ideas about academic writing that the writers bring with them. In *Listening to the World*, Helen Fox tells countless stories about how upper-level undergraduate and graduate students, proficient and sometimes professional writers in their first language, struggle less with the linguistic aspects of English and more with U.S. academic expectations of how writers construct arguments, utilize outside authorities, and even incorporate personal experience and viewpoints into academic texts. Fox suggests that this struggle is not simply an issue of adopting a different style of writing; U.S. academic texts require students to assume different ways of viewing the world and their place in it.[5] Similarly, when Fan Shen discusses his own experiences as a writer moving from a Chinese academic culture to a U.S. context, he explains that making the transition was not as simple as switching pronouns—from *we* to *I*. Instead, he had to learn to create a more individualistic stance for himself when he wrote essays in his English composition course—one that not only used the pronoun *I* but valued it in a different way.[6]

Contrastive rhetoric studies suggest that "not simply rhetorical style but also purpose, task, topic, and audience are culturally informed."[7] Therefore, ESL writers may need resources—"cultural informants"—to help them understand the assumptions and expectations of a U.S. academic audience, assumptions that are not usually directly addressed on the assignment sheet.

The role of informant is an important one for writing center work. It is, in many respects, an extension of the facilitator role where tutors question the students about their texts, the needs of the audience, and how the text might change to meet these needs. As a facilitator, tutors can use these Socratic questioning techniques to elicit knowledge from the writer that the writer may in turn incorporate into the text. Open-ended questions about everything from audience to word choice can push writers to think about and use what they already know. However, for many ESL students as well as inexperienced NES writers, these same techniques may be doomed to fail because no amount of questioning, no matter how clearly and effectively the tutor words it, can elicit language or cultural knowledge the writer doesn't possess. These writers need the tutor to act as informant to provide them with the background they need to successfully negotiate these new writing contexts.

Yet, even the experts don't agree on what tutors should focus on when they take on an informant role. For instance, Susan Blau and John Hall believe that interweaving discussions of language and vocabulary throughout a tutoring session may be more appropriate with ESL writers, particularly those with less experience writing in English.[8] On the other hand, Carol Severino,[9] as well as Muriel Harris and Tony Silva,[10] maintain that higher-order, rhetorical concerns should still come before linguistic concerns. Similarly, many tutor guidebooks, such as *The Longman Guide to Peer Tutoring*, encourage writers to continue to put higher-order concerns first when working with second language writers.[11]

Acting as a cultural informant about U.S. academic expectations—rhetorical or otherwise—and focusing the writer's attention on the text as a whole is vital precisely because no matter what the background of the ESL writer, language can be an overwhelming and blinding concern. Some ESL students have spent time in high school or middle school in the United States. These students may seem to be familiar with aspects of American culture and language, everything from customs to idioms, but they often lack knowledge of U.S. academic culture, just like any inexperienced writer. Because English is not their first language, students may assume that good writing is the same as correct writing.

At the same time, other ESL students may become overwhelmed while trying to write because of the cognitive complexity of the task.[12] These are the students who often cannot see the forest for the trees: They are so focused on the language—on trying to wrestle their complicated thoughts onto paper using language abilities that are not yet sufficient to the task—that they may not realize that the change in language and in culture necessitates a different approach to communicating those thoughts to others. For both sets of students, language concerns can overshadow rhetorical ones, and important conversations about academic culture and expectations may not take place. This is why it can be important to focus on the text as a whole.

What to Do

Tutoring sessions are as individual as fingerprints: They may progress along a familiar pattern only to whorl suddenly off into new and unexpected directions. Therefore, we don't have specific procedures for you to follow, but instead we offer a series of principles and strategies that may help you and your tutee to think and talk about the text in front of you, not just as a series of grammatical constructions but as a complex and rhetorical whole.

Talk Before Text

One of the strengths of writing center conferences has always been the interactive talk between tutor and tutee. Although questions may not work in the same way with ESL writers as they do when working with NES students, we would argue that they can still play a critical role in the writing center conference. One of the ways to incorporate questioning into conferences with ESL students is to talk with the writer *before* turning your attention to the text.

- One way to get the conversation started is to focus first on the assignment. Most tutors have had the experience of discovering at the end of the session that a student had completely misinterpreted the instructor's directions. Oftentimes, this misinterpretation is caused by cultural differences. We forget that the writing assignment itself is cultural; although students might understand the individual words, they still may not have a clear idea of what the instructor expects. Read the assignment. Ask the writer questions about his understanding of the expectations of the assignment and how he tried to meet them. Telling students that they are on the wrong track can be difficult. However, it is even more difficult to tell a student that fact after you've spent forty minutes helping him generate and develop ideas that don't adequately address the assignment.

- Another way to start a conversation before turning to the text is to ask ESL writers what they chose to write about in response to the assignment and why they chose it as the subject for their papers. The simple request "Tell me what your paper is about" can be useful when working with any ESL writer, but it is especially productive when working with students who are inexperienced writers in both English and their native language. These discussions can help both of you notice differences between what the writer has told you and what is on the page—differences you and the writer can negotiate together.

- A third way to start a conversation is to focus on the writer's process. The text is typically what draws writers into the writing center. As a result, we often focus on the product, neglecting the process altogether. To learn about the writer's process, tutors can ask students questions such as "When did you start writing this paper?" "Have you written other drafts?" "Have you received feedback yet?" "What do you plan to do next?" "How can I help you achieve your goals?"

After surveying research on the composing processes of ESL and NES writers, Harris and Silva suggest that

> ESL writers might find it helpful to stretch out the composing process: (1) to include more work on planning—to generate ideas, text structure, and language—so as to make the actual writing more manageable; (2) to have . . . ESL students write in stages, e.g., focusing on content and organization in one draft and focusing on linguistic concerns in another subsequent draft; and (3) to separate their treatments of revising (rhetorical) and editing (linguistic) and provide realistic strategies for each, strategies that do not rely on intuitions ESL writers may not have.[13]

With these ideas in mind, we believe that asking preliminary questions—about the assignment, the topic, and the writer's process—is a critical step in the writing conference. This approach can help you and the writer prioritize and set goals, and it's also a good way to focus the student's attention (and yours) on larger textual issues from the very beginning.

Read (and Read, and Read) with Purpose

If your opening questions are meant to help the writer focus on the text as a whole, we believe it is important for your session to begin with the text as a whole as well. That is, in most situations we recommend reading through the entire essay with your tutee before focusing on the parts. Though there are situations where going through an ESL writer's text paragraph by paragraph or line by line is appropriate, it is difficult to talk about issues of overall focus and organization after reading only the first paragraph or two, especially when the writer may be using different rhetorical strategies than the ones you are used to. It is definitely easier to see patterns—whether they are related to focus, organization, or language—if you approach the paper as a whole first.

Similarly, many tutors find it useful to read through the piece once to get an overall impression, with either tutor or student reading out loud, and then to go through the paper a second time to talk specifically about issues both the tutor and the tutee notice. Because some writers, both NES and ESL, write their way to their main points, this strategy can help tutors address issues of thesis and focus much more effectively. Also, if you notice that a writer consistently employs the same unexpected organizational strategy throughout his paper—putting the main point at the end of each paragraph, for instance—then you can more easily explore the idea that this is something the writer is controlling, which can then be negotiated, as opposed to something that is out of control.

Be Direct, Not Directive

When working with ESL writers, and indeed all writers, we believe it is important to understand the difference between being *direct* and being *directive*. That is, you need to negotiate the fine line between being direct by giving the students information they don't have—about academic expectations, essay conventions, or grammar constructions—and being directive by telling writers what they *have to do* with that information for a specific essay. If you simply tell ESL writers that they need to put a thesis sentence near the beginning of the essay or that they should organize their research paper in a certain manner, you are not helping them understand what you likely know instinctively—the web of assumptions and conventions that shape different writing genres. However, if you talk with ESL writers about the directness of U.S. culture, where phrases like "get to the point" and "time is money" are frequently used and show them how these values are reflected in our rhetorical choices, ESL writers can begin to understand why main ideas tend to be frontloaded at both the essay and paragraph level in U.S. academic writing. It is a thorough understanding of genre(s) including their cultural influences that will help the ESL writer negotiate future writing tasks. One of the best ways to help the student understand is to explore the topic together through interactive discussions where you and the student share your questions and information.

Another reason to be direct, rather than directive, is that it presents opportunities for you to learn. In a truly interactive conference, both the tutor *and* the student learn from each other. When you are directive, the student is forced to be a follower. For example, several years ago a graduate student from Japan was working with an undergraduate tutor on an essay for a course in second language acquisition (SLA). The tutor responded to the writer's use of the terms *production* and *utterance* in regards to language learning by informing her that these were not the expected ways to say these concepts in English. The writer tried to explain that these words were established vocabulary in the field of SLA, but the undergraduate tutor ignored this explanation. The tutor was unable to see the graduate student across the table from her, an individual with specialized knowledge; instead, she saw an ESL student with a vocabulary problem. Rather than asking the writer why she had used these words and then creating a space in the session for discussion and negotiation, the tutor was directive, closed off conversation on this issue, and lost the chance to learn about an unfamiliar discourse community.

As you work with each student on overall textual issues, it is important to remember that although logic is frequently behind the choices a writer has made in a given draft, it is difficult to understand those choices without asking the writer. To put it simply, being direct means understanding when questions might *not* be the most effective way to generate knowledge, but being directive means forgetting about times when they *are*.

Tell . . . and Show

Although questioning is the cornerstone of effective writing conferences, it isn't always enough. When ESL writers seem to be struggling with an assignment—an assessment based either on what they say when talking to you about it or on what you see happening on the page—don't hesitate to address this issue directly. Telling students what a teacher might expect to see in response to the assignment and what you as a reader see happening in their papers is one way to begin the discussion.

For example, a situation we see frequently in our writing center is ESL students struggling in their second composition course—a course that focuses on writing about literary texts. Though some instructors spend a great deal of class time helping students develop strategies for analyzing works of poetry, fiction, and nonfiction, others assume all students will understand their request to "write a literary analysis of _____." Students often come to our center with long summaries of the works they're supposed to analyze and are unsure what the difference is between what they've done and what they're supposed to do. In these kinds of situations, modeling can be a very useful strategy. Try to walk the writer through your own thinking and writing processes if you were given an assignment similar to this. The key is to focus on the *process* you would go through and not the *content* you would generate. Our sessions with these students often involve going back to the story or poem itself and modeling how to look for patterns or themes and then how to move from these things to thinking about them on paper and in an essay format. In doing this, it is important to keep the session interactive. Unfortunately, it can be all too easy to tell writers what to do rather than to relate to writers what they need to know to perform the task successfully themselves.

Don't underestimate the power of textual models. Sometimes instructors will give students a sample paper or two to help them understand the assignment. In other cases, they will provide these samples if the student writer requests them. If the writer has a sample paper, you might consider going through it with him. Models are only helpful, however, if students notice the parts they are supposed to. By asking questions and pointing out textual features, you can help the writer understand the qualities and conventions of the model that she might want to use. For instance, if the sample is a

- narrative essay containing rich description and dialogue, you might ask the student to consider why the author used these techniques and why the instructor might value them.

- book review paper from a history class and the writer keeps the summary of the book separate from the critique, you might highlight and discuss this separation with your tutee.

You can help an ESL writer see a sample as more than a rigid formula to follow. Instead, you can show how it is a specific articulation of larger principles underlying a type of academic writing. These principles may affect every aspect of the piece—from topic selection and organization to the language itself.

Respond as a Reader

Sometimes tutors can get so caught up in what is different about what they see on the page that they forget the most important role they can play with ESL writers—as a reader. Just like their NES counterparts, ESL writers often need feedback on what they're saying—their ideas—and not just on how they're saying it. Some tutors, especially tutors working with older or more experienced students, hesitate to discuss ideas. Sometimes this hesitance stems from a fear of appearing uninformed and thus undermining their credibility or authority. But often tutors shy away from discussing ideas because they don't to offend the student; grammar is safe, neutral territory, whereas ideas are potentially explosive minefields filled with personal beliefs and values.

There are ways to approach ideas with respect and sensitivity:

- Share your own ideas.
- Point out places where an essay suggests connections to your own life or experiences.
- Point out ideas that make you think—or make you think differently.
- Highlight places that are unclear to you; ask the writer to expand her ideas by providing examples or anecdotes that help clarify her thoughts to you.
- Play devil's advocate—help the writer see other sides to his ideas.
- Identify places where the writer could strengthen her argument by acknowledging other opinions or where she could diffuse counterarguments by addressing them directly.

This is one area where the Socratic approach can serve you particularly well. When you're questioning someone gently and are truly interested in what he has to say, it's hard to offend. In fact, the opposite is often the case. Many writers come to the center blocked by their discomfort with the language. Your questions can reassure the writers that although their language skills may not be perfect, they aren't interfering with their ideas, and their ideas are interesting to others.

Use the Power of Paper

It is vital to know when talk is not enough. The spoken word can be extremely powerful, but when placed on a page, writers tend to think of it as permanent. This perceived permanence of words on paper can be intimidating to writers and can especially block ESL writers. However, there are ways you can harness the power of paper to work for the student's benefit.

One of the simplest things you can do for students is to serve as a scribe. Some students who are not fluent speakers of English may be fluent writers if they learned English mainly through writing and reading. On the other hand, some ESL students speak more fluently and have no problems expressing themselves verbally because they don't stop to translate what they want to say; they simply say it. However, when it comes to putting words to a page, their process might be more arduous. Initially, they might write their thoughts in their first language and then translate their ideas. Or, they may write their thoughts in a mixture of both languages, planning to "smooth it out" later. Both of these processes can affect the product. If you suspect this may be the case or if you are having a difficult time understanding what the student has written, ask the student for clarification and write down his response. Although this is a common practice for working with NES writers, it may be even more important for ESL writers who are balancing several complex cognitive tasks at once.

Another way you can use paper to the students' advantage is to get *away* from words. We regularly use outlines or lists with students in the writing center—ESL students should not be an exception. You might also consider graphically illustrating the various elements of a piece of written work (introduction, body, conclusion), showing the relative size and importance of each, along with some notations about what kinds of things might be included in each element. These illustrations can be used to represent both the forms the writer is trying to learn and the actual structure of the writer's text.

The benefits of using a separate sheet of paper are many. You can help loosen up a blocked ESL student by turning her attention from a troublesome sentence or paragraph and helping her *see* the big picture. ESL writers who are visual learners may benefit more from graphic representations than verbal explanations. In addition, by creating a picture or a list or an outline together, you are giving the ESL writer something physical to take with her—an additional reference she can consult as she seeks to revise her writing.

Complicating Matters

In this chapter, we have tried to review one of the challenges you're likely to face when working with ESL students in the writing center: finding ways to pull students' attention toward higher-order concerns such as focus, development, and organization and away from lower-order concerns such as grammar or word choice. It sounds like a simple goal, but it's an extremely complex issue with no easy solutions. To a certain extent, it is this complexity that presented the two of us with unexpected challenges when writing this chapter. We kept getting sidetracked by "what-ifs." We'd like to share some of these "what-ifs" here because they're the kind of complications you may encounter.

What if the student is a repeat customer and has already been to the writing center several times to work on content and organization? What if the student is insistent about working on language only? What if one of the myriad factors that *can* affect the focus of a writing conference (the time pressure of last-minute visits to the writing center, a tutor's awareness of a particular instructor's grading criteria, and/or a tutor's desire to be helpful and student focused) *does* affect the conference? In these situations, it's important for tutors to remember several things:

- You don't have to choose between substance and grammar. Though the goal is to focus as much as possible on higher-order concerns, it doesn't necessarily mean you should focus on these concerns to the exclusion of everything else.

- Most students' time is at a premium: They are students, employees, daughters, fathers, friends, and so on. They need to use their time wisely; if they truly have little need for additional discussion of higher-order concerns (as in the case of the repeat customer), their time—and yours—may be best spent on issues of language. However, even these situations provide room for *conversation.* Try to find out why the student made the language choice she made, and you may discover entirely new areas to discuss. A misplaced comma might lead to a discussion of how punctuation is used in Spanish—or Hindi or Korean—and how that might affect the relationship between author, audience, and text.

- Your students' needs are driven by the situation in which they find themselves. Our preference to focus on higher-order concerns stems largely from our desire to address the majority of our students' needs. We support a community college with a significant ESL population from a wide range of backgrounds—from international students with multiple degrees earned in their native countries to immigrant students who are inexperienced writers in English and their native language—but the majority of our ESL students are inexperienced writers in any language, and they tend to benefit most from assistance with larger textual issues. In environments with upper-level undergraduate or graduate ESL students, it might be more appropriate to shift the balance toward the middle ground between text and language—or shift more toward language.

Finally, remember the cornerstone upon which every writing center is founded: trust. *You* are working with the student. *You* are there to read her body language, inflection, facial expressions, motivation, and intensity. You must trust yourself and your instincts to make the right decision based on the information you have at the time. You must trust the student's knowledge of his own needs and priorities. And ultimately, you must trust in the validity of the ultimate goal of the kind of writing center that Stephen North describes—a place for the "creation of a continuous dialectic that is, finally, its own end."[14] Sometimes this requires a pragmatic approach. You may need to cut a deal now to lure the students back later, so the conversation can continue and the real growth can begin.

One final note: Tutors need to be engaged in another type of conversation as well, and that is the one that all professionals have with the research in their field. We offer some suggestions for further readings we think you will find helpful and interesting:

Ilona Leki, "Twenty-Five Years of Contrastive Rhetoric: Text Analysis and Writing Pedagogies," *TESOL Quarterly* 25(1) (1991): 123–43. In this article, Leki gives a useful overview of the various strands of contrastive rhetoric research and discusses a number of ways that contrastive rhetoric can and should influence writing instruction.

Wayne Robertson, *Writing Across Borders*, DVD (Corvallis: Oregon State University, 2005). In this DVD, theoretical issues of contrastive rhetoric are brought to life as international students and several scholars discuss the cultural and linguistic challenges second language writers face when writing for U.S. academic audiences.

Ruth Spack,"The Acquisition of Academic Literacy in a Second Language: A Longitudinal Case Study," *Written Communication* 14(1) (1997): 3–62. In this research study, Spack follows Yuko, an undergraduate international student from Japan, over the course of three years and explores how Yuko develops academic literacy in English. Spack's research not only highlights the complexities involved in this undertaking but also suggests ways that teachers and tutors can assist international students as they negotiate this process.

Amy Tucker, *Decoding ESL: International Students in the American College Classroom* (Portsmouth, NH: Boynton/Cook, 1995). In this book, Tucker examines how the cultures and cultural rhetorics of both students and teachers influence what happens in the college writing classroom. She demonstrates through multiple examples the need for teachers to learn to "read" and "reread" their students, an idea that is equally important for tutors.

If your writing center does not already have a professional library for tutors, these readings and others cited in this book would make a great start. They will draw you into a conversation you will want to continue for a long time.

Notes

1. Gillespie and Lerner (2008).
2. North, 73.
3. Harris and Silva, 526.
4. Bruffee, 95.
5. Fox (1994).
6. Shen (1989).
7. Leki (1991), 133.
8. Blau and Hall, 23–44.
9. Severino, IV2.3.
10. Harris and Silva, 531.
11. Gillespie and Lerner, 126.
12. Leki (1992), 107.
13. Harris and Silva, 529.
14. North, 83.

Works Cited

Blau, Susan, and John Hall. 2002. "Guilt-Free Tutoring: Rethinking How We Tutor Non-Native-English-Speaking Students." *The Writing Center Journal* 23(1): 23–44.

Bruffee, Kenneth. 1984. "Peer Tutoring and the 'Conversation of Mankind.'" In *Landmark Essays on Writing Centers*, edited by C. Murphy and J. Law, 87–98. Davis, CA: Hermagoras Press.

Fox, Helen. 1994. *Listening to the World: Cultural Issues in Academic Writing*. Urbana, IL: National Council of Teachers of English.

Gillespie, Paula, and Neal Lerner. 2008. *The Longman Guide to Peer Tutoring*. New York: Pearson/Longman.

Harris, Muriel, and Tony Silva. 1993. "Tutoring ESL Students: Issues and Options." *College Composition and Communication* 44(4): 525–37.

Leki, Ilona. 1991. "Twenty-Five Years of Contrastive Rhetoric: Text Analysis and Writing Pedagogies." *TESOL Quarterly* 25(1): 123–43.

—————.1992. *Understanding ESL Writers: A Guide for Teachers*. Portsmouth, NH: Boynton/Cook.

North, Stephen M. 1984. "The Idea of a Writing Center." In *Landmark Essays on Writing Centers*, edited by C. Murphy and J. Law, 71–85. Davis, CA: Hermagoras Press.

Severino, Carol. 1998. "Serving ESL Students." In *The Writing Center Resource Manual*, edited by Bobbie Bayliss Silk, IV2.1–IV2.7. Emmitsburg, MD: International Writing Centers Association.

Shen, Fan. 1989. "The Classroom and the Wider Culture: Identity as a Key to Learning English Composition." *College Composition and Communication* 40(4): 459–66.

8

Meeting in the Middle

Bridging the Construction of Meaning with Generation 1.5 Learners

Jennifer J. Ritter and Trygve Sandvik

A Day in the Writing Center

It's one of those typical dark, winter mornings when we walk into the Writing Center at the University of Alaska Anchorage (UAA). Beatrice is reading Jared's literacy narrative for his freshman composition class. Jared moved to Alaska ten years ago when he was in the air force. After he retired from the service, he decided to stay in the Last Frontier, and he is currently working toward his elementary education degree. Another tutor, Stacy, is working with Natalia, a logistics major and international student from the Russian Far East, who is writing a report for her purchasing and supply management course. Tara is just finishing her tutorial session with Judy, an Alaska Native from Kodiak, who moved to Anchorage in hopes of entering the nursing program. She is working on her digital annotated bibliography from her developmental writing class. Our tutors are much like those in many writing centers. Many are undergraduate students, mostly English majors. Some are graduate student teaching assistants and future composition instructors. Tara, for instance, is an undergraduate English major with plans to teach English overseas, followed by graduate school back in the states.

The next student waiting for a tutor is one who Tara has not seen in the writing center before. When she sits down for the tutoring session, Victor puts his paper on the table in front of them, leans far back in his chair, his legs extended and crossed, and uncomfortably fidgets as he explains his assignment:

> *Victor:* This is my paper. It's a mini-summary response paper. It's a
> summary of the story that we read and thinking about the issue,

how do you feel about it? And supposed to have like complete
sentence and that important stuff and all that.

Victor is what has been identified as a Generation 1.5 learner.

Among ESL students is a group of writers who have been here long enough
that they are not quite considered international or recent immigrant students,
and sometimes they are not considered English as a second language (ESL)
students. They are nonnative speakers of English yet are fluent in spoken English.[1] At the same time, their backgrounds are not like those of native English
speaking (NES) students who were raised speaking and writing in English. In
some cases, unfortunately, these students were directed to take remedial classes throughout elementary and secondary school in the United States because of
their status as minorities.[2] These writers are Generation 1.5.

Victor is Mexican American, and Spanish is his first language. He has
been through the U.S. high school system. He has learned English by living
in the English-speaking world—through social interaction, through the media,
through his teachers—in essence, through his ears. His spoken English is such
that he has no problem understanding and communicating with native English
speakers. He just gets frustrated trying to write with "complete sentence and
that important stuff and all that." We all do. But as a Generation 1.5 learner,
Victor struggles with a distinct set of challenges when it comes to writing in
English. That is, in high school ESL classes, he learned how to write in English
in a way that does not match what he needs to do in his college classes. In high
school, Victor completed fill-in-the-blank exercises and short personal narratives. High school reading involved choral readings during class with little
discussion about the meaning of the texts. In college, Victor needs to write longer assignments that analyze the deeper meanings of essays and short stories,
something that is new to him.

In our writing center, we work with many students, who, like Victor,
are Generation 1.5 writers. Like many U.S. cities, Anchorage is increasingly
multicultural, which is reflected in the student population at UAA. As a diverse campus, our writing center works with a broad spectrum of students,
and at the writing center, the so-called traditional student is in fact a relative rarity. Also, as many of us have noticed, the problem with categorizing
students is that we interact with them as individuals, and individuals do not
fit neatly into categories; instead they tend toward our categorizations. With
this in mind, we have students who tend to fall between the categories ESL
learner and NES learner and who show the characteristics we have attributed
to Generation 1.5 learners.

In an effort to work better with our Generation 1.5 writers at UAA, we
collaborated with a group of six graduate students researching a project in one
of their classes, Conferencing Writers. As part of this project, we all made
video recordings and transcribed several tutorial sessions between our tutors
and Generation 1.5 tutees. After each tutorial, we interviewed the tutor and

student separately to learn more about their perspectives. We then discussed our observations about this population, offered examples from our tutorials, and recommended approaches that might help tutors make the most of such collaborations.

The voices in the tutorials, which we quote in this chapter, are those of our tutors and students and thus represent a variety of styles and accents. That is, the style is informal and conversational, but the tutorials allow you to hear the spoken voices of our tutors and tutees. Because our Generation 1.5 learners are nonnative English speakers, their expressions may seem foreign.

We start our discussion with a few sample profiles of some tutees who we recorded and interviewed and who belong in the category of Generation 1.5 learner:

- Nhia is an eighteen-year-old female student who speaks Hmong as her first language. She came to the United States from a Hmong refugee camp in Thailand during her elementary school years. She lived in Wisconsin until her last two years of high school, at which point her family moved to Anchorage where she graduated from high school. Although she speaks quietly, she speaks English with ease.

- Victor is an eighteen-year old male student who moved to Anchorage from Mexico during his middle school years. His first language is Spanish, and he speaks English fluently but with a slight Spanish accent.

- Ji-Sook is an eighteen-year old female student who speaks Korean as her first language. As a student in Korea, she studied English. When she moved to Anchorage, she was immersed in English in high school. She, like Nhia, is quiet but speaks English well.

All three of these students share the experience of being immersed in English and American culture throughout a portion of their school years. Also, they are first-year students at UAA where they are taking a developmental English composition course for ESL students. In this course, the students learn about the UAA Writing Center, and they all worked with our tutors at least twice during the semester. All three act like typical American college students, and they have high competency in spoken English, albeit with an accent. Even so, we noticed that our tutors tend to categorize these students as ESL learners, meaning those who need help with language concerns. In some cases, these students identify themselves as needing help with language issues. In other cases, they tend to be perceived by tutors as ESL learners because of their seemingly foreign faces or because of their accents.

Though these students are nonnative English speakers, their tutoring needs are often different from other nonnative speakers such as international students (for more on tutoring international students, see Chapter 1). Having practiced writing in their first language, international students often have the advantage that they are familiar with larger rhetorical concerns and the different registers required when communicating in different contexts—spoken, informal, or formal—although with differing culturally specific styles. With immersion in a culture where English is dominant, Generation 1.5 students have the advantage that they are somewhat familiar with the cultural understandings required to communicate in English but doing so on the page is often an unfamiliar challenge.

Moreover, many international students tend to be more familiar with eye learning, such as referring to grammar books in search of rules, whereas Generation 1.5 writers tend to be more familiar with ear learning, such as listening to English to hear the patterns. We have found it useful to focus on Generation 1.5 students' characteristics as ear learners and as competent English speakers who need to develop their writing skills specific to academic contexts. Our subsequent tutorial suggestions encourage tutors to serve as guides in an unfamiliar expressive environment and to use students' existing strengths as a starting point.

Generation 1.5 Writers: Learning English and Writing

Ear Learners

We return to Tara and Victor's tutorial to try to understand the nature of grammatical errors in Victor's paper. In the tutorial, Tara learns that Victor is writing a summary-response of the Flannery O'Conner story, "Everything That Rises Must Converge," which is about the relationship between Julian and his mother. When reading his paper, Tara notices that Victor has some grammar, spelling, and punctuation errors in his writing, such as in this sentence:

> Like in the story above Julian was only thinking on teaching his mother a lesson he never realize how much he loved her he was always critiquing her on what she whore and how she acted etc.

From this example, our discussion of grammatical errors can take many layers. As an example, let's look at the phrasal verb, *think of*, which consists of the verb *think* plus the particle *of*. In his paper, Victor incorrectly writes it as *think on*. First, we might argue that this is a developmental error.[3] That is, Victor still is acquiring English and that includes the correct forms of phrasal verbs, which can be difficult to learn because verbs plus particles take on very different meanings. *Think back* means something different from *think out*, which means something different from *think up*, and so on. Also, Victor's native language, Spanish, does not have phrasal verbs.

Second, we might say that this is an *ear-learning* error.[4] That is, because Victor has a lot of exposure to spoken English, he probably heard the verb, *think of*, in many conversations. Yet, because grammatical elements in English such as particles like *of* are not stressed in the pronunciation, it is difficult to clearly hear the word. As such, Victor may have thought he heard *think on*, and that is how he learned the phrasal verb to express the idea of considering something.[5] This might also explain why Victor makes many phonetically based spelling mistakes in his writing. The example in the previous passage is spelling *wore* as *whore*. During the tutorial, when Tara reads *whore* aloud, Victor laughs, realizing his mistake, and asks how to correctly spell this word. Other spelling mistakes in Victor's writing include "*weigh* reducing class" for "*weight* reducing class," "*minnie* essay" for "*mini* essay," and "human *beans*" for "human *beings*." It may be possible that Victor selected Replace All in spell check and did not inspect each replacement. It may also be possible that Victor makes these spelling mistakes because he is writing the words as he hears them. And, in fact, after the tutorial, Victor told us that he "could hear the paper differently" when Tara read it aloud and that hearing his paper helped him understand where he made some mistakes.

A final layer in this discussion is to move beyond the second language learner aspects and consider the lack of literacy and reading experiences of many Generation 1.5 students.[6] Generation 1.5 writers may have problems with elements of formal writing such as spelling and punctuation. Victor's spelling mistakes, for example, may be the result of hearing these words more often than seeing the words and their correct spelling. This may be a similar issue with his punctuation. Referring to Victor's passage above, we notice that Victor's *sentence* is a run-on containing three independent sentences. Although Victor has periods in his paper, he does not always use them, and other forms of punctuation like commas, correctly. Consequently, punctuation is a common theme in Victor's tutorial. For example, Tara recommends putting quotation marks around the story title and Victor asks, "What do you call those?" Also, Tara points out places to add periods and semicolons to his run-on sentences. Eventually, Victor begins to ask more questions about the punctuation such as "That is a sentence, right?" After the tutorial, Victor told us that he began "to understand things, like a sentence."

Overall, these three layers present the complexity behind learning how to write in English as a Generation 1.5 student. On the one hand, they are not native speakers, and they are therefore still learning the rules of English. On the other hand, they might have learned the grammar, but what they learned is based on what they heard or thought they heard. Finally, they may have limited exposure to reading and writing in English and, as a result, might have limited ability with features more common in written forms such as spelling and punctuation. In any case, these three aspects of being ear learners translate into errors in a Generation 1.5 student's written English.

As a final thought, many of the Generation 1.5 student writers we see in our writing center have learned English as ear learners because they were immersed in English in school and everyday life.[7] In making a distinction between ear and eye second language learners, Joy Reid explains that ear learners "have listened, took in oral language (from teachers, TV, grocery clerks, friends, peers), and subconsciously began to form vocabulary, grammar, and syntax rules, learning English principally through oral trial and error."[8] As a result, they often cannot explain the rules of English grammar. This differs from international student writers who most likely learned English rules and patterns through their eyes. As Reid writes, eye learners "know, understand, and can explain English grammar; they have usually learned grammar through methodologies that focus on rule learning."[9] In the writing center context, these differences between ear and eye learners influence how we assist our Generation 1.5 students with language concerns in their writing.

Academic Writing Skills

One day, Ji-Sook, the Korean American student, comes to our writing center with a paper in which she writes about a student who is applying to Harvard University. In one part of her paper, she describes how this student is waiting for her admittance to Harvard. She expresses this idea with the informal phrase "*gets okay sign* on her application." Beatrice, the tutor, reads this sentence from Ji-Sook's paper and says, "Basically meaning that they were interested in her and gets okay sign." Without further prompting, Ji-Sook is able to self-correct, to an extent, responding to Beatrice, "I don't know. It's informal, right? What should I erase?"

We have tutored other Generation 1.5 writers like Ji-Sook who had similar mistakes in their writing. That is, we see many student writers use language that is more appropriate in spoken rather than written English for college papers. For example, Victor uses the phrase, *etc.*, in his paper, when he writes this list: "new friends, opportunities, meeting great people *etc.*" In another example, Nhia, the Hmong American student, wrote "will get rocks thrown at them *till* they die," in a summary of Shirley Jackson's "The Lottery," in which Jackson writes about a village tradition of stoning people to death. In her paper, Nhia uses the less formal *till* instead of the more formal *until*. So, many of our Generation 1.5 students, like Ji-Sook, write their papers using informal language that we are not used to seeing in academic writing; that is, these students are writing like they speak.

Another problem for our Generation 1.5 writers is the nature of academic writing. As Linda Harklau explains, "Academic writing requires familiarity with complex linguistic structures and rhetorical styles that are not typically used in every day social interactions."[10] Essentially, these students learned by listening to English that does not match the English they need to use in their writing. In addition to the lack of experience with the more formal, written English required in academic writing, some Generation 1.5 writers may not have been socialized into literacy practices that are associated with college writing.[11] Such practices include revision and analytical skills but can even include how to read and understand a writing assignment sheet. So, even though Generation 1.5 writers have the cognitive ability required for their college courses, they may lack the experience with academic writing skills necessary to keep up with their peers.[12]

Tutorial Suggestions

Although all students who come to the writing center bring their unique abilities and backgrounds with language and writing, we recognize that some of our Generation 1.5 writers at UAA learned English as ear learners and learned writing in high school classes that may not have adequately prepared these students for academic writing. Our tutoring suggestions reflect recognition of the Generation 1.5 writer's high competency with spoken English and the tutor's ability to teach the writer how to write in college. Above all, our suggestions offer our Generation 1.5 writers a chance to learn with their ears. With this, we suggest an approach that uses corrective feedback with language concerns and modeling with writing concerns.

Indirect Guidance and Corrective Feedback

Ji-Sook, the Korean American student, brings a paper to the writing center with this sentence: "One of the second generation of immigrants from Korea *apply* to Harvard University" in which she does not have the *-s* suffix at the end of the verb, *apply*. When her tutor, Beatrice, reads this section of her paper aloud, she reads this error with rising intonation, almost as if she is asking a question about the verb:

> *Beatrice:* One of the second generation of immigrants from Korea apply? Um, do you want that in the past or the present tense?
>
> *Ji-Sook:* Do I say *s* after?
>
> *Beatrice:* Yes, you would have *an s* if it's present, and then if you wanted it in past tense you would put a *d*.
>
> *Ji-Sook:* I want present.

With her response, Ji-Sook shows that she is familiar with common grammatical terms like past or present tense. Also, Ji-Sook is able to correct the error when her tutor points it out to her.

In many instances, we observed that Generation 1.5 writers were able to self-correct their errors in response to tutor feedback similar to Ji-Sook's example. In particular, the students engaged in self-correction when their tutor acted as an agent to help the writers bridge the gap between their less proficient written English and their high ability with spoken English. Thus, we recommend that tutors provide feedback to Generation 1.5 writers that does not refer to complex grammatical rules[13] but that also does not put the students on the spot with questions that appeal to native speaker intuitions.[14] That is, as tutors, we should encourage Generation 1.5 writers to draw from their oral competence with helpful guidance from the tutor. With Ji-Sook, for instance, the tutor indicated the error, *apply*, using both indirect guidance, saying the error in a quizzical manner with her rising intonation, and by using corrective feedback by referring to common grammatical forms. Prompted by this feedback, Ji-Sook corrected her error in this tutorial.

Even though Beatrice uses both indirect guidance and corrective feedback with Ji-Sook in the previous example, it is not necessary for tutors to use both in conjunction. One of our tutors, Tara, for instance, uses corrective feedback to prompt the student, Victor, to self-correct. In this tutorial, Victor makes a similar error to Ji-Sook's by excluding the -s suffix on his verb. In one of his sentences, he writes "He *make* mean comments about her." Tara responds to his error with corrective feedback:

> *Tara:*   Is this the right verb form?
>
> *Victor:*   He makes, makes.

The corrective feedback that Tara uses is posed as a question with reference to language elements. Using manageable terms and without directly correcting it, this type of corrective feedback points out the nature of the language error. The key to this type of feedback is that it avoids overt error correction.

Like corrective feedback, tutors can use indirect guidance exclusively to encourage Generation 1.5 writers to self-correct. Indirect guidance can take several shapes such as when a tutor pauses during the reading of the student's writing and, as seen with Beatrice and Ji-Sook, when a tutor rereads a section in the student's writing in a quizzical manner. These moves indicate to the student that a part of the writing rings problematic in the reader's ear. In some cases, this is sufficient for the student to notice and, if capable, to self-correct. In other cases, this prompts the student to comment about the error. Returning to the tutorial between Tara and Victor, Tara pauses after reading Victor's phrase, "he was always *critiquing* her." Tara's pause allows Victor to step in and comment, "I wanted to say *criticizing*," which then leads into a discussion on how to spell criticizing. Although the word *critiquing* is an appropriate use of the word in this sentence, by reading slowly and pausing, Tara provides Victor the chance to talk about what he wants to do with his writing. As such, it opens the door for student direction in the tutorial.

The use of corrective feedback applies to more global writing concerns as well. In the following example, Tara guides Victor to clarify his meaning with a more careful use of pronouns and their referents. Victor's sentence is "One day *she* is punched by a Black woman because *she* got irritated and gave *her* son a penny so *she* got irritated and punched *her*." Tara's response directly addresses the ambiguity in terms that highlight the readers' reaction to this type of problem.

> *Tara:*   The only thing . . . is that there is a lot of shes and hers. It's
>   tough to remember who is who.

Tara gives Victor time to think. As he writes notes on his paper, he makes a few suggestions. He begins by asking Tara, "If you say, because Julian's mother gave her a penny?" After this, Victor scribbles notes on his paper while he and Tara verbalize possible changes. Then, he says, "So the Black woman got irritated." Victor wrote his corrections on his paper. Later in the same tutorial, Victor asks questions about other pronoun usage, showing an increased awareness of the larger writing concern. In his revision, this sentence says, "One day she is punched by a Black woman because *Julian's mother* gave her son a penny so the *Black woman* got irritated and punched her."

Feedback, whether in the form of indirect guidance or corrective feedback, can encourage Generation 1.5 writers to self-correct their language errors or teach the students how to bridge the gap between their oral language and the more formal, written language, required in their papers. Sometimes our Generation 1.5 writers may bring to the tutorial other concerns such as how to approach a writing assignment. In these situations, we recommend that tutors model what good academic writers do.

Modeling Academic Writing: Tutors as Models and Scaffolds

When Tara works with Victor on a close reading assignment based on the short story "The Lottery" by Shirley Jackson, she notices that he seems unsure of the assignment and how to approach the writing. She watches Victor as he keeps shifting in his chair and flipping through his textbook. To add to his body language, Victor repeats the expression, "I don't know" many times as she asks him about the story and the assignment. With his reactions, Tara decides to ask Victor questions about the assignment and story as a means not only to help him understand how to write this assignment but also to model behaviors that are a part of academic writing.

For instance, she puts the assignment sheet at the center of the table and refers to it on several occasions when the topic of discussion relates to the assignment. Here is what the assignment sheet says:

> Write a short essay. You will want to choose one central issue that is raised in the story, provide a detailed example (close reading) that shows the issue in the story, provide your stance on the issue, and examine the importance of the issue in our society.

After the first review of the assignment sheet, Tara asks Victor if he knows what issue he wants to give his opinion on, and Victor responds by sitting back in his chair, throws out a few ideas, but also says, "I don't know" and "I don't like the story." Tara then tries to make this assignment more manageable for Victor by asking him, "Why don't we look at the story and find a paragraph that you can discuss." After this question, Victor takes some time to think about a paragraph to use as an example. At first, he flips through the story, skimming through some passages. As Victor skims through the story, he begins to focus on a paragraph. At this point, Tara asks a more specific question: "Is this something you want to focus on?" Victor responds with some ideas that he has about a character in the story, Old Man Warner. With this, Tara narrows the focus and asks, "What do you like about what it says in the story?"

With these questions, Victor begins to open up and discuss what he thinks about the story, and in particular, what he thinks about the character, Old Man Warner. In the story, this character supports the annual village tradition of stoning a villager to death. The villager is chosen by chance in a lottery drawing. When Victor talks about this character, he says,

> Well, he's an older man in the village and when they are talking about giving up the lottery, he's like, crazy fools. If there is no lottery, it makes no sense. And that if there had no lottery, they'd be living like cavemans and eating grass and stuff like that. And he's really biased towards it no matter what.

Tara listens and when he finishes, she brings his attention back to the assignment. She suggests that Victor use that information he just spoke about as an example of his close reading, and then she helps him write an outline of information to match the writing assignment. Acting as a scribe, she writes what he said on a piece of paper:

Paragraph: Old Man Warner

- oldest in village
- biased toward the lottery
- says without it, villagers like cavemen
- tradition not like it used to be (maybe worse)

In his final draft of this paper, Victor adds this sentence based on the Old Man Warner discussion:

> Old Man Warner seems to be bias towards this kind of lottery. He says he couldn't imagine the village with out the lottery.

Throughout the rest of the tutorial, Tara and Victor dance between the reference to the assignment sheet and her questions about the story and issues. Tara notices that he responds with uncertainty to the questions that have to do with the assignment language but can address general questions regarding the story more easily. After the tutorial, Victor told us that the most difficult part of the assignment was to "describe how the author makes her stance on the issue clear." When Tara focuses on this part of the assignment sheet toward the end of the tutorial, she says to Victor, "In your conclusion, tell us what you think she is saying." In the ensuing conversation, Victor bounces around a few ideas, while Tara listens and attempts to connect those ideas to his writing:

Victor: I think she is just crazy.

Tara: There's always that option.

Victor: It's just no sense . . . I just don't know what to use. I know my point in the story is that I don't like it.

After some discussion, Tara brings the discussion back to the assignment and states, "You need a thesis in your first paragraph. It's going to be your opinion on what she thinks and what you think her opinion of the story was." Victor responds by thinking aloud, and he considers how he can write his essay:

> *Victor:* Could I say like this proves that in the world there still is horrific traditions that other cultures might not understand?

After this, Tara agrees with this idea and Victor brainstorms a few ideas of how to make the connection with cultures and horrific traditions. Although Victor is still unsure of what to do and says, "I don't know what to put there, but I will think of it," he later adds some sentences to his final draft that attempt to describe Shirley Jackson's stance on the issue. In his final draft, he adds this sentence to his introduction paragraph:

> I think Shirley tries to prove that traditions are really strong in any culture and that's what makes them unique.

He also adds these sentences to his third paragraph:

> The way I personally see this story is that maybe she was going threw a tuft time which they way to express it better was to write something like this. Or it could be that there were wars or conflicts in the world that she was inspirited on to write this story.

Essentially, these questions facilitate Victor's process in understanding and analyzing the story. Moreover, the outline and notes that Tara and Victor keep provide him a tool that helps him write his essay after the tutorial session. With this, Tara is acting as a scaffold in that she is working with Victor's abilities with the task at hand and helping him bring his writing skills to the next level. After this session, Victor spoke to us about how Tara's questions were very helpful for him to understand the story, especially her questions related to the author's stance on an issue. He stressed that he still did not like the story but that at least he learned how to write about it. When we read his revisions of his paper after the tutorial, the information that Tara and he outlined on a piece of paper were included in his essay. Also, most of the things that Victor talked about, but he did not write down, were in his paper, too.

Terese Thonus writes that "many writers come to the tutorial table [without] the specialized language to talk about writing."[15] In this example, Victor is not able to talk about the writing in terms of the language on the assignment sheet. Victor responds with uncertainty to expressions like "provide your stance on the issue" and "examine the importance of the issue in our society." As a means to move beyond his uncertainty, Tara assists Victor through the assignment by asking him questions that relate to the assignment but are in terms that Victor can understand, such as, "Why don't we look at the story and find a paragraph that you can discuss." With these questions, Victor demonstrates that he is thinking about the meaning and significance of this story. Moreover, Tara acts as a model of what academic writers do by referring to the assignment sheet to understand what the writer needs to consider for this assignment. As such, she is teaching Victor how to write.[16]

Validating Cultural Heritage

We would like to add that in addition to facilitating Generation 1.5 students with academic writing skills that tutors acknowledge the students' cultural heritage. In doing so, tutors can bridge the gap between the students' content knowledge and their ability to write an academic essay. With this close reading assignment, for instance, the teacher recommended that the students refer to their own cultural traditions to contrast the traditions presented in the story. Nhia, the Hmong American student, incorporates this suggestion in the essay she brings to the writing center. In her paper, she writes about the Hmong New Year celebration. With this inclusion in the essay, her tutor, Stacy, learns about the food and clothing the Hmong people traditionally wear during this celebration and even how to pronounce the word *Hmong* in which the *h* is silent. The learning relationship here is mutual because the discussion of Hmong culture provides a platform for Stacy and Nhia to discuss writing strategies of including examples to support the analysis presented in the essay.

A valuable strategy to bridging the gap between Generation 1.5 students' oral and cultural strengths and their need to write more formally is offered by Thonus. Her recommendation that tutors should "validate students' cultural . . . heritage" not only serves to reduce the sense of marginalization experienced by many students who were not born in this country—particularly for Generation 1.5 students who can feel split between cultures—but also provides significant teaching opportunities. The practice offers tutors a platform from which to guide students through the lexicon of academic writing. Further, it opens the conversation to identification of culturally specific rhetorical styles and even discussion of how students can use their backgrounds in a positive way in their writing. For example, in her paper analyzing "The Lottery," Nhia makes a comparison between the customs portrayed in the story and those of Hmong culture. Her tutor, Stacy, strongly affirms the value of the comparison and asks questions about the Hmong traditions that indicate genuine interest. Nhia is thus provided with an immediate and positive reader response.

Simplifying Matters

The Generation 1.5 students we see have accomplished a fairly remarkable feat of adaptation in moving to a new country and developing the skills required to go to college. In the midst of this process, they often live suspended between cultures, with a home life and language more closely aligned with their country of origin and a school life more closely aligned with English and American culture. Usually, by the time we see them, they are pretty good at communicating in their new environment; however, the process of adaptation continues as they are challenged to use their acquired language in new ways.

With their limited backgrounds in academic literacy and writing in English, Generation 1.5 students may have the added challenge of unlearning language habits even as they learn new ones. Tutors require particular sensitivity to finding the appropriate level of support in order to facilitate learning. Finding the balance between too much help and too little help is a delicate process—which depends on reading, listening, and speaking skills distinct from those required when tutoring traditional, international, or recent immigrant students—but the overlap between these categories makes development of these skills valuable for almost any tutoring session. The oral fluency and familiarity with the academic setting possessed by Generation 1.5 learners is a major asset and aids the communication between tutor and learner. Such students are equipped to meet the tutor more than halfway as they work together to bridge the gap between students' abilities and needs. Our overwhelming conclusion is that awareness of the particular *needs* of students, although useful, should not overshadow our awareness of Generation 1.5 learners' particular *strengths* in a bridged perspective on language, writing, and culture.

Notes

1. Thonus, 17.
2. Thonus, 18.
3. Reid, 78.
4. Reid, 78.
5. The phrase *think on* used in this way is consistent with southern dialect in the United States, but we believe that Victor's usage is idiomatic rather than dialectal.
6. Reid, 77.
7. Reid, 76.
8. Reid, 77.
9. Reid, 79.
10. Harklau, 2.
11. Harklau, Siegal, and Losey, 9.
12. Harklau, 3.
13. Ferris, 150.
14. Thonus, 22.
15. Thonus, 18.
16. Thonus, 18.

Works Cited

Ferris, Dana. 1999. "One Size Does Not Fit All: Response and Revision Issues for Immigrant Student Writers." In *Generation 1.5 Meets College Composition: Issues in the Teaching of Writing to U.S.-Educated Learners of ESL*, edited by Linda Harklau, Kay Losey, and Meryl Siegal, 143–57. Mahwah, NJ: Lawrence Erlbaum.

Harklau, Linda. "Generation 1.5 Students and College Writing." *ERIC Clearinghouse on Languages and Linguistics*. Retrieved July 26, 2005, from www.eric.ed.gov.

Harklau, Linda, Meryl Siegal, and Kay Losey. 1999. "Linguistically Diverse Students and College Writing." In *Generation 1.5 Meets College Composition: Issues in the Teaching of Writing to U.S.-Educated Learners of ESL*, edited by Linda Harklau, Kay Losey, and Meryl Siegal, 1–16. Mahwah, NJ: Lawrence Erlbaum.

Reid, Joy. 1998 "'Eye' Learners and 'Ear' Learners: Identifying the Language Needs of International Students and U.S. Resident Writers." In *Grammar and the Composition Classroom: Essays on Teaching ESL for College-Bound Students*, edited by Patricia Byrd and Joy Reid, 3–17. New York: Heinle and Heinle.

Thonus, Terese. 2003. "Serving Generation 1.5 Learners in the University Writing Center." *TESOL Journal* 12(1): 17–24.

9

A(n)/The/Ø Article About Articles

Sharon K. Deckert

Although articles are small words, they are not without consequence in English; and because of this, they pose a particularly interesting challenge for writing center tutors. To create a writing center–oriented parody of Churchill's famous quote, "Never in the history of writing centers have so many problems been created by such little words." On one hand, teachers often teach[1] and tutors are often encouraged to address higher-order writing concerns. On the other hand, as Fei-Yu Chuang argues, article misuse is an English as a second language (ESL) difficulty that is often neglected by tutors, and this can have negative consequences for writers.[2] As Dana Ferris has shown, what evaluators view as typical ESL errors may negatively affect the grading of second language (L2) writers' work.[3] In addition, L2 writers, particularly advanced ones, are concerned with making their writing sound more "nativelike," and many insist on help with their article usage. As one L2 writer put it, "I have many problems with the little words like articles and prepositions. In the first draft, I don't care too much about articles and prepositions, but I go to my tutor for going over it for articles."

This chapter provides a discussion of the English article system and offers insights into why articles are a difficult puzzle for many L2 speakers/writers. This chapter also provides useful strategies for tutoring both beginning and advanced L2 writers. Ultimately, one-on-one meetings with a tutor are valuable because they create opportunities for writers to discover that their overall knowledge of English is often better than their compositions indicate, and writers can be reinforced to trust this instinct as part of their editing process. For example, one valuable exercise is for writers to hear their work read aloud. What L2 writers know about the sound patterns of English often can be used to help them hear missing elements in their own written product. There are, of course, two ways that this can occur.

The first is for the tutor to read the writer's work out loud for the writer. As Paul Kei Matsuda and Michelle Cox (Chapter 4) have noted, this allows the writer to hear where "the reader stumbles, pauses, fills in missing articles and modifiers, or reads smoothly" (47). Even the opportunity to watch a reader's face to see when he seems to have difficulty with a passage can be a useful experience for a writer.

A second way for writers to hear their work is to read it out loud to their tutor. On one level, this can create difficulties for some writers. They may, as Matsuda and Cox also note, shift their focus to issues of pronunciation. For others, however, this can still be a useful tool. In particular, it can be a useful tool for those writers who are in acquisition stages in which they may produce articles in speaking that they do not yet consistently produce in writing. In fact, as many advanced L2 writers like Takashi have experienced, when they read out loud, their reading often includes articles that were not on the page.[4] As Takashi said, "One tutor said to me that when I read, I added articles which I missed on the pages." This chapter also addresses the idea that L2 speakers frequently need reassurance that context usually can provide their readers with enough information to interpret meaning without article production perfection.

The Challenge of Articles

One reason articles may be particularly challenging is that they occur with such incredible frequency in English. *The*, for example, is the most frequently used word in the language.[5] In fact, *the* occurs so frequently in actual language use that in the British National Corpus, which is made up of multiple collections of both spoken and written types of language, *the* accounts for approximately 6.18 percent of the overall words used.[6] *A* and *an* are not far behind, making up 2.68 percent of the overall words used.[7] The articles, *the*, *a*, and *an*, then, account for nearly 9 percent of all words used.[8]

Articles, Determiners, and Noun Phrases

Articles occur so frequently simply because they are a class of words that modify nouns and most sentences are made up of multiple noun phrases. *Noun phrases* consist of a noun and any modifiers it may have. An important part of all noun phrases are *determiners*, the larger part of speech to which articles like *a*, *an*, and *the* belong. As a quick example of the frequency of noun phrases in a sentence, look at the first sentence of this paragraph again. It only contains twenty-five words but has seven noun phrases: *articles*, *they*, *class of words*, *words*, *nouns*, *most sentences*, and *multiple noun phrases*. At first glance, it appears to have only one article (*a*), but this will be addressed shortly.

Before jumping straight into a discussion of the challenges that articles pose for many L2 writers, some explanation of how articles work in English may be useful. Many older, traditional grammar books often grossly oversimplified their treatment of words that come before nouns by classifying all such words as "modifiers." In those old grammar books, words like *the*, *that*, *all*, *my*, and *yellow* were all said to "modify" the head noun and were often lumped into one large category called "noun modifiers." But more specificity than this is needed to help L2 writers understand how noun phrases work and to understand their own language production.

The first need is some basic facts related to the structure of noun phrases. We can say, for example,

"I like that yellow cat," *or* "I like the yellow cat."

But we cannot say

*"I like that the yellow cat," *or* *"I like yellow the cat."

(The asterisk is used to mark a sentence that seems generally unacceptable in English.)

As mentioned, articles belong to a grammatical class of words called determiners. A discussion of this grammatical class of words can begin with a simple syntactic strategy.[9] A determiner is any word that can fit into the following slot and make the following sentence grammatical:

"I want _____ cat."

If we use an article like *the*, *a*, or *an*—in this case *a*, due to phonological factors—before *cat*, the sentence is grammatical: "I want the cat with the white paws," *or* "I want a cat." But there are other words like *my*, a specific type of pronoun, and *this/that* that can be used in the same position before *cat* to make a grammatical sentence: "I want my cat," or "I want this/that cat." Traditionally, *this* and *that* (and their plural forms *these* and *those*) are referred to as *demonstratives*.[10]

In summary, English has three types of words in the determiner class:

- articles—*a*, *an*, and *the*[11] (Grammars of English define *a* and *an* as indefinite articles and *the* as a definite article.)

- *my* series of pronouns (possessive determiners)—*my*, *our*, *your*, *his*, *her*, *its*, *their*

- demonstratives—*this/these* and *that/those*

Making a distinction between the three types of determiners in English explains why words from these sets do not occur together in a noun phrase—noun phrases, in English at least, can only have one determiner.

Other Languages, Articles, and Acquisition

Although it has been argued that all languages have determiner phrases,[12] this does not mean that all languages cut up the article portion of the determiner pie in exactly the same way that English does. Many other Indo-European languages, such as German, Spanish, Italian, and French, have both definite and indefinite articles. Other languages, such as Arabic, have definite articles but not indefinite ones. And many other languages, such as Chinese, Japanese, and American Sign Language,[13] have ways of communicating definiteness or indefiniteness, but this is done without articles. Articles, then, can provide a particular challenge for many L2 writers.

Articles and L2 Acquisition

The frequency hypothesis of second language acquisition states that "the order of L2 acquisition is determined by the frequency with which different linguistic items occur in the input."[14] Since *the*, *a*, and *an* are incredibly frequent in English, one could assume that they should be rather early acquired. But this is not the case—as anyone who tutors ESL writers for any length of time discovers. Research has shown that English articles are a particular challenge for L2 speakers of English, particularly those whose language backgrounds have no articles.[15] In examining fifty essays of Chinese English-for-academic-purposes students, Chuang found that the top three types of errors that students produced were related to article use, and these accounted for 27.4 percent of the errors she coded.[16] In Chuang's study, article usage errors far exceeded even the subject–verb agreement (2.4 percent) and wrong tense and aspect errors (3.84 percent) that are so typically focused on.

Articles and Meaning

Articles belong to a class of words that are often called *function words* because one reason they exist is to function in some grammatical way. One purpose of these types of words is grammatical, so defining these words in the same way that we might define a content word is very difficult. Try defining the article *the* to a writer. You'll probably say something like, "Well, it's the word that you use when you are trying to talk about something that the reader already understands or something you've already established with the reader. . . ." It can get very messy. This does not mean, however, that function words, including articles, do not contribute to meaning.

When it comes to talking about meaning and articles, the most important idea to understand and convey to writers is that meaning does not exist simply in individual words such as nouns—it exists in noun phrases; more important, it exists in sentences as they interact within their extended context. Articles are a very important part of how contextual meaning is signaled to a reader.

A *Versus* An

The distinction between *a* and *an* is based on the beginning sound of the following word. Because this distinction is typically taught as soon as articles are introduced, it would seem to be a fairly straightforward rule. But here is where real life in the writing center differs from rules in a grammar book. Although there can be rather explicit, easily explained "rules" about how a particular grammatical feature should behave, this does not mean that the particular grammatical feature is easily acquired. Even an advanced student, like Takashi, will occasionally bring a tutor a sentence like, "I said I did not object to these tendencies of using new acronyms and emoticons because they are very convenient and have a intimate implications." As a general rule, if the difficulty is simply the choice between *a* or *an* and because this distinction is related to the sound system of English, a strategy for dealing with an occurrence of an *a* or *an* distinction is to read aloud with the writer so that the phrase in question can be heard and evaluated according to its sound. But negotiating this particular sentence out loud might not solve the underlying problem; the writer's intended meaning must be considered.

Articles, Count Nouns, and Meaning

Clearly, Takashi is not trying to talk about a specific type of intimate implications, so his inclination to choose the indefinite article is an appropriate one. What must be negotiated with Takashi is whether he wanted to communicate the idea that multiple implications were involved. Basically, as obvious as this may seem, implications can be counted; nouns that have either singular or plural forms are called, appropriately enough, *count nouns*. Nouns that are not used as singular or plural forms are called *noncount nouns*.[17] If we use Takashi's noun phrase to create a slot to consider, we find the following potential indefinite options:

a. Have *an* intimate implication (singular)

b. Have _____ intimate implications (plural).

This alteration makes sense when considering that historically, *a* and *an* developed from the word *one*,[18] and it still carries with it the same kind of singularity that *one* has. It can only be used to modify a single count noun. A strategy for helping writers with *a* and *an* is linked to its underlying meaning connection to *one*. It can only be used if there is only one of something that can be counted.

This is not the most important point of Takashi's example, however. The most important thing to notice about this set of options is what is *not* there. For Takashi to show that he wanted the meaning of indefinite multiple intimate implications, he would have to signal this meaning by using no article at all. In other words, the alternation between the article *a* or *an* and no article has meaning. Most grammar books deal with this by proposing what is called the *null*, or *zero*, *article*. It is most often represented by a null sign, Ø.

Articles, Noncount Nouns, and Meaning

With noncount nouns, article choice would appear to be much simpler. Either the writer has a definite meaning signaled by *the* or an indefinite, general meaning signaled by Ø. In many grammar books, this is summarized in a chart like the following:

	COMMON NOUNS			PROPER NOUNS
	Count Nouns		**Noncount Nouns**	Definite in and of themselves
	SINGULAR	PLURAL		
Indefinite	*a(n)*	*Ø*	*Ø*	No article is needed to mark definiteness
Definite	*the*	*the*	*the*	

Unfortunately, although charts like this are very helpful when the first language and English have certain similarities, using one is not quite as simple as it would seem.

Difficulties with Proper Nouns

This chart predicts, for example, that Takashi's production "Sometimes I cannot catch their utterance at all even though they come from the same area in United States," is perfectly correct. *United States* is a proper noun, and according to the chart, proper nouns do not get articles. As a tutor, you have probably come across this rule-generated difficulty many times. So what do you do? Actually, sometimes it's just easier to tell students to memorize the fact that *United States* needs an article and that their professors will definitely notice this one, than it is to spend the time explaining the intricacies of the plural-or-collective-geographical-names pattern of English. Take the easy way out, and have the L2 writer make a note to memorize this one; but for student's who are real grammar buffs, you can recommend a good grammar text like Marianne Celce-Murcia and Diane Larsen-Freeman's *The Grammar Book*.[19]

A second difficulty a writer might have with a chart like the one above is related to how the writer interprets the structure of a noun phrase and uses that interpretation in relation to article choice. Consider a condition in which Takashi incorrectly interprets the context of the article to be one modifying a proper noun: "The other day, one young woman spoke to me at the library since she was just interested in Japanese person." Clearly *person* is a singular count noun in this case, but the proper noun *Japanese* got in Takashi's way. A quick reminder that articles modify the head noun of a phrase would help here. Asking Takashi to identify which noun was actually the head noun would get him to recognize that the word *Japanese* was not the head noun and that the general rule about proper nouns did not actually apply here. Also having Takashi listen to or read this sentence out loud could trigger his unconscious head-noun recognition, and Takashi may have added the article on his own.

Missing Definite Articles

Probably the most common article difficulty that you will encounter when working with writers is missing definite articles. Missing indefinite articles, *a* or *an*, is much less frequent then missing definite articles, possibly due to the fact that indefinite articles are still somehow seen as more clearly being connected to the singularity of a noun phrase. The meaning of definite articles is most often a contextualized one. This context can include the immediate use in the written piece of discourse. Take, for example, a sentence from earlier in this chapter:

> Although there can be rather explicit, easily explained "rules" about how a particular grammatical feature should behave, this does not mean that the particular grammatical feature is easily acquired.

Notice that when the concept "particular grammatical feature" is first introduced, it is modified by the article *a*. But on its second reference, after the noun phrase has been established in the context, it is modified by the article *the*.

Context, however, can also include specific and general as well as local and cultural knowledge.[20] Consider Takashi's production of the following sentence: "Main editor is Albert Valdman." *Editor* is not a noun that is specific enough to on its own take an article, but the immediate context of the word *main*, which adds uniqueness with the mention of a unique individual, creates a context in which a definite article is needed. Talking to Takashi about how a noun phrase like "main editor" is specific enough to identity a unique individual, even if the name is not mentioned, allows Takashi to think of this noun phrase as a specific identifier.

Difficulties with Count/Noncount Noun Distinctions

If you are an L2 speaker of English or of any other language, you know that seemingly equivalent words in two different languages can refer to meaning in very different ways. And this is true for the count noun and noncount noun distinction. The Spanish *los muebles*, for example, refers to multiple pieces of furniture, and it is a plural count noun. But the English word *furniture* refers to pieces of furniture as a set, and it is a noncount noun. In academic writing, the English noun *research* presents a similar dilemma for many L2 writers. It is not uncommon to see a sentence such as "In a research done by Dana Ferris . . . ." In discussing examples like this one with writers, it is tempting to say that there is not supposed to be an article here and tell them to simply delete it. This does not, however, really address the actual underlying difficulty.

Consider the writers' understanding of the noun. This writer understands *research* as a count noun, and so his use of the article is understandable. What needs to be addressed is that in English—despite the fact that pieces of research can be counted—*research*, in its most common use, is a noncount noun. With this understanding, you can now offer at least two solutions. Remember that, for writers, meaning is important. If writers are trying to refer to research that they found in a particular article, you can offer the option of replacing "a research" with "a piece of research." If they intend to discuss a set of research, then point out that the English word *research* already has this quality of meaning and that is why it cannot take an article that is used with singular count nouns. This also resolves the difficulties of writers who write something like "Not a lot of researches have been done in this area." Because *research* is a noncount noun, it cannot be pluralized in this way. In my field, *vocabulary* is another noun that is commonly misunderstood as a count noun.

Articles as Part of the Prosodic Pattern of English

In the process of acquisition, it is typical for individuals' perceptions and understanding of language to precede their conscious production of language. Because articles, like other function words, tend to be unstressed in sentences, they can be seen as less salient items when working on a second language. But even though articles are unstressed, they still add to the overall prosodic pattern of spoken English. Because perception often precedes production, L2 writers who are not consciously producing writing that contains a consistent production of articles can still often recognize that something is different with the prosodic pattern of a phrase when they hear a sentence read out loud. Tutors should reinforce writers to trust this instinct as part of their editing process. As noted earlier, it can also be a valuable exercise for tutors to have writers read their work out loud. Quite often what they know about prosody can be used to help them hear missing elements in their own production, and learning that they can listen and recognize where some articles are missing can be encouraging.

Reassurance

It is important to reassure writers that context is a useful tool for their readers. Although every advanced reader of English has probably suffered a few awkward twinges when reading a sentence like "they come from the same area in United States," it does not keep a reader from figuring out that the writer is talking about *the United States* as a country. A missing or added article here or there is not going to completely throw a reader off track. There are examples where the difference between the presence or lack of an article makes a significant difference in meaning. A sentence like "I like dog," for example, when a basic writer means "I like dogs" can produce an unexpected meaning for the writer and reader, but readers read in context. If the sentence is written in a narrative about childhood pets, most readers, though possibly amused by the triggering of the unintentional meaning,[21] can figure out that the writer is not talking about food preferences. Finally, it is most important to reassure writers that they unconsciously know more about articles than is currently showing up in their writing. A more advanced production of articles will occur over time as their production catches up with their perception and acquisition.

Notes

1. Chuang (2005).
2. Chuang (2005).
3. Ferris (2002).
4. I would like to thank Takashi Kurata, an advanced L2 speaker who allowed me to use examples of actual texts that he took to the writing center for help.
5. World-English (1999).
6. Leech, Rayson, and Wilson (2001).
7. Kilgarriff (1996), like Leech, based his frequency list on the British National Corpus, which contains multiple corpora of both spoken and written discourse.
8. When one considers that the Ø article is not coded for in these corpora, the overall percentage of frequency for articles is even higher.
9. Slager and Deckert (1991).
10. There is some argument about whether demonstratives are determiners in other languages, but for the purposes of clarity in discussing English, I define demonstratives as determiners as many ESL grammars do. See (among others) Celce-Murcia and Larsen-Freeman (1999).
11. Many grammars include unstressed versions of *some* and particular cases of *any* in their classification of articles. An example of this would be the use of *some* in "Some man was running down the street." See Quirk and Greenbaum (1973) and Pinker (1994).
12. Some linguists argue that essentially all noun phrases are headed by determiners even if these are not overt. See, for example, Abney (1987) as cited in Uriagereka (1998).
13. MacLaughlin (1997).
14. Ellis (1994).
15. For a good summary of articles related to this topic, see Trenkic (2008).
16. Chuang (2005).
17. Noncount nouns are also often referred to as *mass nouns*.

18. Baugh and Cable (1978). See also, for example, Fries (1940).
19. Celce-Murcia and Larsen-Freeman (1999). Another valuable way of ex-
    amining articles looks at them as differentiating between notions of clas-
    sification and identification. An in-depth discussion of this analysis can be
    found in Master (1990).
20. For a more in-depth discussion of each of these types of uses, see Celce-
    Murcia and Larsen-Freeman (1999).
21. Research has shown that words with multiple meanings undergo *exhaus-
    tive access*. In other words, all of the possible meanings of the word are
    accessed at the same time. It is only downstream in the process of under-
    standing a sentence that a particular meaning gains salience. See Onifer
    and Swinney (1981).

Works Cited

Abney, Stephen Paul. 1987. As cited in Uriagereka (1998).

Baugh, Albert C., and Thomas Cable. 1978. *A History of the English Language*. 3rd ed. Englewood Cliffs, NJ: Prentice-Hall.

Cairns, Helen Smith. 1995. *The Acquisition of Language*. 2nd ed. Austin, TX:
Pro-Ed.

Celce-Murcia, Marianne, and Diane Larsen-Freeman. 1999. *The Grammar
Book: An ESL/EFL Teacher's Course*. 2nd ed. Boston: Thomson
Heinle.

Chuang, Fei-Yu. 2005. "Article Misuse: A Neglected Problem in Chinese
EAP Student Writing." Retrieved October 3, 2007, from www.reading-
matrix.com/conference/pp/proceedings2005/chuang.pdf.

Ellis, R. 1994. *The Study of Second Language Acquisition*. Oxford: Oxford
University Press.

Ferris, Dana R. 2002. *Treatment of Error in Second Language Student Writing*. Ann Arbor: University of Michigan Press.

Fries, Charles Carpenter. 1940. *American English Grammar: The Grammatical Structure of Present-Day American English with Especial Reference
to Social Differences or Class Dialects*. New York: Appleton-Century-
Crofts.

Kilgarriff, Adam. 1996. "English Word Frequency List." Retrieved December 27, 2007, from www.eecs.umich.edu/~qstout/586/bncfreq.html.

Leech, Geoffrey, Paul Rayson, and Andrew Wilson. 2001. "Word Frequen-
cies in Written and Spoken English." Retrieved December 26, 2007,
from http://ucrel.lancs.ac.uk/bncfreq/lists/2_2_spokenvwritten.txt.

MacLaughlin, Dawn. 1997. *The Structure of Determiner Phrases: Evidence
from American Sign Language*. Boston: Boston University.

Master, Peter 1990. "Teaching the English Articles as a Binary System." *TESOL Quarterly* 24(3): 461–78.

Onifer, William, and David A. Swinney. 1981. "Accessing Lexical Ambiguities During Sentence Comprehension: Effects of Frequency of Meaning and Contextual Bias." *Memory and Cognition* 9(3): 225–36.

Pinker, Steven. 1994. *The Language Instinct.* New York: Harper Perennial.

Quirk, Randolph, and Sidney Greenbaum. 1973. *A Concise Grammar of Contemporary English.* San Diego: Harcourt Brace Jovanovich.

Slager, William, and Sharon Deckert. 1991. "Expanding the Noun Phrase." Unpublished manuscript.

Trenkic, Danijela. 2008. "The Representation of English Articles in Second Language Grammars: Determiners or Adjectives?" *Bilingualism: Language and Cognition* 11(1): 1–18.

Uriagereka, Juan. 1998. *Rhyme and Reason: An Introduction to Minimalist Syntax.* Cambridge, MA: MIT Press.

World-English. 1999. "The 500 Most Commonly Used Words in the English Language." Retrieved December 26, 2007, from www.world-english .org/english500.htm.

10

Editing Line by Line

Cynthia Linville

Dinuba greets Tang at the door of the writing center with a smile, and as they get started on their session, Dinuba asks Tang what she can help him with today. Tang replies, "My professor said my paper cannot pass because it has so many errors in it. I need to fix every one of them. Please help me so that I can pass!" Nearly every experienced tutor has faced a situation like this one. Tang's goals for the session are very clear: line by line editing until the paper is error free. Dinuba is facing a dilemma because, after glancing at Tang's paper, she knows that even if she corrected every error for him, one session would not be enough time to effectively edit his paper. The first task of a tutor in this situation, then, is to negotiate a more realistic goal with her student.

A collision of student goals and tutor goals during writing center sessions is not uncommon. Students are often focused on the short-term goal of earning a passing grade on the assignment at hand, while tutors are often focused on teaching the students portable skills that can be applied to any assignment. This situation is exacerbated by varying concepts of what is expected in academic writing, including how many errors and what kind of error is acceptable. In addition, when faced with editing English as a second language (ESL) papers for errors line by line, tutors are often at a loss to determine how skillful an ESL student might realistically become in editing his own errors, knowing that he lacks the *native ear* for the language. Frustrated tutors are often tempted to either give the student too much help correcting errors or none at all, directing the student's attention to rhetorical issues instead. Most would agree that neither of these solutions is satisfactory. To help tutors with this dilemma, this chapter explores concrete strategies for providing appropriate and realistic help in editing ESL papers for errors, line by line.

Chris Thaiss and Terry Myers Zawacki's research has shown that students tend to view their professors' expectations for academic writing as "idiosyncratic and unpredictable," including expectations for "good grammar."[1]

Indeed, Thaiss and Zawacki demonstrate that both rhetorical and grammatical expectations vary from discipline to discipline and even from professor to professor and that these expectations are influenced by sociocultural factors as well. For example, the researchers were surprised to discover that university instructors often valued originality of voice over conventional standards. Tutors, therefore, need to keep in mind that their own concepts of "what is good writing" may vary from what individual professors expect.[2] Nevertheless, student papers with serious and frequent errors rarely earn students the passing grades they expect.

Fortunately, research has shown that college-level ESL students can and do learn to become proficient editors of their own texts when given the necessary instruction. For example, Dana Ferris conducted a semester-long study of ESL university freshman and found that twenty-eight out of thirty students were able to significantly reduce their errors over time as they practiced self-editing strategies.[3] When a student can learn what her most frequent errors are and learn to recognize and correct her own mistakes, then she will be a proficient self-editor.

Convincing a student that learning to edit her own papers is both possible and necessary, however, is a difficult task for a tutor, a task that will require persistent and consistent effort. Despite the difficulty, I believe that teaching students to become effective self-editors is absolutely vital to fulfilling the writing center's mission of helping students become independent writers. The alternatives are unacceptable: providing a proofreading service, which creates the kind of unhealthy dependency Carol Severino discusses in Chapter 5, or not providing the service at all. Most tutors don't need to be convinced that teaching ESL students to self-edit is a worthwhile goal; they simply aren't sure how to go about it.

Just as ESL students need to learn how to diagnose and correct errors, their tutors need to learn how to do so as well. This is more difficult than it seems because tutors will need resources beyond their native knowledge of English to carry out these tasks. When faced with a paper riddled with grammatical and lexical mistakes, tutors need strategies for spotting *patterns* of reoccurring errors, pointing those patterns out to the student, and providing rules about how to correct those errors. In addition, tutors need to know which kinds of errors are most important to address. This chapter explores six types of major errors that ESL students and their tutors can correct together. Focusing on this limited set of errors will not enable students to produce error-free writing, but this narrow focus will enable students to improve their writing. I find it important to note, however, that a tutor is not a grammar teacher. His ability to help is limited. Sometimes a tutor will find it necessary to refer a student elsewhere for more instruction, as discussed later in this chapter.

Before examining these issues in more depth, a summary of goals discussed so far might be helpful.

Goals for the Student

- Acknowledge the need to become a proficient self-editor.
- Learn what his most frequent patterns of error are.
- Learn how to recognize these errors.
- Learn how to correct these errors.

Goals for the Tutor

- Teach the student how to become a proficient self-editor.
- Learn how to diagnose frequent patterns of error.
- Learn how to correct (and teach students to correct) six major error types.
- Learn when to refer students elsewhere for more instruction.

Error-Correction Research

Some researchers note that while proofreading is usually against writing center policy, many students request this service and some tutors do provide it. In one study, Jon Olson, Dawn Moyer, and Adelia Falda suggest that the writing centers should consider lifting the ban against proofreading.[4] Research has shown, however, that direct error correction (crossing out errors and writing in corrections) does not prevent students from making the same errors in the next paper, nor does it seem to promote student learning.[5] In addition, scholars generally agree with writing center pioneer Steven North: The overarching purpose of writing center tutoring is to "intervene in and ultimately alter the composing process of the writer"[6]—that is, to *improve* students' writing skills toward the goal of making them independent writers. Accordingly, most writing centers have a policy against tutors acting as proofreaders. Teaching students to become self-editors, then, is the best alternative.

Ferris has demonstrated a successful approach in teaching students to become effective self-editors through "(a) consciousness-raising about the importance of editing in general and of each particular student's areas of need; (b) training in recognizing major error types; (c) teaching students to find and correct their own errors."[7] ESL writing specialists agree that error diagnosis should focus on those that are the most frequent, serious, and treatable.[8] Serious errors are usually defined as those that interfere with the clear communication of meaning; treatable errors are those that students can most readily learn to self-correct.

Clearly, some students will evidence serious errors not included in the six error types presented here. When *any* error is interfering with communication, it should be addressed. Tutors should be aware, however, that some language features, such as prepositions, articles (see Chapter 9), and precise word usage, take many years to learn; thus, while such errors may be serious, they may not be treatable. This will vary depending on the fluency of the student.

Six Error Types

Six error types that are treatable and are often frequent or serious in ESL college compositions are subject–verb agreement, verb tense, verb form, singular/plural noun endings, word form, and sentence structure.

Subject–verb agreement errors occur when the subject does not agree with the verb in person or number. These errors can be as simple as "He *walk* every morning" or as complex as "Every teenager knows how to choose clothes that *flatters* her figure."

Verb tense errors occur when an incorrect time marker is used. For example, "I *was* working on my paper since 6:00 a.m.," or "Even though this is my first day on the job, I have already found out that there *were* some difficult people here."

Verb form errors occur when a verb is incorrectly formed as we see in the following sentences: "I *will driven* to the airport next week," and "I *was cook* dinner last night when you called."

Singular and plural errors often occur when there is confusion about which nouns are countable and which aren't. For example, "I have turned in all my *homeworks* this week," and "I set up six more *desk* for the afternoon class."

Word form errors occur when the wrong part of speech is chosen: "I'm happy to live in a *democracy* country," and "I feel very *confusing* this morning."

Sentence structure errors occur for a variety of reasons: A word (often a *to be* verb) is left out; an extra word (often a duplicate subject) is added; word order is incorrect; or clauses that don't belong together are punctuated as one sentence. For errors like the following, asking the student for the intended meaning is key: "As a result of lack of moral values being taught by parents and the reemphasis by school many children have little respect for authority." Note that sentence structure errors often contain other types of errors within them.

While these six error types *are* rule based and thus treatable, it is important to note that the rules behind these errors are much more complex than tutors may first believe. This will quickly become apparent in line-by-line editing sessions. In addition, there are exceptions to every rule, exceptions that ESL students will demand explanations for. Because of this, effective tutors will need to study, discuss, and even debate grammatical rules together.[9]

Tutor Resources

Successful tutoring sessions begin behind the scenes with the appropriate tutor resources and training. One resource that every writing center needs is an ESL grammar handbook. If you can only choose one, I suggest Janet Lane and Ellen Lange's *Writing Clearly: An Editing Guide*.[10] A handbook and workbook combined, this text provides clear rules, strategies, and practice exercises helpful to both students and tutors. In addition, the unit topics correspond to the errors I discuss here (with additional errors covered as well). *Writing Clearly* is also a helpful resource in developing ESL grammar handouts for use in tutoring sessions.[11] At the end of this chapter are six sample tutorials and worksheets, and I recommend that tutors and their trainers work together to develop more.

Another valuable handout is a list of ESL resources available *outside* the writing center. There will be times when a tutor cannot be of help in line-by-line editing because the student does not yet have the level of language acquisition necessary for such a task. In those times, a referral to an ESL grammar class or lab on campus or in the community prevents the student from leaving the writing center empty handed. A list of interactive ESL grammar websites is also helpful.[12]

The handbook, tutorial worksheets, and referral sheet make it possible for tutors to follow the strategies suggested below without any additional training; however, additional training and practice in ESL error correction will help tutors feel more confident and be more effective during tutoring sessions. Ask a tutor trainer for suggestions.

Tutoring Strategies

At the opening of this chapter, Dinuba is beginning a tutoring session with Tang, who has unrealistic goals for their hour together. Dinuba's first task is to negotiate a more realistic goal with Tang. She might begin by reflecting back and affirming his stated goal: "I understand that correcting the errors in this paper is very important to you, and we will certainly spend most of our time during this session focusing on your errors." Next, she might gently inform him that the goal of an error-free paper at the end of the hour is not possible, but let him know what is: "I do need to tell you, though, that we won't have time today to correct *all* of your errors, so we're going to focus on your most frequent and serious errors here. Is that okay with you?"

Tang might need time for this point to sink in. He may become angry, depressed, or difficult as he feels his hopes being dashed. It would be best for Dinuba to pause until Tang has conceded this point. (Role-playing practice outside the session is very useful for situations such as these. Tutors need practice maintaining calm confidence even when the negotiations go awry.) A reminder that the clock is ticking might be helpful in persuading a stubborn student to move ahead.

Before Dinuba begins diagnosing Tang's paper, however, another step in the negotiation is needed. Dinuba needs to outline the procedure, especially if Dinuba and Tang have not edited together before. Dinuba might say, "I'm going to take a look at your paper and point out what some of your most serious errors are. Then we'll review the rules behind those errors and correct your paper together." Once they are in agreement on the procedure, Dinuba is ready to begin diagnosing Tang's patterns of error, focusing only on the six error types outlined above.

A paragraph from Tang's paper might look something like the example here:

> Jackson applied for a job and was given an interview since he had all the necessary skills for the job; however he *does* [verb tense] not have the moral values *suck* as *respect other people or when not to use abusive language* [sentence structure]. So during Jackson's *interviewed* [word form], he interrupted and used foul language toward his interviewers, and *a as* result he did not get the job. However, with the *institute* [word form] of moral values as part of the school *academic* [singular/plural], *it will* [sentence structure] *improves* [verb form] or *built* [verb form] on to the moral values each student already *possessed* [verb tense].

After marking the errors as shown here, Dinuba asks Tang to read the paragraph aloud, correcting any mistakes he sees.[13] Dinuba is quickly able to determine that words such as *suck* instead of *such* and the word order problem of *a as result* are typographical mistakes, but Tang is not able to correct any of his other errors. After glancing through the rest of his essay, Dinuba notices many more word form errors like the two above, so she decides to focus on those first, marking them throughout the essay.

After Dinuba shows Tang his pattern of word form errors and reviews some rules for word formation with him, they are ready to begin editing Tang's paper together. Dinuba points to the first error, reads it aloud, and asks Tang, "How can we correct this?"

during Jackson's *interviewed*

This point in the session is frequently one of the most difficult for the tutor because she must repress her urge to give too much help. I suggest that tutors put down their pencils and wait patiently and silently for the student to give a response. This is quite difficult but very necessary. It is important for tutors to remember that an unhealthy dependence on the tutor will be formed if the tutor is willing to supply the correct answers.

After a few moments of silence, Tang gives the answer *interviewing*, which of course is not quite right. Even still, Dinuba does not supply the correction. She directs Tang's attention back to the rules they have reviewed together and asks him to determine what part of speech the word should be (verb, noun, adjective, or adverb). On the second try, Tang gets it right: *interview*. Dinuba then asks Tang to write in the correction and double-checks to see that he wrote down his correct verbal answer. They proceed onward exactly this same way until all word form errors are successfully edited. If there is more time, Dinuba and Tang can move on to verb tense or verb form. After repeated sessions like these, the student can be led to recognize his own errors and correct many of them on his own, as discussed below. Editing sessions like the one portrayed here become the foundation on which students become proficient self-editors.

Granted, this method of editing is excruciatingly slow. To follow these suggestions, tutors will need to fight down their own sense of urgency. It is only natural to feel that too little is being accomplished in a session as slow moving as this. Yet simply by marking a pattern of error and providing Tang with the information to correct those errors, Dinuba is providing a valuable service. By refusing to give corrections, Dinuba affirms Tang's ownership of the paper, encouraging him to become a proficient self-editor. To implement these strategies, tutors must be convinced of the benefits of this approach. If a tutor is not sure that he *is* convinced, I suggest he discuss these ideas with a tutor trainer.

The scenario described here between Tang and Dinuba is a successful one. At times the session will be faster moving because the student is already skilled at correcting his own errors once they are pointed out. But more frequently, a session can move even slower than the one described. A tutor might wonder how slow is too slow. What can a tutor do if, after waiting patiently between each guess and reviewing the rules several times, it becomes clear that the student is not able to correct her own work? That is the time to bring out the ESL referral sheet and point the student toward a class or lab that can help her learn the skills she needs.

The tutor might say something like this: "It looks to me as if you need to brush up on your English grammar before we can edit together. Here are some places where you can do that." Again, role playing outside of the session can help tutors navigate difficult situations like this one. If the tutor is convinced that it would be unethical for him to correct the student's errors and that teaching ESL grammar exceeds his limitations, he will be confident in referring the student elsewhere. However, that doesn't mean the session has to end there. If the student is willing, the tutor can then refocus the session on rhetorical issues.

More often than not, however, tutors will find that their line-by-line editing sessions with students *are* successful. After the student has become aware of what his frequent patterns of error are, has learned the rules needed to correct those errors, and has become fairly proficient in correcting the errors his tutor marks for him, he is ready to begin finding errors on his own. An interim step toward that goal is for the tutor to be less direct in pointing out errors. In a future session between Dinuba and Tang, for example, Dinuba might say, "I see several word form errors in this paragraph. Can you find them?" If Tang has trouble finding them, Dinuba might say, "I see two on this line." If Tang still doesn't spot them, Dinuba could read that line out loud, exactly as it is written. Again, patient silence is needed while the student struggles to find the errors. Gradually, the student will become more proficient in finding his own errors; then he will be ready to learn how to proofread his own papers.

Clearly the student won't be able to proofread for every kind of error, so knowing her most frequent patterns of error is important. The tutor can ask the student to underline the types of words she has the most trouble with.

For example, if the student has difficulty with subject–verb agreement, the tutor can ask the student to single-underline every subject and double-underline every verb, one paragraph at a time. This is something that can be practiced together during tutoring sessions until the student gains proficiency. Once the student has no trouble marking the frequent trouble spots in her paper, she is ready to start proofreading on her own, assisted by the grammar resource sheets she has already been working with. When a student reaches this stage of independence, her tutor should rejoice in the knowledge that she has played a big part in fulfilling the writing center's mission of helping students become proficient, independent writers.

Sample Grammar Tutorial Worksheets

Subject–Verb Agreement Grammar Tutorial Worksheet

For the Tutor

When struggling with subject–verb agreement errors, ESL writers often have trouble identifying the correct subject of the sentence, just as native English-speaking writers do. This can be especially difficult when *there is* or *there are* is used and when a word like *that* is the subject of a relative clause.

When the words *there, that, which, who,* and *what* stand in as the subject of a clause, encourage your writer to look for the real subject elsewhere in the sentence to determine agreement. For example, in the sentence "There are fifteen students in the room today," the real subject is *students*, so the word *there* is treated as plural. However, in the sentence "There is a penny on the sidewalk," the real subject is *penny*, so the word *there* is treated as singular.

For the ESL Writer

Study these examples.

Corrected Examples

- There *is* three prerequisites for this class. (incorrect)
- There *are* three prerequisites for this class. (correct)

In the above example, the word *there* is standing in for the real subject *prerequisites*.

- Every teenager knows how to choose clothes that *flatters* her figure. (incorrect)
- Every teenager knows how to choose clothes that *flatter* her figure. (correct)

In the above example, the word *that* is standing in for the real subject *clothes*.

Correct the following.

PRACTICE SENTENCES

- Alexina found two online articles that *is* good for her assignment.
- Who *are* Sergey's and Mohammed's English teacher this semester?
- There *is* two sorority sisters in my class, Fatima and Thoa.
- My grandmother knows the Latin name of every plant that *grow* in her garden.
- Which *are* older, Enrique or Miguel?

Verb Tense Grammar Tutorial Worksheet

For the Tutor

Many second language (L2) writers have the misconception that all verbs in a paragraph should be in the same tense, yet shifting tense is usually necessary in a piece of writing to communicate information clearly. Learning to shift tenses, especially when the perfect tenses are involved, is a challenge for many ESL writers.

For the ESL Writer

Study the following passage, which demonstrates logical shifts in verb tense:

> Yesterday I *went* [simple past] to Admissions and Records to pay my fees; today I *am going* [present progressive] to the University Transportation Office to pick up my free bus pass; tomorrow I *will go* [simple future] to the bookstore to buy my texts and to the health center to get my flu shot. I usually only *do* [simple present] one or two errands per week, but I *have discovered* [past perfect] that I always *have* [simple present] too much to do at the beginning of the semester.

Here is another example showing incorrect and correct shifts in verb tense:

INCORRECT EXAMPLE

> The Chemistry Dept. has just changed the prerequisites for Chem 200. Now instead of taking it after Chem 101, students must also have completed Chem 102 before they *have enrolled*. In addition, students must have declared a Chemistry major and concentration before they *have been allowed* to take Chem 200. This has been problematic for many students because the office often has taken up to six months to process students' declaration of major.

CORRECT EXAMPLE

> The Chemistry Dept. has just changed the prerequisites for Chem 200. Now instead of taking it after Chem 101, students must also have completed Chem 102 before they *enroll*. In addition, students must have declared a Chemistry major and concentration before they *will be allowed* to take Chem 200. This has been problematic for many students because the office often has taken up to six months to process students' declaration of major.

Although most of the paragraph is in *past perfect tense*, some verbs need to be in other tenses to convey correct meaning. Note that the last sentence could be written in present tense if the writer wished to show a general trend: "This *is* problematic for many students because the office often *takes* up to six months to process students' declaration of major.

Correct the following:

PRACTICE PARAGRAPH

> The Office of International Studies has just started a Partner Program that pairs American students with international students who will only *have been* in the United States for a short time. Both students and professors are happy with this program. The students are happy because the program has proven to be a great way *to have met* new friends and *learned* about other cultures. The professors are happy because they have been able to assign their students to discuss certain topics with an international partner to gain a broader perspective and a better understanding of the curriculum.

Verb Form Grammar Tutorial Worksheet

For the Tutor

Some verbs are limited by the forms they can combine with. For example, some verbs are followed by infinitives, as in "I *agreed to look over* the article." Other verbs are followed by gerunds, as in "Do you *deny telling* her that?" Some verbs can be followed by infinitives or gerunds, as in "Lixin *likes skiing* or Lixin *likes to ski*." A more limited list of verbs is followed by the base form, as in "*Let* me *help* you carry that."

This type of verb formation is not rule based but must be learned through careful listening and reading, emphasizing the point that much of grammar is illogical and harder to master than native English speakers may realize.

Because of the difficulty that ESL writers may find in mastering this, a tutoring session may be limited to focusing on just one or two of these verbs at a time. Although the slow pace may be frustrating for both tutor and tutee, such sessions are valuable nonetheless.

For the ESL Writer

NONRULE-BASED VERB FORMATION

Study the verbs below that must be followed by infinitives, gerunds, or either infinitives or gerunds:

INFINITIVES	GERUNDS	EITHER INFINITIVES OR GERUNDS	BASE FORM
agree	deny	like	let
offer	finish	try	have
decide	suggest	begin	make
hope	dislike	remember	
plan	discuss	start	

CORRECTED EXAMPLES

- Aradhna *began study* chemistry in high school. (incorrect)
- Aradhna *began to study* chemistry in high school. (correct)
- Aradhna *began studying* chemistry in high school. (correct)

In the above example, the verb *began* must be followed by either an infinitive or a gerund.

- Dhiren *hopes finding* the bookstore before he goes back to the dorms. (incorrect)
- Dhiren *hopes to find* the bookstore before he goes back to the dorms. (correct)

In the above example, the verb *hope* must be followed by an infinitive.

Correct the following:

PRACTICE SENTENCES

- Svetlana plans *finish* her degree by 2012.
- Kaulana's and Sliman's relatives suggest *to plan* a June wedding.
- Giovanni remembers *ride* an elephant when he was younger.
- Yumi makes her sister *to do* her homework every night.
- Luu tries *run* for 30 minutes every day.

Singular Plural Grammar Tutorial Worksheet

For the Tutor

Some nouns are both countable and noncountable, depending on the meaning of the word and situation in which the word is used. Generally, if a noun can be made plural, it is countable—but not always. For example, *intelligence* is generally considered to be noncountable. Yet is it now common to discuss Howard Gardner's *theory of multiple intelligences* in an academic atmosphere. This can cause confusion for your ESL writers. Distinguishing between nouns that are countable, noncountable, or both is a lengthy and difficult task for most L2 writers of English and must be learned by experience.

For the ESL Writer

Study the following:

SOME NOUNS THAT ARE BOTH COUNTABLE AND NONCOUNTABLE

water	hair	work
truth	light	soda
money	intelligence	email
candy	cake	room

EXAMPLES

- Would you like some of this chocolate *cake*? (noncountable)
- We baked three *cakes* for the fundraiser. (countable)

- This room needs more *light*. (noncountable)
- In some *lights*, Pa looks blonde. (countable)

- *Email* is Sothea's preferred method of communication. (noncountable)
- How many *emails* did you receive when you were on vacation? (countable)

Correct the following:

PRACTICE SENTENCES

- How many *soda* did you order?
- Have you read the complete *work* of Emily Dickinson?
- Does Huii have enough *rooms* at the end of the table?
- Shakiba had her *hairs* cut and styled yesterday.
- Ricardo strongly believes in telling the *truths*.

Word Form Grammar Tutorial Worksheet

For the Tutor

Some words have more than one form for the same part of speech. Such subtle distinctions can be troubling for your L2 writers. For example, *bored* and *boring* are both adjectives, but their meaning is different. "The student is bored" indicates that something outside the student is causing the boredom (such as the classroom lecture). "The student is boring" indicates that the student herself is causing the boredom (possibly by talking for too long). In general, the past participle form is used to indicate an outside cause, and the present participle form is used to indicate an internal cause.

Other differences in word form are nonrule based and must be acquired by paying attention when listening or reading. For example, *discriminating* may be considered positive, as in the ability to make wise choices, whereas *discriminatory* is certainly negative, indicating prejudice.

For the ESL Writer

Be aware that although words may share the same root and even the same part of speech, word meaning changes when form changes. Use an ESL dictionary (such as *Longman Advanced American Dictionary*) to determine the differences in meaning in these words. Study the following:

Differences in Meaning

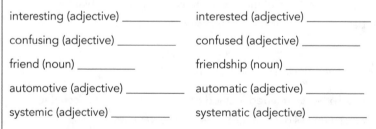

interesting (adjective) _____   interested (adjective) _____

confusing (adjective) _____   confused (adjective) _____

friend (noun) _____   friendship (noun) _____

automotive (adjective) _____   automatic (adjective) _____

systemic (adjective) _____   systematic (adjective) _____

Correct the following:

Practice Sentences

- Alma feels *boring* when she listens to long lectures.
- Gregorio is *concerning* about global warming.
- The senators attacked each others' *characteristic* during their political campaigns.
- Yesterday it was hot; today it is cold. The weather has been *various*.
- This class is *comparative* to the class you are taking at city college.

Sentence Structure Grammar Tutorial Worksheet

For the Tutor

Sentences missing subjects often occur in ESL writing when prepositional phrases are present. When this type of error occurs, remind your L2 writer that main subjects do not occur in prepositional phrases. The solution is often as simple as eliminating a preposition. For example, in the following sentence, either the preposition *in* or *by* can be eliminated: "In the article ~~by~~ Smith states that crime has increased 50 percent over the last year."

For the ESL Writer

Study the following:

SOME COMMON PREPOSITIONS

in	to	by	after	except	despite
on	out	from	along	upon	during
of	at	as	with	across	among

CORRECTED EXAMPLE

- *In* the painting by Dali shows melting clocks. (incorrect)
- The painting by Dali shows melting clocks. (correct)

In the above example, a preposition had to be removed in order to provide a subject for the sentence.

Correct the following:

PRACTICE SENTENCES

- In the article *by* Singh supports this point.
- *During* a long lecture by my cousin Suk is boring.
- *With Yusef and me to the park* is fun.
- *At* Josiah's house is filled with many photographs.

Notes

1. Thaiss and Zawacki, 7, 109
2. Thaiss and Zawacki (2006).
3. Ferris (1995).
4. Olson, Moyer, and Falda (2002).
5. For a summary of error correction studies, see Leki (1990) and Ferris (2003).
6. North, 28.
7. Ferris (1995), 45.
8. For example, see Harris and Silva (1993) and Ferris (1995).
9. An excellent comprehensive reference for such study is Celece-Murcia and Larsen-Freeman (1983).
10. Lane and Lange (1999).
11. Also useful is Master (1996).
12. I recommend these interactive grammar websites: The ESL Quiz Center at www.eslcafe.com/quiz/, The English Page at www.englishpage.com/index.html, and Self-Study Grammar Quizzes at http://a4esl.org/q/h/grammar.html.
13. This method is suggested by Bartholomae (1980).

Works Cited

Bartholomae, David. 1980. "The Study of Error." *College Composition and Communication* 31(3): 253–69.

Celece-Murcia, Marianne, and Diane Larsen-Freeman. 1983. *The Grammar Book: An ESL/EFL Teacher's Course*. Boston: Heinle and Heinle.

Ferris, Dana. 1995. "Can Advanced ESL Students Become Effective Self-Editors?" *CATESOL Journal* 8(1): 41–62.

——————. 1999. "The Case for Grammar Correction in L2 Writing Classes: A Response to Truscott (1996)." *Journal of Second Language Writing* 8(1): 1–11.

——————. 2003. *Response to Student Writing: Implications for Second Language Students*, Chapter 3. Mahwah, NJ: Lawrence Erlbaum.

Harris, Muriel, and Tony Silva. 1993. "Tutoring ESL Students: Issues and Opinions." *College Composition and Communication* 44(4): 525–537.

Lane, Janet, and Ellen Lange. 1999. *Writing Clearly: An Editing Guide*. Boston: Heinle and Heinle.

Leki, Ilona. 1990. "Coaching from the Margins: Issues in Written Response." In *Second Language Writing: Research Insights for the Classroom*, edited by Barbara Kroll, 57–68. New York: Cambridge University Press.

Master, Peter. 1996. *Systems of English Grammar: An Introduction for Language Teachers*. Englewood Cliffs, NJ: Prentice Hall.

North, Steven. 1984. "Writing Center Research: Testing Our Assumptions." In *Writing Centers: Theory and Administration*, edited by Gary Olson, 24–35. Urbana, IL: National Council of Teachers of English.

Olson, Jon, Dawn Moyer, and Adelia Falda. 2002. "Student-Centered Assessment Research in the Writing Center." In *Writing Center Research: Extending the Conversation*, edited by Paula Gillespie, Alice Gillam, Lady Falls Brown, and Byron Stay, 111–31. Mahwah, NJ: Lawrence Erlbaum.

Thaiss, Chris, and Terry Myers Zawacki. 2006. *Engaged Writers Dynamic Disciplines: Research on the Academic Writing Life*. Portsmouth, NH: Boynton/Cook.

11

Tutoring ESL Students in Online Hybrid (Synchronous and Asynchronous) Writing Centers

Lee-Ann Kastman Breuch and Linda S. Clemens

Tutoring English as a second language (ESL) students online presents a challenge because of the range of language and sometimes cultural differences that tutors must negotiate while working in a technology-mediated environment. This challenge is part of an emerging area of scholarship and practice that we believe represents a broadening of what writing centers and writing tutors do. In addition to helping ESL students become better writers and more familiar with American academic discourse, American tutors and directors must now learn to engage in substantive *online conversations* about writing with ESL students—in writing.

In this chapter, we discuss how our thinking has evolved with regard to tutoring ESL students in online environments. We specifically discuss the transition that the University of Minnesota (UMN) made to tutoring ESL and other students online. As we will explain, UMN previously offered online tutoring through an online writing center in an asynchronous-only environment—in other words, students submitted a paper electronically through a Web interface and later received feedback typed into the document by an online tutor. Now, online tutoring resides in the UMN Center for Writing and is named Student Writing Support online, or SWS.online. SWS.online is a *hybrid* model consisting of two phases: an asynchronous phase in which the tutor reads and responds online to a student's document and a subsequent synchronous phase in which tutor and student meet online for a scheduled chat to discuss writing. This shift in online tutoring has changed our thinking about what is possible in online tutoring sessions with ESL students, especially in terms of balancing higher-order and lower-order tutor comments. We have found that a hybrid model offers excellent opportunities for tutors to interact with students, prioritize comments, and address ESL concerns of expression and grammar. In the remainder of this chapter, we discuss these possibilities more fully. We believe this discussion can illustrate new opportunities for tutors who work with ESL students online.

We begin by reviewing key issues involved in online tutoring of ESL students. We then introduce an online hybrid model of tutoring, discuss its potential benefits and challenges, and provide sample tutoring transcripts for consideration.

Issues Involved in Tutoring ESL Students Online

There are precious few resources that address the specific intersection of online tutoring and ESL students, and most of those resources address asynchronous-only tutoring or static online resources. However, in the accounts we found, one thing is clear: Managing a balance between higher-order and lower-order concerns is a dominant and recurring theme. Specifically, many articles discuss the degree to which online writing tutors should focus on grammar and mechanics when working with ESL students. Consider this quote from Suzan Moody of the University of Kansas, who observed in 1996 that several online writing resources for ESL students at that time focused on grammar instruction and handouts: "The greatest number of existing ESL resources in these eight OWLs center on English grammar. Only half provide information on how to write essays, most of which were written for native English speakers. While these OWLs are useful resources for ESL students, more on-line writing resources should be developed for non-native English writers."[1] She calls for online resources for ESL students that extend beyond grammar and mechanics.

Since 1996, online writing centers have included more asynchronous tutoring services for ESL students. But as many tutors and administrators have noted, ESL students who use asynchronous tutoring continue to ask for help with grammar. When tutors receive specific requests from ESL students to focus on "lower-order" concerns like grammar, to what degree should online tutors comply? This recurring issue presents a dilemma for online tutors who work with ESL writers. If tutors focus on grammar and sentence-level concerns, they feel they are ignoring their training and writing center policies; if tutors focus on higher-order concerns, they feel they are ignoring the requests from ESL writers. This dilemma is intensified in asynchronous-only tutoring situations (like email tutoring) where there are fewer opportunities to interact and explore these concerns with students directly. To illustrate, consider the following request that we recently received from an online ESL student: "I need to criticize this case study so that I put a lot of my opinions in this paper. Please let me ask your thought in terms of the content's flow. . . . I'm concerning about grammar in English."

How Should an Online Tutor Respond to Such Queries?

The accounts of online tutoring of ESL students that we found offer different approaches to this dilemma. Some celebrate the potential of online environments to provide ample feedback to ESL students. For example, in reports of the online asynchronous tutoring resource for ESL students at Kent State University, Sarah Rilling, assistant professor of English, observes that tutors can use the technology to insert intertextual comments related to higher- and lower-order concerns, with the written feedback providing "an advantage to students who may not remember all the oral comments a tutor in a face-to-face tutoring session may provide."[2] Rilling advocates focusing on error feedback—comments about organization and development of ideas as well as sentence-level issues—rather than error correction or comments only about grammatically correct expression.[3]

In another account of asynchronous tutoring, Virginia Pyle, ESL program graduate student at the University of Minnesota, studied a small group of ESL writers who used the asynchronous Online Writing Center (OWC) formerly in place at UMN. She noted that the ESL writers in her study reported needing and receiving help with grammar, word choice, and similar lower-order issues, but that tutors in the study were encouraged to focus their comments on higher-order issues. In light of her research results, she recommended that the online tutoring staff include an ESL specialist who received training in differences between ESL and native English speakers. She also suggested "perhaps giving the 'ESL specialist' tutor(s) more leeway to go ahead and give the L2 [ESL] students who submit papers more robust feedback in the arena of expression [e.g., grammar and word choice], as well as training these tutors in how best to do so, is in order."[4]

These two accounts suggest that online tutors can and should provide ESL students with feedback on both higher-order and lower-order concerns. However, others warn against moving too much in this direction. As Ben Rafoth suggests in Chapter 12, online tutors should read ESL student papers through an accommodationist stance, resisting the urge to correct sentence-level errors. He offers the useful advice that online tutors should not overwhelm ESL students with too many written comments: "Writing lots of feedback items in online responses is ineffective. We discovered that tutors who responded in this way called attention to more points than writers actually followed through on when they revised." Rafoth suggests that tutors select two priority items in an online tutorial rather than attempt to address all potential issues online.

Our stance is that online tutoring of ESL students, like face-to-face tutoring, must be flexible to the individual needs of the learner. We agree with the advice shared by Jennifer Staben and Kathryn Dempsey Nordhaus (Chapter 7), who assert that "the dichotomy itself is false: Tutoring objectives are rarely as simple as *either* grammar *or* the whole text" and "tutoring sessions are as individual as fingerprints." We advocate that, as the situation suggests, online tutors provide ESL students with feedback on higher-order concerns as well as error feedback (rather than error correction) on lower-order concerns—especially when ESL students request such feedback. However, we also support Rafoth's suggestion that tutors must be selective in their comments in order to make an online tutorial manageable. It would be virtually impossible for tutors to highlight each higher-order or lower-order concern in a paper (there simply is not enough time; see Chapter 10). Online tutors must be prepared to look for priority issues and offer feedback on those issues. Like Rafoth, we suggest that tutors can be purposefully selective by articulating one to three focal points for the student. A good place for this kind of statement is at the end of an online tutorial when a tutor summarizes his or her comments. Returning to our earlier example in which an online ESL student requested help for grammar, here is the tutor's response, in which the tutor selected two aspects of the paper to address (content and grammar):

> As far as the content's flow in the paper is concerned, I did wonder if you had organized your paragraphs under individual topics or there was any other kind of organization pattern you have to use for this paper? I had some difficulty trying to follow all the data because I couldn't grasp if there were several big topics, each with one section or if you were just listing flaws in the study in no particular order. In terms of grammar, I had some trouble in areas where you use passive voice construction; for more on active and passive voice usage, you may find our website useful: www.writing.umn.edu/sws/quicktips/style_grammar/activepassive.htm.

This response is a good example of how a tutor can selectively address both higher-order and lower-order concerns in an asynchronous tutorial.

Another way that online tutors can maintain a balance between higher-order and lower-order issues is by articulating their approach, often within a written greeting at the top of a student's paper. To illustrate, here is a response from the same tutor regarding the ESL student's request to review grammar:

> I see that you would like help with grammar so I have to begin by letting you know that [we are] happy to help you with your writing, but we do not edit papers in the sense of finding all the errors and correcting them. Our aim is to interact with the students and help them improve their writing in terms of content and structure. . . . We can point out some examples of errors in mechanics but we hope that we can help you learn to identify those errors for yourself in the future so that you become your own proofreader.

We have found this strategy to work well in shaping the direction of a tutorial and maintaining balance of higher-order and lower-order issues—while also maintaining a helpful, consultative tone in our online interactions with students. (See Chapter 10 for more on helping students become competent self-editors.)

Another way to increase and/or maintain balance and flexibility in online tutor feedback is to offer (or at least consider offering) synchronous (chats) as well as asynchronous (email or the Web), tutoring sessions for ESL students. In making this suggestion, we do not mean to say that asynchronous-only (such as email) tutoring is not useful for ESL students. On the contrary, there are several benefits that asynchronous tutoring affords ESL students. For example, students can benefit from (archivable) written tutor comments that include questions about clarity and meaning or highlighted error patterns. In addition, asynchronous tutoring may appeal to those ESL students who feel less comfortable talking with a tutor face-to-face. (Such discomfort can be an issue among students from some cultures who see being tutored as a sign of weakness or who worry that asking for help is an imposition. See Chapter 18 for more on this issue.) The convenience of asynchronous tutoring is also an appealing benefit: Students can submit writing for review at any time. In our experience, the accumulation of these benefits led to a strong ESL student population in our asynchronous-only tutoring center where consistently 30 percent of all clients were nonnative speakers of English. ESL clients particularly liked the convenience of asynchronous tutoring and the ability to archive tutor comments.

However, there are also ESL students for whom asynchronous-only tutoring is not helpful. Some students may find it difficult to articulate questions about their writing (as seen in the student example). And, as Rafoth points out, some ESL students might be completely overwhelmed by the volume of online comments provided by a tutor; in addition, some ESL students might not be able to prioritize tutor comments ("Which online comments are most important to address?"). Furthermore, tutors might be frustrated working with ESL students in asynchronous-only environments because of the limited opportunities to interact with students. This was certainly true in our experience: Tutors were often quite unhappy in asynchronous-only tutoring environments and felt isolated. It was difficult for tutors to gauge in this environment how helpful their sessions with ESL students had been. These frustrations make sense, given that asynchronous-only tutoring limits tutor response to the texts at hand. In our experience, these frustrations intensified during busy times in a semester when several students would submit writing for tutor review all at once (and expect tutors to immediately respond). In these times, tutors had to limit the amount of time they spent on each submission. This was a disadvantage for tutors who would prefer to have more time, not less, to focus on ESL written work.

In the spirit of Staben and Dempsey Nordhaus' assertion that each tutoring session is individual, we have found it useful to think about the possibilities beyond asynchronous-only tutoring for ESL students so that we have more flexibility in working with them and a better shot at understanding their needs. In the next section, we provide more details about hybrid online tutoring models.

What Is Hybrid Online Tutoring?

A hybrid model of online tutoring includes both asynchronous and synchronous components, both conducted entirely online (no face-to-face interaction) and configured as a seamless, interactive tutorial. The asynchronous component occurs across time, meaning that the student and tutor do not interact at the same time. An asynchronous tutoring component usually consists of some variation of the following process:

1. A student submits a paper (or parts of a paper) to a Web- or email-based online tutoring service.

2. The student asks questions about the paper she would like the tutor to discuss.

3. At a later time, the tutor downloads and reads the paper and writes a comment at the beginning of the paper in which he greets the student and explains how he will approach the tutorial.

4. The tutor often provides intertextual comments throughout the paper, usually in the form of questions or comments. These comments are made using word processing features such as "Track Changes," "Comments," or simple textual markers such as an asterisk [*], a bracket [], or *italics* or **bold** typeface.

5. The tutor may provide a written, summarizing comment in which they review priority issues for further consideration.

6. The tutor sends his feedback to the student via email or the Web.

Variations of this process are common among many asynchronous-only writing centers, including email tutoring.

An online hybrid model of tutoring takes online interaction further by adding a synchronous follow-up online chat between the tutor and student.[5] To illustrate, we share the hybrid tutoring process used in SWS.online, which consists of the following steps:

1. A student submits up to five pages of text for an online tutor to review.

2. The tutor spends up to forty-five minutes reading and commenting on the text (see Figure 1).

3. The tutor sends the text with comments back to the student, and then they participate in a forty-five-minute online chat about the paper (see Figure 2).

During the chat, as shown by Figures 1 and 2, our interface facilitates a shared view of the student's document with consultant comments. In addition, student and tutor can engage in live revision of the document during the chat.

Certainly, hybrids can take different forms than the internal, custom software our institution has created. For example, the software NetMeeting or

Consultant response

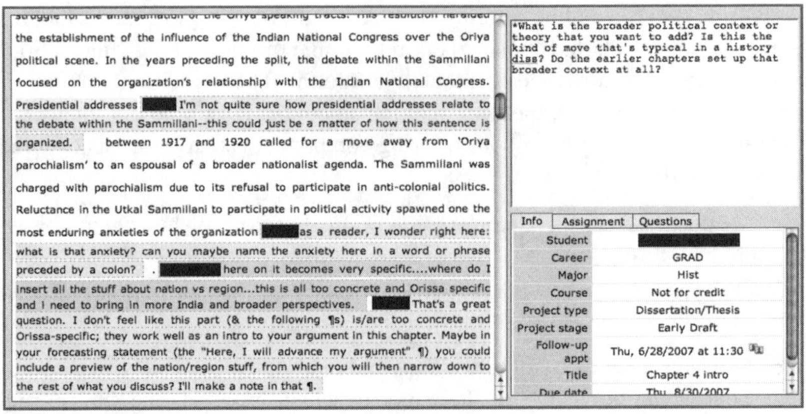

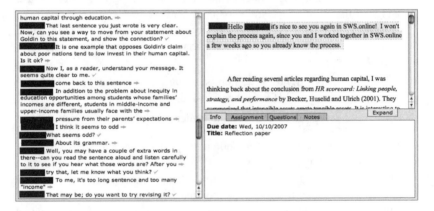

Figure 1: Sample Asynchronous Consultant Response

Figure 2: Sample Synchronous Chat to Accompany
an Asynchronous Response

Windows Meeting Space allow for shared viewing of a document with a simultaneous chat. Another hybrid option is the use of instant messaging (IM) to talk with students after submitting asynchronous-only comments. A third option is the use of chat rooms—possibly supported by Web courseware packages such as WebCT or Blackboard—that supplement asynchronous comments on texts. In short, there are many ways to create hybrid environments.

    Whatever technology is used, we favor a two-phase process in which tutors spend forty-five minutes commenting asynchronously and forty-five minutes conversing with the student synchronously. This approach places realistic (and even generous) parameters on tutor time while also creating a structure for the hybrid tutorial. We have found that students like aspects of the hybrid model, too. In a survey of students and tutors about our hybrid service, students reported that they like the following features of SWS.online:

- the written response and chat transcripts they received
- the additional time consultants had to craft responses
- the additional time students had to think about consultants' responses
- the flexibility of participating from their own locations

We discovered that tutors in SWS.online also appreciated having two scheduled forty-five-minute sessions for each writer—one session to read and respond to the draft and one session to chat with the writer of that same draft. This two-phased system eliminated the time-crunch problems that occurred in asynchronous-only environments and allowed tutors the opportunity to thoughtfully read and reflect on student writing. In addition, tutors reported that they felt less pressure to comment on everything because they knew they would have the chance to further discuss concerns and issues with the student directly in the chat.

What Can Hybrid Models Offer ESL Students?

Our hunch about an online hybrid model was that it would provide more flexibility for both tutor and student to further discuss concerns that ESL students might have. To explore this hunch further, we conducted a focus group and interviewed a small group of tutors in SWS.online who had experience working with ESL students using the hybrid format.[6] The tutors reported a range of benefits of the hybrid model in working with ESL students, and all of them said they would continue to use the hybrid format. Here are some of the things they had to say:

- In a hybrid format, ESL students can participate in written conversation with the tutor, allowing them to practice writing and "speaking" English with a native speaker. Tutors commented that the chat format especially immerses ESL students in language and encourages writing practice. Students can archive the transcripts to further examine the conversation.
- In a hybrid format, ESL students can practice revising or editing with tutor guidance. Sentence-level issues can be discussed and clarified, and ESL students can return to the draft to implement changes, all during the chat.
- In a hybrid format, ESL students have time to read and reflect on the asynchronous comments that tutors provide in advance of the chat. They can formulate questions and then pose those questions in the chat. This factor is particularly helpful to ESL students who must deal with the cognitive challenges of thinking and writing in a nonnative language.

- A hybrid format increases opportunities for tutor and student to interact and clarify details of an assignment.
- A hybrid format allows tutors to respond to both higher-order and lower-order concerns with greater flexibility. Asynchronously, tutors can highlight sections of the text that may need attention but then reserve commentary on those sections for the synchronous chat. This supports a minimalist approach for written commentary and a chance for students to ask questions about highlighted sections.
- A hybrid format allows tutors to prioritize revision suggestions.

Another possible advantage of including chat as a component of ESL online tutoring is that this hybrid structure accommodates "reformulation" along a continuum. In Chapter 5, Carol Severino describes an ESL tutoring option in which a tutor helps the ESL writer replace second language features with native language features, to a degree ranging "from slight to extensive." Reformulation of this type could occur more easily in a chat rather than an email exchange.

However, tutors in our focus group also noted some potential challenges of the hybrid model, especially regarding the chat. One issue reported by tutors was that some ESL students may feel uncomfortable in a chat environment responding on the spot. For example, one tutor described a chat in which she explained thesis statements and provided some examples; the student's comment indicated she understood the information, and she summarized a thesis statement she thought she would use. The tutor asked if the student would write the actual sentence to practice writing a thesis statement, but after pausing the student replied, "No, I cannot write it right now. Sorry." As the chat continued, it became increasingly clear that the student was having difficulty conversing in writing. The tutor realized that the student was using a dictionary during the chat, resulting in long pauses in the chat discussion. In recounting this situation, the tutor suggested that it might be important for tutors to simply help ESL students become comfortable in the chat environment.

Another potential challenge is lack of connection in the chat. If language barriers are extreme, tutor and student may have a difficult time understanding one another. Another tutor in the focus group shared an experience in which the student did not appear to respond to the tutor's questions at all during the chat. The tutor described the chat experience as one in which the tutor and student "were at cross purposes." Despite these possible downfalls, tutors who we interviewed unanimously endorsed the use of a synchronous chat as simply another online tool that tutors can use with ESL students; they especially appreciated the interaction it provided between student and tutor.

To illustrate the range of issues that tutors articulated, we offer three examples from actual transcripts of online tutoring sessions with ESL students.[7]

Example 1. Clarifying Assignment Expectations

An ESL student submitted a draft of a personal statement for a fellowship application. The student identified several issues: "I have problems with my grammar and long sentences. I also want feel back in the strength of my statement and if it is clear to the lector what I want to transmit." In the asynchronous response phase, the consultant used intertextual and end comments to suggest clarity-related content and structural issues that the student might think about. The final asynchronous comment by the tutor addressed how the student might rearrange information in the statement to highlight academic experience rather than personal experience: "I think that one thing you may want to consider revising is moving the information about your studies toward the top of the essay. This will help readers understand why you're applying for a fellowship and what you hope to do with it."

In the chat, however, the student immediately questioned the tutor's final comment about organization of information on "academic studies" and clarified information about the application essay ("but the thing is that in the scholarship webpage the clarify that they want to know about your life").

Client:	I read your comments (some of them)
Consultant:	how are you feeling about them?
Client:	but the thing is that in the scholarship webpage the clarify that they want to know about your life
Consultant:	Okay, so that's why you're thinking you want to stick with your same order?
Consultant:	of your life first and then your studies?
Consultant:	Is that what you mean?
Client:	this is what they say
Client:	We want to know you better. Tell us about your family and why education and service to others is important to the person you are now and the person you hope to become.
Client:	they have a different form where you talk about your studies.
Client:	there you have to described what you've done and what you're planning to do next.
Consultant:	Oh okay, I see

Note that the student directly quotes information from the fellowship application and shares this with the tutor: "this is what they say . . . 'We want to know you better. Tell us about your family and why education and service to others is important to the person you are now and the person you hope to become.' . . . they have a different form where you talk about your studies."

This example demonstrates how a follow-up synchronous chat can stimulate interactions that can help clarify assignments or other important information that the student wishes to share with a tutor. In this way, the chat reflects the kind of interaction you might find at the beginning of a face-to-face tutorial when a tutor and student discuss an assignment for the first time, clarifying expectations about the assignment and about the tutorial.

Example 2. Providing Sentence-Level Feedback

This example shows how a tutor addressed comma usage (a lower-order concern) in a follow-up synchronous chat. Unlike the previous example, where lower-order concerns were simply highlighted, this session demonstrates how the tutor explained a punctuation error and helped the student work through it. In this example, the consultant stated, "There is one specific type of comma that you miss" and provided a link to a Center for Writing reference sheet about punctuation. The tutor then explained the need to use a comma after introductory phrases and clauses. After using one of the student's sentences to demonstrate and explain that concept, the consultant identified additional individual sentences with that punctuation issue and asked the student to indicate where she would put a comma in each; the student corrected each sentence.

Consultant: I also wanted to talk real quickly about commas.

Consultant: There is one specific type of comma that you miss

Client: where?

Consultant: One second, I'm grabbing a link

Consultant: http://writing.umn.edu/sws/quicktips/punctuation/commas.htm

Consultant: that is a website that will tell you a lot about commas. [tutor finds example sentence]

Consultant: Since I was little, I decided I wanted to make a difference in this world.

Client: ohh, ok

Client: yeah Im not very good a this

Consultant: You can pick these out because, if you took away "Since I was little," you would still have a complete sentence.

Consultant: See what I mean? It would say "I decided I wanted to make a difference in this world."

Consultant: that's a complete sentence all by itself. So, the extra information at the front is some sort of phrase, which means it should have a comma after it.

Consultant: here's another one

Consultant: During all my years of college I was a volunteer in the ambulance helping in the transportation and treatment of people severely sick or who suffered accidents.

Client: After college, right?

Consultant: Yes, perfect!

In this example of lower-order feedback, the consultant helped the student learn to recognize and correct the error, ending that portion of the online chat conversation by commenting, "Yes, that is great. You've got that down. So, watch for those in your papers." Tutors are using a similar approach to addressing other grammatical and punctuation issues as well as errors of word usage, syntax, and other sentence-level issues that ESL students encounter.

Example 3. Balancing Higher-Order and Lower-Order Concerns

This final example demonstrates how a tutor and student can discuss higher-order concerns while also addressing lower-order concerns on the sentence level. The student in this example is a graduate student in environmental health in a course on public health risk assessment; she is writing a case study. The student's native language is Korean. The student requested the tutor's perspective on content and grammatical issues. In the following excerpt of the asynchronous component of the tutorial, the student provides a statement about the case, which the tutor does not fully understand. Note the tutor's comment in brackets and italics:

> I believe that it should be discussed of uncertainty and variability to confirm the DCT level of exposure, as I mentioned above. Confidence about the hazard and dose response are integrated with those from the exposure assessment, it needs include the information about the uncertainties associated with each aspect of the assessment in the final risk summary. [*Consultant: In this sentence, are you only pointing out flaws in the study or are you saying that some of it is okay and other things needs to be improved? If there are two different judgments you are making, you might need to use transition words to highlight that contrast.*] There are several categories of uncertainty, and each merits consideration, for instance, a substantial amount of uncertainty is inherent in air, water or soil sampling. [*Consultant: Are you making a general statement for all studies or pointing out a problem in this study?*] The data gap is broad such as the absence of information on the effect of exposure to DCT on populations or on the biological mechanism of action of an agent.

These paragraphs and tutor comments came up in the chat that followed the student's writing submission. Note that in the chat, the student points out this example and asks for help. The tutor and student clarify pronouns and verbs and suggest revisions to clarify meaning.

Consultant: what shall we talk about next?

Client: shall we talk about uncertainty?

Client: like . . .

Client: I believe that we discuss the uncertainty and variability to confirm the DCT level of exposure, as I mentioned above.

Client: I changed the sentenses as above.

Consultant: let me find that

     (*Pause*)

Consultant: okay, who is "we"?

Consultant: I think you need a subject

Consultant: to help readers

Client: risk assessors

Consultant: okay

Consultant: great!

Consultant: can we say that instead of a pronoun?

Client: sure.

Consultant: pronouns confuse the reader

Consultant: if there is no noun to refer to

Consultant: the second thing is,

Consultant: in that sentence are you stating a fact: that risk assessors look at uncertainty and variability?

Consultant: or is that what you think is ideal?

Consultant: in other words, do you want to use the word "should" or not?

Client: actually risk assessors who wrote in this case study.

Consultant: okay

Consultant: so they "should"?

Client: Right.

Client: should discuss

Consultant: okay, got it?

     (*Pause*)

Client: yes.

Client: I think I need insert "should discuss"

Consultant: it sounds like a critique, when you do; which is what you want this paper to do, right?

Client: Exactly!

Consultant: i get a better sense of that with "should"

In this example, the hybrid format allowed the tutor and student to suggest sentence-level changes that would clarify meaning. They focused on one sentence but revealed problems with a pronoun and verb. The revised sentence would read "I believe that risk assessors should discuss uncertainty and variability to confirm the DCT level of exposure, as I mentioned above." The chat allowed the student and tutor to discuss those areas and brainstorm ways to clarify meaning. Throughout this tutorial, the tutor identified similar sentence-level problems with pronouns, verbs, and use of passive voice. This exchange led to a closing discussion between the tutor and student about higher-order concerns such as organization.

Consultant:	I think I mentioned that I was slightly unsure about overall organization
Consultant:	it might help the reader
Consultant:	if you
Consultant:	have major topic sentences
Consultant:	for each paragraph
Consultant:	but I don't know if there is any particular organization needed in such a paper in your field
Client:	Let me ask to my professor.
Client:	Thanks for good point.
Consultant:	yeah, that might be ideal
Consultant:	or even look for examples
Client:	I even didn't realize that I need to organize this paper.
Consultant:	of such papers if you can find any
Consultant:	typically
Consultant:	you want each paragraph to have a main idea
Consultant:	that you mention right away
Client:	Right!
Client:	Thanks a lot, Consultant!

These examples from actual asynchronous and synchronous tutorials demonstrate a final strength of the hybrid tutorial structure: Rather than focusing primarily on a text (which tutors tell us is a risk in asynchronous-only tutorials), the tutor can more easily focus on the student and his writing. When working in an online hybrid setting, tutors explain that, during the asynchronous phase, they are thinking about laying the foundation for what the student will think about after receiving the document with response and also setting the stage for the online synchronous chat; they are not thinking about "giving feedback on a paper." The difference may seem subtle, but we believe it is an important factor in conducting effective online tutorials, especially with ESL writers. During the asynchronous phase, tutors often identify an issue and then write a comment such as "Perhaps we can discuss that when we meet online" or "Shall we talk about that in the chat?" or "Do you have time to revise that and bring the new version to the chat?" In that way, they establish the seamless connection between the two phases for the student, emphasize the nature of the dialogue about writing, and keep their attention on the student.

Concluding Thoughts

In this chapter, we have explored new possibilities for working with ESL students in online tutorial settings. One of the central issues revealed in literature about online tutoring of ESL students is balancing higher-order and lower-order concerns. We believe that a combination of asynchronous and synchronous technologies in a hybrid tutoring model offers excellent opportunities for tutors to highlight, discuss, and clarify a range of writing concerns with great flexibility. In addition, we appreciate the ways that hybrids invite ESL students to interact with the tutor and encourage writing practice. We know we have much more to learn about the ways ESL students and tutors can work together in online tutorials. Some of our remaining questions include the following:

- How can we effectively prioritize the writing and language issues that we address online with ESL students?
- What are strategies for effectively linking the asynchronous and synchronous phases of a tutoring session?
- How much should we encourage ESL students to revise "live" during a chat?
- How can we identify situations that are particularly suited for online tutoring and those most suited for face-to-face tutoring?
- What approaches to online tutoring do ESL students find helpful?
- What aspects of the hybrid model of online tutoring do ESL students value most? Least?

We are encouraged by our experiences working online with ESL students as well as by the research we find. Our parting advice to fellow tutors and administrators interested in online tutoring of ESL students is to take every opportunity to gather information from tutors and students about how online tutoring is working. Such data collection might start with a short (five- to ten-item) online survey with questions about the online tutoring experience. Questions might address preferences regarding technology, comments about the helpfulness of tutor feedback, comfort level in chat and document modes, or anything else of interest. It is only through feedback from tutors and students that we continue to learn about how online tutoring is working, the possibilities it affords, and ways it can be made more useful. We look forward to continuing this conversation about the possibilities of online tutoring for ESL writers.[8]

Notes

1. Moody, paragraph 6.
2. Rilling, 363.
3. Rilling (2005).
4. Pyle, 56.
5. This model is certainly not new: versions of it have been adopted in the past by Utah State University, University of Wisconsin–Madison, and SMART THINKING.com, a national online tutoring service. However, hybrids are not yet commonplace among online writing centers because they require time, money, and personnel willing to make them work. At the University of Minnesota, we are fortunate to be a part of a team piloting a hybrid model for online tutoring called Student Writing Support Online (SWS.online) that supports asynchronous and synchronous tutor-student interaction in an open-source interface that the team created internally. The team is led by the director and assistant director of the Center for Writing and includes a computer programmer, eight online tutors, and an affiliate faculty member of the Writing Studies Department; one tutor and the faculty member previously worked with the Online Writing Center (OWC) discussed earlier in this chapter. This hybrid model is a departure from our previous asynchronous-only online writing center in that it is designed to reflect the pedagogy of a face-to-face conference.
6. Institutional review board approval at our institution was obtained for tutor interviews. Participating tutors signed consent forms allowing their comments to be included in this chapter.
7. In actual chats and transcripts, the students' and tutors' names appear. We replaced names with Client and Consultant to preserve anonymity in this chapter. Students and tutors signed consent forms allowing their examples to be included in this chapter.
8. A special thank you to Center for Writing and SWS.online director, staff, and tutors who supported and/or participated in this project: Kirsten Jamsen, Katie Levin, Huy Hoang, Kim Strain, Debra Hartley, and Linda Clemens.

Works Cited and Suggested Readings

Blau, Susan, John Hall, and Sarah Sparks. 2002. "Guilt-Free Tutoring: Rethinking How We Tutor Non-Native-English-Speaking Students." *The Writing Center Journal* 23(1): 23–44.

Carlson, David A., and Eileen Apperson-Williams. 2000. "The Anxieties of Distance: Online Tutors Reflect." In *Taking Flight with OWLs: Examining Electronic Writing Center Work*, edited by James A. Inman and Donna N. Sewell, 129–40. Mahwah NJ: Lawrence Erlbaum.

Curtis, Andy, and Tim Roskams. 2000. "Language Learning in Networked Writing Labs: A View from Asia." In *Taking Flight with OWLs: Examining Electronic Writing Center Work*, edited by James A. Inman and Donna N. Sewell, 29–40. Mahwah NJ: Lawrence Erlbaum.

Gillespie, Paula, and Neal Lerner. 2003. *The Allyn and Bacon Guide to Peer Tutoring*. 2nd ed. New York: Pearson Longman.

Hobson, Eric H. 1998. "Straddling the Virtual Fence." In *Wiring the Writing Center*, edited by Eric H. Hobson, ix–xxvi. Logan: Utah State University Press.

Moody, Suzan. 1996. "OWLs and ESL Students." *Kairos: A Journal for Teaching Writing in Webbed Environments*. 1.1 at http://english.ttu/kairos/1.1/owls/moody.html.

Pyle, Virginia. 2005. "Where Online Writing Centers and Second Language Writers Meet: A Closer Look at the University of Minnesota's Online Writing Center." Double Plan B Project, University of Minnesota.

Rilling, Sarah. 2005. "The Development of an ESL OWL, or Learning How to Tutor Writing Online." *Computers and Composition* 22: 357–374.

Shadle, Mark. 2000. "The Spotted OWL: Online Writing Labs as Sites of Diversity, Controversy, and Identity." In *Taking Flight with OWLs: Examining Electronic Writing Center Work*, edited by James A. Inman and Donna N. Sewell, 3–16. Mahwah NJ: Lawrence Erlbaum.

12

Responding Online

Ben Rafoth

About 3.5 million students, or 20 percent of all students in higher education in the United States, are enrolled in at least one online course, according to the most recent survey available.[1] We do not know how many of these students are nonnative speakers of English, but we do know that online education is most firmly established at large public institutions that serve many immigrant, international, and Generation 1.5 students and that large numbers from this population seek help in writing centers. This trend is sure to grow, and writing centers that offer some form of online tutoring—whether it is based on instant messaging, discussion groups, bulletin boards, white boards, informational websites, or email with attachments—are adapting to new media for instruction. For writing centers that have been involved in online tutoring, fundamental questions remain: When the writer is not present to answer questions, how should tutors respond? What does experience tell us works best? Although there are no easy answers, experience can be a good teacher. The tutors at my university learned a few lessons as we developed our online service:

1. Less is more when it comes to writing comments.
2. Focus and consistency are paramount.
3. Direct but polite feedback is regarded as most helpful.
4. How tutors read a writer's paper affects the responses they write.

This last point is significant because tutors bring to each tutorial their own ways of reading, and so responding effectively begins with an awareness of the many different ways one can read a paper. By looking closely at what tutors do and how writers respond to their feedback, we can learn a lot.[2] This chapter closely explores a short sample of ESL writing in order to illustrate some of the lessons we learned from our online experience.[3]

Below is a key paragraph from one paper an English as a second language (ESL) writer submitted to our online writing center as an email attachment (we do not know his native language). Before sending the paper, the writer asked for help with grammar and organization but offered little additional direction. As you will see, it is possible to infer most of what the writer is trying to say in this paragraph, but doing so is a struggle, and most readers would find it difficult to read the entire paper. The writer of this paper could definitely benefit from a tutor who understood what he was trying to say and could help him make the meaning clearer and the style more readable. Where should the tutor begin? The paragraph consists of only sixty-seven words but poses a number of challenges that are made especially difficult when the author is not available to clarify his intentions or guide the tutor's attention. Let's take a look at the paragraph the writer wrote:

> India and Nigeria are not democracy that share internal conflicts between diverse ethnics and religion groups. Two countries faced the same path of colonialism and created parliamentary democracy. At a time of independence, they were not ready to control over the country, since then they faced several difficulties to maintain the democracy. Their positions as democracy are not stable, moreover, the possibility to fail is likely today.

What exactly is this writer trying to say about India and Nigeria? Does he want to explain why he believes the history of both countries is responsible for their unstable governments today, or does he want to talk about their future and the possibility that their governments could fail? How would a passage like this be handled if the writer and tutor were face-to-face? Since they are not face to face, what should the tutor look for when she reads this paragraph in order to be most helpful to the writer?

Reading Papers, Reading Responses

Like most writing centers that use asynchronous tutoring (in our case, an email message with the paper attached), students on our campus were asked to respond to a few questions when they submitted their papers:

1. Please tell us your name, course, instructor, and due date for the paper.
2. What is the assignment?
3. Tell us one or two areas you would like a tutor to help you with and try to be as specific as you can.

At the time we conducted this study, we logged the incoming requests and forwarded them to tutors working at home or in the writing center. They wrote their responses directly in the file and sent them back to the students as attachments. As the writing center director, I received a copy of each response and used it to give feedback to the tutors and to assess the program. We also asked most students to complete a brief survey and to participate in a follow-up interview. We interviewed four ESL writers and used their comments along with those of our native English speakers to learn more and to improve the tutors' responses.

Initially, the biggest challenges tutors faced were responding to ESL students' papers that contained lots of language problems, papers that were long, and papers in which the writer offered little guidance about the assignment. Instead of focusing their feedback on one aspect of the paper, the tutors tended to insert lots of comments into the text, especially when students gave vague or incomplete requests for help.[4] The tutors' comments were far ranging; they asked questions about the author's intended meaning, suggested ways to relate the thesis statement to the rest of the paper, and gave punctuation rules or links to further explanations and examples. The tutors tried hard to be helpful, but there was little focus to their feedback. The many comments inserted throughout the paper showed that they were reading closely, but to what end was not always clear.[5]

In addition, we could see that the feedback did not have the feel of the open-ended and collaborative sessions we conducted face-to-face every day in our writing center. In the online environment, tutors began with a greeting and a self-introduction ("Hi _____, I'm Marie, a tutor at the writing center, and I'll be reading your paper today.") and then delved into the paper. The outcome for many of these sessions was a mix of questions, comments, suggestions, and corrections inserted into lines and paragraphs, usually in bold or italics. Upon examining this feedback, one could see that it was rich in detail but weak in focus. Sometimes comments shifted between lower- and higher-order concerns even within the same sentence. Given this, where should the writer begin? What was the tutor's most important comment? The answers to these questions were hard to find in the tutors' feedback.

As we eventually learned in our staff meetings, tutors responded in these ways because most of the ESL students' papers presented frequent opportunities to give this type of feedback; in other words, the writers usually asked for word- and sentence-level assistance when they submitted their papers, and these problems were not hard to spot. Besides, tutors believed that lots of feedback is helpful. They reasoned this way: In place of the assistance they were accustomed to giving in face-to-face meetings—carrying on conversations, reading carefully, smiling, nodding, questioning, affirming, and so on—they felt that being helpful in online sessions meant making lots of comments. Their sense of responsibility in this case was shaped by the online environment. As one tutor remarked, "I wanted to show them I worked on their paper." Without the writer to speak to, tutors went out of their way to demonstrate their diligence. For them, it was a natural and conscientious thing to do.

Tutors inserted comments directly into the writer's text. To illustrate, here is the writer's paragraph again, but this time with a tutor's comments, in brackets and italics.[6]

India and Nigeria are not democracy [*do you mean* democracies? *demo-cratic countries?*] that share internal conflicts between [due to? *I'm a little confused here*] diverse ethnics [ethnic *is an adjective and doesn't take an* s] and religion [*the adjective form of* religion *is* religio*us, and that's what you want to use before the noun* groups] groups. [*You need to begin this sentence with the article* the *here*] Two countries faced [*need* the *here, too*] same path of colonialism and created parliamentary democracy. [*I'm not that familiar with this part of history, so maybe I'm missing something, but . . . are you saying that colonialism created parliamentary democracy? If so, then you might want to explain how colonialism brought this form of government about. Just a thought.*] At a time of independence, they [*who was not ready?*] were not ready to control over [*you could omit the word* over, *or you could say* they were not ready to exercise control over] the country, [*you probably want to end the sentence here.*] since then they faced [*it's interesting to read about the link between present-day problems and past history—could you say more about this?*] several difficulties to maintain [*it's better to say* in maintaining] the democracy. Their positions as democracy [*the plural form is* democracies] are not stable, moreover, the possibility to fail is likely today.

Many writers might consider this to be a helpful response, as most of our tutors did. It appears to give the student the help with grammar and organization he asked for, reflects an inquiring tone, provides explanations, encourages the writer, shows frankness, and demonstrates a close and careful reading. Comments are embedded in the text because tutors found it cumbersome to point to specific parts of the paper and impossible to read more than one screenful at a time. Still, the number of inserted comments is daunting. The tutor gives no indication of priorities for what is most and least important, and the isolated comments make it hard for readers to discern the tutor's tone.

This approach is not as helpful as it might seem because responses that provide lots of feedback to students run the risk of being *too* helpful. Too much help can involve "demotivating" ESL writers as Andy Curtis and Tim Roskams discovered,[7] appropriating the student's text as Carol Severino discusses in Chapter 5, or overtaking the session and overwhelming the writer as Molly Wingate writes about.[8] We discovered that the problem wasn't exactly too much help but not the right kind of help. What eventually put tutors on the right track, after studying the feedback that we received from writers and modifying our training, was not merely writing less but writing more selectively. This in turn depended on how tutors read the papers to begin with.

Within a few weeks, tutors began to change the ways they responded to papers submitted by ESL and native English-speaking (NES) students alike. They did this not by simply changing what they wrote in their feedback but by reading the papers from a new perspective. In Chapter 4, Paul Kei Matsuda and Michelle Cox describe three approaches readers can take to ESL texts:

Assimilationist: When we apply this notion to tutors reading an ESL student's paper, we can see that with an assimilationist stance, the tutor reads the ESL writer's text with an eye toward some ideal form of native-like writing and defines her task as one of making the flawed text conform to the flawless ideal.

Accommodationist: With an accommodationist stance, the tutor is more accepting of differences between NES and ESL texts and tries to let the writer decide how native-like he wants his text to become.

Separatist: With the separatist stance, the tutor reads differences sympathetically and tries to help the ESL writer express her ideas clearly without dwelling on the rules and conventions of standardized English.

These three approaches form a continuum of acceptance of differences, with the assimilationist approach being the least accepting, the separatist being the most, and the accommodationist falling somewhere in the middle.

The tutor's response above probably reflects an assimilationist stance toward language differences, and this competed with her attempts to read for meaning. In terms of language, the tutor read the text against a type of ideal text that she thought a native speaker might write. Although it is hard to know exactly what ideal the tutor had in mind—and this is one of the problems with reading a text in this way—we can suppose it was something like the following, a paragraph that most college-level instructors would consider generally clear, logical, and error free.

India and Nigeria are not entirely democratic countries; they also share similar internal conflicts due to their diverse ethnic and religious groups. The two countries faced a history of colonialism, which eventually led to the parliamentary democracies that govern these countries today. When the two states became independent of their colonial rulers, however, they were not ready to control their own countries. Ever since then, they have faced difficulties in maintaining democratic elements in their systems of government. As a result, their status today as democracies is not stable, and there is the likely possibility of failure.

When we compare this "ideal" text to the writer's original, the contrast is so great that the ideal seems rather preposterous. It is likely that no amount of diligence on the part of the ESL writer would produce this ideal text and no amount of expert tutoring could prepare him to write in this manner because the two texts emanate from such different sources, culturally and stylistically. Moreover, we cannot even be sure this is the meaning that the writer intended for the paragraph. For these reasons, it is fruitless to read this ESL writer's own text against an ideal, and any response based on such a reading cannot be helpful. Instead, it can only distract the writer from building on his own abilities (see Tseng's discussion of Vygotsky's concept of zone of proximal development in Chapter 2).

A Revised Example

One can imagine, for example, how the feedback might have looked if the tutor's response had attended to grammatical problems but refrained from comments pertaining to superficial surface forms. In the case of the ideal text, for instance, surface forms like the inclusion of definite articles serve more to improve smoothness and signal a polished academic register than to carry the burden of meaning (see Chapter 9). In other words, we can imagine a reading of the text that leaves surface problems alone while focusing on the writer's intended meaning.[9] This reflects an accommodationist or perhaps even a separatist stance on the part of the tutor, as the following example illustrates. Though the response still has some problems, as we will see, it says less but achieves more focus.

India and Nigeria are not democracy that share internal conflicts between [*due to? I'm a little confused here*] diverse ethnics and religion groups. Two countries faced same path of colonialism and created parliamentary democracy. [*I'm not that familiar with this part of history, so maybe I'm missing something, but . . . are you saying that colonialism created parliamentary democracy? If so, then you might want to explain how colonialism brought this form of government about. Just a thought.*] At a time of independence, they [*who was not ready?*] were not ready to control over the country, since then they faced [*it's interesting to read about the link between present-day problems and past history—could you say more about this?*] several difficulties to maintain the democracy. Their position as democracy are not stable, moreover, the possibility to fail is likely today.

When comments about superficial forms unrelated to meaning are taken out, as in this example, what remains are two requests for clarification and elaboration of ideas: *I'm not that . . .* and *it's interesting to read . . .* and two comments about grammar and form:

1. Choice of preposition: *due to?*
2. Pronoun reference: *who was not ready?*

The point is that one way to honor an ESL writer's request for feedback on grammar or language problems is to focus on problems that involve unclear meaning.[10] This approach stops short of trying to make the style flawless, an unrealistic goal for most of us anyway.

Consider what would happen if we were to remove the comments about prepositions, pronouns, and sentence boundaries from the ESL student's paragraph. Would this enhance or diminish the effectiveness of the tutor's feedback? Look at the following:

India and Nigeria are not democracy that share internal conflicts between diverse ethnics and religion groups. Two countries faced same path of colonialism and created parliamentary democracy. [*I'm not that familiar with this part of history, so maybe I'm missing something, but . . . are you saying that colonialism created parliamentary democracy? You might want to explain how colonialism brought this form of government about. Just a thought.*] At a time of independence, they were not ready to control over the country, since then they faced [*it's interesting to read about the link between present-day problems and past history—could you say more about this?*] several difficulties to maintain the democracy. Their position as democracy are not stable, moreover, the possibility to fail is likely today.

An interesting thing about this version is that both comments make the same point. They both refer to the connection the writer seems to be trying to make between India's and Nigeria's colonial governments of the past and their parliamentary democracies of the present. With only these two comments in the paragraph, their common message stands out. Now imagine the paragraph once more, this time with just one comment at the end:

India and Nigeria are not democracy that share internal conflicts between diverse ethnics and religion groups. Two countries faced the same path of colonialism and created parliamentary democracy. At a time of independence, they were not ready to control over the country, since then they faced several difficulties to maintain the democracy. Their position as democracy are not stable today, moreover, the possibility to fail is likely. [*It sounds like you are trying to make an important point about the link between present-day problems and past history. If so, I think it is important for you to include more facts and examples about the past and present because this point needs more support in your paper.*]

With this comment, the tutor shows that she recognizes the writer is attempting to make a point and tries to confirm what it is. But the comment does something else, too. It helps the writer see that communicating his main idea is the most important thing to attend to in this paragraph. To reach this point, however, the tutor has to ignore the many other opportunities for comments that she sees and concentrate on helping the writer get his main idea across. Similarly, the writer must ignore for the time being language edits that are not essential. For tutors, learning to respond in this way means that they must read the student's paper more for meaning than for errors, and they must respond in ways that enhance the clear expression of ideas. This is one of the lessons we learned from our online tutoring experience. I would like to conclude this chapter with a few others and some advice for online tutors who face challenges similar to our own.

Lessons Learned from the Online Experience

The following are based on our experiences tutoring online for both ESL and NES writers.[11]

1. Writing lots of feedback in online responses is often ineffective. We discovered that tutors who responded in this way called attention to more points than writers actually followed through on when they revised. In our follow-up interviews, writers explained that they appreciated the detailed feedback that tutors provided but often did not follow through and revise the areas their tutors raised questions about. When asked why he made only a couple of changes and did not address the rest, one writer felt he should have done so but said he didn't get around to it before the paper was due. Another said she did not agree with the tutor's comments. Comments like these warrant further research.

   The advice to tutors working online, then, is to streamline comments. Good feedback is time-consuming to write, challenging to prioritize, and easy to ignore. Although writers appreciate the effort a tutor makes, they are not always prepared to follow through on all of them. Writers, ESL or not, get better little by little, and frequent tutorial sessions that focus on small changes are probably better than one or two sessions that try to cover many at once.

2. Writers who receive detailed feedback, with suggestions ranging from minor editing to global revision, often make the editing changes but not the global revisions. In follow-up interviews, some students did not see a distinction between a suggestion to change a word or phrase and a suggestion to develop an idea or revise a thesis. This is consistent with the findings of Nancy Sommers, who wrote, "On every occasion when I asked students why they hadn't made any more changes, they essentially replied, 'I knew something larger was wrong, but I didn't think it would help to move words around.'"[12]

   Although it sometimes seems as though writers are interested only in word- or phrase-level revisions because these are the easiest to make, beginning writers may in fact be focused on this level because they see it as the *only* level, as Sommers observed. Moreover, feedback that mixes comments directed at occasional surface errors with comments about larger rhetorical matters such as organization, focus, and the development of ideas may lead writers to assume they can mitigate rhetorical problems by correcting surface problems or by simply moving words around. But if they cannot see how moving words around makes any difference, then they may assume the rhetorical problem cannot be fixed, at least not by them.

   The advice to tutors, then, is to keep comments about rhetorical matters distinct from other comments. Unless a word, phrase, or sentence is clearly preventing the writer from conveying a key point, let it go and focus on those places where key points are getting lost. Identify confusing areas of the text that need to be worked on. When a paper contains many places where key points are unclear, then pick one or two and focus on them, leaving the rest alone. If you believe it is necessary to comment about a word or phrase when no key point is at stake, then tell the author what the relative priority of this comment is. Carol Severino (Chapter 5) adds this important qualification:

> The assignment, focus, argument, development, and organization are usually more important than expression unless some language clarifications and corrections are needed simply to understand whether the student has followed the assignment and to understand her points. In the case of language completely obscuring argument, the level of language would be considered a higher-order and global concern. Otherwise, there is no point in working carefully and slowly to reformulate language that should not or probably will not appear in the next draft because the student needs to refocus or revise her entire argument.

3. Writers assess their tutors' trustworthiness. We tend to take for granted that students value the feedback they receive from tutors, and most do. At the same time, they view feedback with a consumer's eye, mindful that the quality of advice they receive depends on their tutor's knowledge and skills. Our follow-up interviews indicate that tutors who acknowledge unfamiliarity with a topic sow seeds of doubts in some writers' minds. Tutors who indicate frankly that they don't know much about the topic—as the tutor did in one response when she wrote "I'm not familiar with this history, so maybe I'm missing something . . . "—may cause some writers to doubt the value of the tutor's comments on other aspects of their writing and make them hesitant to make revisions. Writers sometimes read tentativeness as wishy-washy, we found, as when tutors wrote statements like "You might want to think about changing . . ." or "I wonder if some readers might think this means . . . ." Because the tutor seemed unsure about her own idea, they reasoned, they would leave that part of the paper alone.[13]

   The advice here is that honesty is essential. Tutors should disclose their limitations when they feel it is necessary. At the same time, when tutors do have something constructive to offer the writer, they should say it plainly and confidently and explain why. Writers hear tentativeness or hesitation in phrases like "you might want to think about . . ." or "I wonder if . . . ." We might think we sound polite and nondirective, but writers might hear wishy-washy.

4. Finally, writers often avoid revisions because they do not hear a consistent message. We found that writers perceived inconsistencies in their tutors' message. At the beginning of one paper, the tutor had written the following:

> I really enjoyed reading your paper, Jo. You picked an interesting topic to write about. As you can see, I just made a few comments for you. I hope they make sense. These changes shouldn't be too hard to make, so don't cancel your plans for the weekend. Good luck with this assignment!

When Jo read the tutor's comments, however, she saw that they involved making global revisions that would indeed take time. But the tutor had said they shouldn't be too hard to make, Jo reported in a follow-up interview, and so she decided to make a few edits and that's all. In other words, the writer responded more to the tutor's attempt to be reassuring and comforting than to the real need for revisions the tutor had identified.

Another time, there was inconsistency between the tutor's advice and the instructor's. In this paper, following the greeting, the tutor identified a paragraph near the end that did not seem to fit with the overall flow of ideas. When asked in the follow-up interview why he had decided not to make any changes to that paragraph before he handed it in, the writer replied that his instructor had said this was a particularly good paragraph in a previous draft of the paper, and so he did not want to change it. In this writer's mind, a good paragraph is a good paragraph, and because the tutor's advice seemed to conflict with his instructor's, he followed the instructor's advice.

The advice here is to make suggestions clear to the writer and don't try to sugarcoat them. More important, deliver a consistent message and reinforce it throughout the paper so that the writer can see how important it is.

In the end, our tutors learned to improve their responses to all papers submitted online in much the same way we all learn to write, by drafting their responses, giving and listening to feedback, and improving their work as they went along. It is a process that can improve all tutoring with ESL or NES writers, face-to-face or online.

Notes

1. Allen and Seaman (2007).
2. For an account of tutors' experiences with face-to-face versus online conferencing, see Carlson and Apperson-Williams (2000).
3. We began online tutoring in January, 1999, thanks to the assistance of Jennifer Ritter, Dennis Ausel, and a grant from the Indiana University of Pennsylvania Faculty Professional Development Council. After grant funding ended, we continued to conduct online tutoring on an occasional basis with one or two classes each year.
4. Although some students provided assignment details and a clear sense of direction for tutors to work with, most did not. They tended to write requests like "Please look over my paper. Any help you can give me with grammar or whatever you see would be appreciated." or "I need help with organizing my thoughts, and punctuation."

5. For a good discussion of protocols for inserting comments into a paper, see Bell (2006); Cooper, Bui, and Riker (2005); and Monroe (1998).

6. The tutor's comments in this paragraph reflect a composite of responses we developed for training, after studying many students' papers and tutors' responses.

7. Curtis and Roskams (2000).

8. Wingate (2005).

9. See Ritter (2005).

10. The question of how to go about helping ESL writers correct grammar is discussed in Leki, Chapter 10.

11. For another list of valuable lessons learned from online conferencing with English language learners, see Hewett and Lynn (2007).

12. Sommers (1980).

13. The mixed messages that nondirective feedback can create are confirmed by Ferris and Hedgcock, 144–45.

Works Cited

Allen, I. Elaine, and Jeff Seaman. 2007. *Online Nation: Five Years of Growth in Online Learning*. Needham, MA: Sloan Consortium and Babson Survey Research Group. www.sloan-c.org/publications/survey/index.asp.

Bell, Lisa Eastmond. 2006. "Preserving the Rhetorical Nature of Tutoring When Going Online." In *The Writing Center Director's Resource Book*, edited by Christina Murphy and Byron Stay, 351–58. Mahwah, NJ: Lawrence Erlbaum.

Carlson, David A., and Eileen Apperson-Williams. 2000. "The Anxieties of Distance: Online Tutors Reflect." In *Taking Flight with OWLs: Examining Electronic Writing Center Work*, edited by James A. Inman and Donna N. Sewell, 67–89. Mahwah, NJ: Lawrence Erlbaum.

Cooper, George, Kara Bui, and Linda Riker. 2005. "Protocols and Process in Online Tutoring." In *A Tutor's Guide: Helping Writers One to One*, 2nd ed. Edited by Ben Rafoth, 129–39. Portsmouth, NH: Boynton/Cook.

Curtis, Andy, and Tim Roskams. 2000. "Language Learning in Networked Writing Labs: A View from Asia." In *Taking Flight with OWLs: Examining Electronic Writing Center Work*, edited by James A. Inman and Donna N. Sewell, 91–101. Mahwah, NJ: Lawrence Erlbaum.

Ferris, Dana, and John S. Hedgcock. 1998. *Teaching ESL Composition*. Mahwah, NJ: Lawrence Erlbaum.

Hewett, Beth L., and Robert Lynn. 2007. "Training ESOL Instructors and Tutors for Online Conferencing." *The Writing Instructor*. Retrieved April 21, 2008, from www.writinginstructor.com/esol.

Leki, Ilona. 1992. *Understanding ESL Writers.* Portsmouth, NH: Boynton/ Cook.

Monroe, Barbara. 1998. "The Look and Feel of the OWL Conference." In *Wiring the Center*, edited by E. Hobson, 3–24. Logan: Utah State University Press.

Ritter, Jennifer. 2005. "Recent Developments in Assisting ESL Writers." In *A Tutor's Guide: Helping Writers One to One*, 2nd ed. Edited by Ben Rafoth, 54–62. Portsmouth, NH: Boynton/Cook.

Sommers, Nancy. 1980. "Revision Strategies of Student Writers and Experienced Adult Writers." *College Composition and Communication* 31: 378–88.

Wingate, Molly. 2005. "What Line? I Didn't See Any Line." In *A Tutor's Guide: Helping Writers One to One*, 2nd ed. Edited by Ben Rafoth, 9–16. Portsmouth, NH: Boynton/Cook.

13

Raising Questions About Plagiarism

Kurt Bouman

Maybe it's a word that stands out or a phrase that seems out of place. Maybe a sentence sounds as though it must have been written by a native English speaker. Perhaps it's just an inkling that something about the writing is incongruous, that one or two passages seem inconsistent with the rest of the paper, and with the English as a second language (ESL) writer sitting next to you. What happens now? Do you set aside your feelings and continue with the tutoring session, worrying that your suspicions might offend the writer? How do you respond if you recognize the paper from another consultation with a different student? Maybe you feel a flush of embarrassment, confusion, or indignation; perhaps you look for a reason to step over to a fellow tutor, or to your director, for a quick consultation of your own: "I'm not sure what to do; I don't think this student wrote these words!"

Questions about plagiarism can leave students hurt, alienated, or confused, even when they have cited all of their sources correctly and completely. Feelings of social and psychological distress may be especially acute for ESL writers, who often work very hard to produce the kinds of writing that their professors expect. Fortunately, as a peer writing tutor, you are in a good position to help ESL students learn more about your institution's rhetorical values and conventions regarding using sources in writing, and to help them practice the particular textual skills—paraphrasing, summarizing, and quoting—that accompany these values. In the context of a one-on-one writing consultation, you can feel comfortable raising questions about plagiarism and discussing the conventions, beliefs, and values that make some people react to it so strongly.

Understanding Plagiarism

Before you enter into a discussion about it, it is important to think about just what plagiarism is. *Plagiarism* is commonly defined as presenting the words or ideas of another person as though they are the writer's own. Although this definition seems straightforward, it raises important questions about cultural and academic values and textual practices:

- How can a person "own" abstractions like words or ideas?
- How many words can a writer safely copy from a source?
- What is it about plagiarism that can make someone describe it as "the worst academic sin of all"?[1]

To begin with, plagiarism does not have a single, clear-cut meaning. Instead, people use the term to describe a range of textual practices:

- using ideas from a source without acknowledging it
- copying specific words or phrases without using quotation marks
- doing a word-for-word substitution in an attempt to paraphrase a source, but keeping its basic ideas and sentence structure intact[2]
- "patchwriting," or building a paper by patching together sections of text from one or more sources[3]
- submitting a paper downloaded off the Internet or written by a friend or classmate

As a writing center tutor, you will encounter ESL writers with a wide range of rhetorical skills and experiences, and each of them will come from a unique cultural and educational background. At my school, for instance, some of the second language writers who visit the writing center have already earned an academic degree. These students have spent years working in professional positions in their home countries as teachers, accountants, and physicians. Most have experience writing from sources, yet the citation conventions they learned in their home countries may be different than those we are used to.

Most writers who have studied in American or Western European colleges know that their academic audiences expect them to use a standard citation system such as MLA (Modern Language Association) or APA (American Psychological Association) to clearly differentiate their words from their sources' language. People often spend years practicing these conventions before they can use them confidently and correctly as they weave together their own thoughts with ideas from their sources. Yet some of the writers you work with will get it wrong. Many ESL students are also academic newcomers, and they may be learning advanced literacy practices as they develop their English language skills. Many of these writers will try hard to avoid accusations of plagiarism by mentioning their sources in a bibliography or by only copying from texts their instructors will be familiar with. But their developing English can make summarizing and paraphrasing difficult, and they might be shocked to learn that "unattributed textual borrowing is considered an academic 'crime' in Western academic contexts."[4] For many writers, plagiarism is a particularly confounding concept.

Plagiarism and Culture

Ideas about plagiarism are driven by a particular understanding about what it means to write. Many Western cultures, for instance, place a strong value on individuality and independence, and writers are encouraged to develop and use their "authentic voice," a way of writing that is uniquely their own.[5] Most Western cultures expect writers to express themselves in their own voices rather than through the voices of others. So, when one considers *why* voice might matter so much in writing, one reason for strong attitudes toward plagiarism becomes clear: Plagiarism misrepresents voice, a unique, individual, and essential characteristic of a writer.

While individuality is an important value in Western education, so, too, is originality. Many teachers expect writers to say things that are original, not simply to parrot ideas and words they've found elsewhere.[6] Western audiences expect writers to build on source texts as they contribute their own ideas to the discussion, and U.S. students "are rewarded for their own creativity and fresh voice."[7] However, as Ali Abasi, Nahal Akbari, and Barbara Graves point out, "ESL students' view of their role as writers may not be congruent with what successful academic writing . . . calls for."[8] Purdue University's OWL (Online Writing Lab) neatly sums up some of the clashing expectations that students face when writing for an American academic audience:

> Show you have done your research, but write something new and original;
>
> Appeal to experts and authorities, but improve upon or disagree with [them];
>
> Improve your English by mimicking what you hear and read, but use your own words . . . ;
>
> Give credit where credit is due, but make your own significant contribution.[9]

By design, American citation practices favor individuality. Each of our three main referencing systems—MLA, APA, and Chicago—ensure that readers will be able to clearly delineate between the writer's words and ideas and those of the author of a source.[10] These conventions are established to ensure "transparency"—a clear separation between writer and source.[11] Many international students, however, come from academic backgrounds that aim to strengthen communal ties rather than unique individual identities. These cultures, according to Glenn Deckert, "emphasize close allegiance to a few acknowledged authorities with resulting convergence of perspective and greater social harmony."[12] Yet even as collectivist cultures and economies evolve—as they permit and adopt aspects of Western individualism—their writing conventions continue to be influenced by deeply ingrained habits of thought and textual practices that have been developed and refined over centuries.

These different cultural values lead to different writing practices. For example, in China, where knowledge is based on "collective wisdom and social norms"[13] rather than in the mind of any particular individual person, writers are expected to suppress their individuality rather than celebrate it. There, "Confucianism still promotes the use of proverbs to carry on age old messages about morality and universal truths. In Korea, students are graded highly by their teachers if they imitate classic writers,"[14] and in some cultures, success is measured on the accuracy of a student's memorization of standard texts. However, such imitation and memorization are not regarded as plagiarism. As Dilin Liu points out,

> Memorizing good writing to help one learn to write better is not the same thing as copying and claiming it as one's own . . . . In fact, a major role of memorizing good writing in Chinese is to help the learner appreciate and become familiar with effective rhetorical styles and useful writing techniques . . . .[15]

Just like all writers, ESL students rely on what they have been taught about writing; that knowledge, however, sometimes contradicts the expectations of a Western audience. Indeed, the belief that ESL writers (particularly Asian students) plagiarize regularly has "become conventional wisdom in some circles."[16] For instance, Deckert asserts that many Chinese students plagiarize (unintentionally) by repeating source material verbatim: "They are the proverbial rote memorizers or recyclers," he writes. "In the school setting, they are unaccustomed to deriving and expressing their own insight into academic issues."[17] Sometimes, then, particular ways of writing that violate basic Western conventions may be seen as correct and appropriate by other (non-Western) audiences.[18] As one Chinese student reports,

> If the English teacher required me to write a long English essay . . . I would turn to famous sayings and sentences derived from famous writers and essays on the same topic. I would imitate what other people say and use their sentences in my essays. I would at most change a single word but I would not change the main frame or structure. . . . If my English teacher required me to write long English essays, I would use famous sayings, proverbs, and quotable phrases quite often, just as I use them very often in writing Chinese essays, for I consider they are essential in writing Chinese and English essays.[19]

A researcher who compared essays by American and Chinese students did find significant differences in how each group of writers incorporated source text in their papers. Ling Shi reports that the Chinese students borrowed source words more frequently and cited them less often than the American students whose writing she analyzed.[20] It is not the case, though, that Asian cultures tolerate plagiarism, as many people assume. Liu, a native Chinese researcher/teacher at an American university, notes that "the concept of *plagiarism* as an immoral practice has existed in China for a very long time."[21] He explains, "Chinese has two terms for plagiarism and they are both derogatory: *piao qie*, which literally means to rob and steal someone's writing, and *cao xi*, which means to copy and steal."[22] And Phan Le Ha, a Vietnamese writer and teacher, writes,

> If the term plagiarism in English is "laden with negative moral connotations," the Vietnamese terms for plagiarism, *dao van* and *an cap y/van*, have the same or even more negative connotations. These two terms clearly and straightforwardly condemn the act of cheating in writing.[23]

We expect that the students who seek success in American classrooms will adopt and master not just our language but also our beliefs, values, and conventions regarding authorship and source use. When a writer violates our rhetorical rules, we may assume that the problem is a simple matter of enculturation. However, Colin Sowden reminds us that "groups defined by nation, culture or language are not homogeneous, but composed of individuals who are not all alike," and that "while maintaining an awareness of cultural predispositions on the part of multilingual students, we must be careful how we interpret the behaviour."[24] Sometimes, cultural differences are the best explanation for plagiarism, but other factors influence students' writing decisions as well.

One reason for some ESL writers' plagiarism is familiar to all students: time pressure. Pat Currie writes about Diana, a native Cantonese speaker from Macau. To cope with the challenges of being a nonnative speaker with a heavy load of classes in an English language business school, Diana intentionally plagiarized several assignments for one of her more difficult courses. Currie argues that Diana did not set out to "violate Western cultural norms" but rather that she copied "with the intent to learn, to keep her head down, and to pass the course."[25] Currie explains that although Diana's copying was "neither appropriate nor justifiable in a Western academic context, it was at least understandable" in that it allowed Diana to successfully pass her class (the instructor did not detect the plagiarism).[26]

As Diana's case shows, even intentional plagiarism cannot be dismissed as a simple lack of ethics. Often there are deeper explanations, especially for second language students. A student from Kyrgyzstan describes plagiarizing assignments at her central Asian university because she felt that her instructors didn't care about her as a student or about her writing: "Professors required us to show that we were familiar with the subject and they were happy . . . . They didn't care whether we just copied all these texts or wrote it by ourselves."[27] Alastair Pennycook offers an interpretation for some of the deliberate cheating that occurs in institutional contexts such as this (the Kyrgyz student was attending a state-run university in a post-Communist country). He explains that for many nonnative and World English speakers, English represents imperialism, and when students feel that discourse is forcing them to think and act in certain ways, "plagiarism might then be seen as a justifiably cynical form of resistance."[28]

The Challenge of Paraphrasing Properly

The complexity of academic English presents a formidable challenge for many ESL writers (as it does for many native English-speaking students as well). Even professional scholars sometimes plagiarize as they struggle with writing in English. A Taiwanese computer scientist states,

> After working hard in research, locally trained researchers with poor English writing skill still need to struggle very hard for translating their research findings into English [so that they can be published in Western academic journals]. It is even more disappointing when their papers are rejected simply because of writing problems.[29]

"If faculty have difficulty comprehending and manipulating the languages of the various academic cultures," Rebecca Moore Howard asks, "how much more difficult a task do undergraduate students face as they are presented with a bewildering array of discourse, none of which resonates with the languages of their homes and secondary schools?"[30] Think about some of the difficult texts you have been asked to read in college and remember some of the ways you have struggled with academic discourse; now, imagine how much more difficult these tasks would be if you were reading and writing in a second (or third) language.

When students write in academic settings, David Bartholomae points out, they must "learn to speak our language, to speak as we do."[31] For some ESL writers, changing a few words of a source text but keeping intact the structure and tone of the original represents a starting point—an entryway into a new language community. Yet most plagiarism policies require students to paraphrase well and appropriately—that is, that they effectively recast a source text in their own voice, using their own words. However, paraphrasing is one of the most complex writing skills there is.[32] To paraphrase well and correctly, writers must employ a number of high-level language skills:

- They need to understand the meaning of all of the words and ideas in a source text.
- They need to accurately discern the author's tone and stance in the writing.
- They need to come up with lexical and syntactic equivalents of the source text (alternative words and sentence structures) so that they can express the source's meaning in original language.

Successful paraphrasing requires that a writer "both master his sources and break his connection to their language and structure."[33] If an attempted paraphrase fails to break away sufficiently from its source, a writer's text will appear plagiarized despite any efforts he made to avoid it. Diane Pecorari's research with postgraduate ESL writers demonstrates this situation. Even though their papers appeared to contain some plagiarism, the students' explanations of their writing and Pecorari's analysis of their texts "strongly suggest the absence of intention to plagiarize."[34] When one's vocabulary is limited or when her familiarity with the syntax of a language does not allow her to draft alternate versions of a sentence, a writer may have no options other than patching together source passages in an attempt to compose an acceptable college-level paper.[35] Sometimes, then, when ESL writers make a too-close paraphrase, or even when they copy patches of source text directly into their papers, what appears as plagiarism may in fact represent the beginning of their participation in a new academic language and culture rather than an attempt to subvert that culture's expectations about originality and authorship. When this happens, we should welcome the attempt to move into a new terrain, and we should do all we can to help the writer negotiate the complexities of academic writing in English.

Plagiarism and Citation Conventions

Many students know the surprise and confusion they experience when they're given contradictory advice about documentation by different instructors. On one level, the important question is "MLA or APA?" Yet questions about referencing and attribution are often more complex than this.

Shi, the researcher who compared Chinese and American students' essays, explains that first and second language writers often credit their sources in different ways.[36] Based on her experience as a teacher and student, Phan Le Ha notes that in Vietnamese universities undergraduate writers are not expected to provide full in-text citations for sources they use in their essays. She explains that this is not considered plagiarism "as long as students acknowledge all the authors whose ideas they have referred to in the bibliography"at the end of their papers.[37] Yet because Western academic audiences expect writers to explicitly acknowledge their sources in their texts, the Vietnamese conventions that Phan Le Ha describes might be branded plagiarism in an American classroom.

ESL students, Shi claims, may need to employ more direct attribution practices in their source-based writing in English than they use when writing in their other languages.[38] But the expectation that nonnative writers must leave behind their other rhetorical practices when they write in English is a controversial one, as Eric Prochaska explains:

> Though Americans, in particular, are fortunate that English is the current world language, we have gone so far as to demand that when someone uses our linguistic features that they must also adopt our ideology, in the form of our rhetoric. . . . In the process of globalization and world dominance of one language, we eradicate not only native tongues, but also rhetorical patterns and ideologies.[39]

Suggestions for Tutoring ESL Writers

Many tutors do not feel comfortable raising questions about plagiarism. We don't want to risk offending students, particularly those who have worked diligently on their assignments. We should keep in mind, however, that there is nothing inherently shameful in the topic,[40] and it is both appropriate and important to discuss source use with a writer when there are any questions about whether the writer has plagiarized, intentionally or not.

Be Direct and Explicit When Discussing Problems with Using Sources

To open a conversation about suspected plagiarism, you might simply ask the writer, "Did you consult any sources as you wrote this paper?" If she answers yes, you might follow up by asking her to indicate in her paper any words, phrases, or ideas from her sources. If she replies no, you can show her why you asked the question, pointing out which parts of her paper caught your attention, and helping her find ways to make those parts fit more smoothly.

During this conversation, remember to maintain a supportive, encouraging, nonjudgmental role. You might do this most easily by keeping in mind that source use, like any other aspect of writing, represents a developmental continuum, and that some writers will be better at it than others. You might also consider alternatives to the "*p*" word, which for many people causes more confusion than clarification.[41] Using terms such as *borrowed words* or *too-close paraphrase* can help you talk about what's going on in a second language writer's text with more precision—and, importantly, with less moral baggage—than simply using the catch-all term *plagiarism*.

Several resources can facilitate your conversations about plagiarism. First, familiarize yourself with your school's plagiarism policy. (This can usually be found in the student handbook.) Discussing the specific wording the policy uses to describe plagiarism can make the institution's expectations clearer to ESL students who may not fully understand the language of the policy on their own. You might also consult one or two composition handbooks; reviewing various descriptions of plagiarism and citation will offer alternative explanations as well as examples illustrating correct and incorrect use of sources. Finally, invite your writing center to build up an archive of sample papers from different disciplines, written and documented according to different styles (MLA, APA, Chicago, etc.). Such a corpus will allow tutors and writers to analyze real writing samples to discover different ways to integrate source information into a paper.[42]

Ask the ESL Writer About His Understanding of Plagiarism and How He Is Accustomed to Writing with Sources

One effective way to raise the topic of plagiarism in a tutoring session is to invite the writer to talk about some of the writing conventions he learned in his home culture.[43] Christine Pearson Casanave suggests, "If you, your colleagues, or your students are from non-Western cultures, compare your views on copying, imitation, and memorization as (a) instructional techniques in the writing class and (b) practices that are or are not allowed in academic writing."[44]

Consider asking some of the following questions about academic writing in terms of the student's home culture. The writer's responses to these questions will provide points of comparison through which you can better understand cultural and rhetorical differences regarding source-based writing:

- What have you been taught about how academic writers should use sources?
- Are writers expected to consult sources as they write papers, or are they expected to base their writing on their own ideas?
- Are writers expected to use direct quotes from sources? If so, how do they separate the source's words and ideas from their own?
- How do writers acknowledge their sources to their readers? Do they use footnotes, in-text citations, or a "works cited" page?
- Is it ever appropriate or expected for a writer to copy words or ideas directly from a source without citing the source?
- Does your home/native language have a word for *plagiarism*? If so, what does it mean? What have you been told about U.S. academic conventions regarding plagiarism and source use?

During a Consultation, Look at a Writer's Sources
Side-by-Side with Her Paper

One of the best ways to help a writer learn to use sources effectively and appropriately is to look at the writer's sources alongside her text. Begin by asking the writer to indicate where in her paper she used words or ideas from sources; for instance, she might underline all of the source words that appear in her paper. Using highlighters to color-code sources works well, too, especially to distinguish between direct quotes and paraphrases or summaries. If computers are available, you might suggest the writer display her source's words and ideas in a different font. Whatever your method, the point is the same: to draw the writer's attention to the traces of her source texts in her own paper. Even first language writers sometimes find it difficult to summarize or paraphrase a source text without drawing too heavily on the source's original language or sentence structure; looking at source and paper side-by-side will allow immediate, accurate comparisons and will make any too-close paraphrases (and missing citations) readily apparent.

In addition to making it easier for the writer to pick up inadvertent plagiarism, highlighting source text will help you focus on the writer's use of her sources and will let you focus on the following questions:

- Does the writer do a good job of weaving the source information into her paper?
- Does she vary the way she incorporates source information by drawing on summary, paraphrasing, and direct quotation?

- Does she choose appropriate times to include direct quotes from her sources, or does she overuse them, failing to develop an original argument?

One way to help ESL students incorporate sources effectively is to teach them to use "reporting verbs,"[45] also called *signal phrases* or *attributional tags*. A reserve of even five or six stock phrases (such as "The author *acknowledges*" or "As Connor *suggests*") can help ESL writers incorporate source information into their writing. So with the writer's sources in front of you and with a list of signal phrases at hand, you and the writer can best ensure that her paper employs and acknowledges source material accurately and correctly, in academically acceptable and rhetorically powerful ways.

Responding to Plagiarism

Most students who plagiarize do so unintentionally. Yet some students, native and nonnative English speakers alike, knowingly disregard citation conventions or sometimes deliberately pass off someone else's writing as their own. This kind of plagiarism—what Rebecca Moore Howard urges us to call "fraud"[46]—puts writing tutors in a difficult and uncomfortable position. The best way you can prepare for such a situation is to consider your options ahead of time. With your writing center director and with fellow tutors, discuss how you might respond to the following scenarios:

- An ESL student brings in a paper for a second consultation with you. As you read the paper, you notice that the writing is much clearer and more complex than it was in a previous draft. When you mention this to the student, she tells you that she asked her roommate, an English major, to edit the paper for her and to make any needed changes to her wording and sentence structure.

- As you read over a student's paper, you notice that several paragraphs are printed in a slightly different font than the others. When you ask the student about this, he says that he was having trouble coming up with ideas for the paper, so he copied a few paragraphs from a website into his paper. "It's okay, though," he says, "because I wrote the website's URL on my Works Cited page. But I'll change the font."

- At the beginning of your tutoring session, you ask your tutee to tell you a little bit about her paper. She isn't able to describe her topic very clearly, and she can't restate some of the specific points she made. When you ask her about particular words she used in her paper, she doesn't seem to know what they mean. Her paper has a few grammatical errors, but it is generally clear, fluent, and well-written—which is unexpected given how she talked about it.

If you suspect a student of intentional plagiarism, the most appropriate response might be to handle it in the same way you would handle inadvertent plagiarism: Offer to help the student understand your school's plagiarism policy, and offer to work with the student on appropriate ways to use source texts. Because tutors work with writers in the drafting and revising stages of writing—generally before work has been submitted for final evaluation—there may still be time for the writer to complete the assignment on his own, showing that he knows and can follow the rules of documentation as well as those of academic integrity.

As you have these conversations in your writing center, ask your director if there are any established procedures you should follow if you suspect that a writer has plagiarized. In particular, discuss whether (and, if so, how) you should document your conversation with the writer. Because some instructors are suspicious of writing center assistance (thinking that writing centers help students plagiarize) and because some colleges have honor codes that require students to report suspected plagiarism, it will be helpful to have clear guidelines that tutors can follow consistently.

A Final Word

What a challenge writers face when they move into a new academic culture: They must adapt to a new language, new ways of developing and organizing papers, and new ways of engaging with the texts they read. As you work with ESL writers, keep in mind that this new academic environment may be quite different than those they are accustomed to, and remember that the rules of Western academic culture and its conventions for using sources may seem quite foreign. As insiders to the academic community, writing tutors are in an ideal position to serve as "cultural/rhetorical informants,"[47] helping ESL writers understand the citation and documentation conventions that are so important to their academic success.

Sowden writes,

> The usual way of responding to the perceived culture gap . . . is to encourage [multilingual students] to adopt the norms of their host culture, including those relating to the issues of plagiarism, and to become adept at the skills that this involves. . . . Perhaps instead multilingual students would benefit from preserving what they find most useful from their own vernacular culture, both general and academic, while also striving to assimilate what is best from their new context.[48]

It is not naïve to think that we can learn about source use from the students we work with; discussing and practicing citation conventions can help all writers avoid plagiarism, regardless of their language backgrounds. It will also help ESL writers develop the kind of original, independent voice that many of their English language instructors expect them to use. It will result in better writing, too—not just more correct writing but also writing that uses sources in more complex and rhetorically effective ways.

Notes

1. Elbow, 330.
2. Howard (2000), 82.
3. Howard (1992), 233.
4. Casanave, 170.
5. Elbow, 334–35.
6. Spigelman, 4.
7. Graff (2002).
8. Abasi, Akbari, and Graves, 114.
9. Purdue OWL (n.d.).
10. Pecorari, 324. For a "useful distinction between the writer of a new text and the author of a source text," Pecorari credits G. Thompson and Y. Ye, "Evaluation of the Reporting Verbs Used in Academic Papers," *Applied Linguistics* 12 (1991): 365–82.
11. Pecorari, 324.
12. Deckert, 132. Here, Deckert is paraphrasing L. K. Hsu, *Americans and Chinese* (Honolulu: University Press of Hawaii, 1981).
13. Cai, 281.
14. Graff (2002).
15. Liu, 237.
16. Pecorari, 318.
17. Deckert, 133.
18. Cai, 280.
19. Ho, p. 234, cited in Ramanathan and Atkinson, 54–55. Here, Ramanathan and Atkinson are quoting from I. Ho, "Relationships Between Motivation/ Attitude, Effort, English Proficiency, and Socio-Cultural Educational Factors and Taiwan Technological University/Institute Students' English Learning Strategy Use" (Auburn University, unpublished dissertation, 1998).
20. Shi, 181.
21. Liu, 235.
22. Liu, 235.
23. Phan Le Ha, 76. Phan Le Ha cites Chandrasoma, Thompson, and Penny-cook, 172, for the embedded quotation.
24. Sowden, 228.
25. Currie, 11.
26. Currie, 11.
27. Minett (2002).
28. Pennycook, 282.
29. Myers, 14.

30. Howard (1992), 233.
31. Bartholomae, 134.
32. Myers, 9.
33. Dossin, 129.
34. Pecorari, 317.
35. Howard (1992), 240.
36. Shi, 191.
37. Phan Le Ha, 79.
38. Shi, 191.
39. Prochaska, 72.
40. Hyland, 380.
41. Chandrasoma, Thompson, and Pennycook, 172.
42. Thompson and Tribble (2001).
43. Crowley, 3.
44. Casanave, 187.
45. Hinkel, 186–192.
46. Howard (2002), 488.
47. Powers, 42.
48. Sowden, 229.

Works Cited

Abasi, Ali R., Nahal Akbari, and Barbara Graves. 2006. "Discourse Appropriation, Construction of Identities, and the Complex Issue of Plagiarism: ESL Students Writing in Graduate School." *Journal of Second Language Writing* 15(2): 102–17. Retrieved August 2007 from Science-Direct database.

Bartholomae, David. 1985. "Inventing the University." In *When a Writer Can't Write*, edited by Mike Rose, 134–65. New York: Guilford Press.

Cai, Guanjun. 1999. "Texts in Contexts: Understanding Chinese Students' English Compositions." In *Evaluating Writing: The Role of Teachers' Knowledge About Text, Learning, and Culture*, edited by Charles Cooper and Lee Odell, 279–97. Urbana, IL: National Council of Teachers of English.

Casanave, Christine Pearson. 2004. *Controversies in Second Language Writing: Dilemmas and Decisions in Research and Instruction*. Ann Arbor: University of Michigan Press.

Chandrasoma, Ranamukalage, Celia Thompson, and Alastair Pennycook. (2004). "Beyond Plagiarism: Transgressive and Nontransgressive Intertextuality. *Journal of Language, Identity, and Education* 3(3): 171–93.

Crowley, Catherine. 2001. "'Are We on the Same Page?' ESL Student Perceptions of the Writing Center." *Writing Lab Newsletter* 25(9): 1–5.

Currie, Pat. 1998. "Staying Out of Trouble: Apparent Plagiarism and Academic Survival." *Journal of Second Language Writing* 7(1): 1–18.

Deckert, Glenn D. 1993. "Perspectives on Plagiarism from ESL Students in Hong Kong." *Journal of Second Language Writing* 2(2): 131–48.

Dossin, Mary Mortimore. 2000. "Using Others' Words: Quoting, Summarizing, and Documenting Sources." In *A Tutor's Guide: Helping Writers One to One*, edited by Ben Rafoth, 127–34. Portsmouth, NH: Boynton/Cook.

Elbow, Peter. 1999. "Individualism and the Teaching of Writing: Response to Vai Ramanathan and Dwight Atkinson." *Journal of Second Language Writing* 8(3): 327–38.

Graff, Sarah. 2002. E-mail post reprinted in *"TESL-EJ* Forum: Perspectives on Plagiarism in the ESL/EFL Classroom," edited by Karen Stanley. *TESL-EJ* 6(3): 5. www.writing.berkeley.edu/TESL-EJ.

Hinkel, Eli. 2004. *Teaching Academic ESL Writing: Practical Techniques in Vocabulary and Grammar*. Mahwah, NJ: Lawrence Erlbaum.

Howard, Rebecca Moore. 1992. "A Plagiarism *Pentimento*." *Journal of Teaching Writing* 11(2): 233–45.

———. 2000. "The Ethics of Plagiarism." In *The Ethics of Writing Instruction: Issues in Theory and Practice*, edited by Michael E. Pemberton, 79–90. Stamford, CT: Ablex.

———. 2002. "Sexuality, Textuality: The Cultural Work of Plagiarism." *College English* 62(4): 473–91.

Hyland, Fiona. 2001. "Dealing with Plagiarism when Giving Feedback." *ELT Journal* 55(4): 375–81.

Liu, Dilin. 2005. "Plagiarism in ESOL Students: Is Cultural Conditioning Truly the Major Culprit?" *ELT Journal* 59(3): 234–41.

Minett, Amy. 2002. "Plagiarism and Pedagogy: Central European Perspectives and Practice." Paper presented at European Association for the Teaching of Academic Writing Conference, June 17–20, Groningen, the Netherlands.

Myers, Sharon. 1998. "Questioning Author(ity): ESL/EFL, Science, and Teaching About Plagiarism." *TESL-EJ* 3(2). www.writing.berkeley.edu/TESL-EJ.

Pecorari, Diane. 2003. "Good and Original: Plagiarism and Patchwriting in Academic Second-Language Writing." *Journal of Second Language Writing* 12(4): 317–45.

Pennycook, Alastair. 1994. "The Complex Contexts of Plagiarism: A Reply to Deckert." *Journal of Second Language Writing* 3: 277–84.

Phan Le Ha. 2006. "Plagiarism and Overseas Students: Stereotypes Again?" *ELT Journal* 60(1): 76–78.

Powers, Judith K. 1993. "Rethinking Writing Center Conferencing Strategies for the ESL Writer." *The Writing Center Journal* 13(2): 39–47.

Prochaska, Eric. 2001. "Western Rhetoric and Plagiarism: Gatekeeping for an English-Only International Academia." *Writing on the Edge* 12(2): 65–79.

Purdue OWL (Online Writing Lab). n.d. Purdue University. *The Contradictions of American Academic Writing*. Retrieved March 21, 2005, from http://owl.english.purdue.edu/handouts/print/research/r_plagiar.html.

Ramanathan, Vai, and Dwight Atkinson. 1999. "Individualism, Academic Writing, and ESL Writers." *Journal of Second Language Writing* 8(1): 45–75.

Shi, Ling. 2004. "Textual Borrowing in Second-Language Writing." *Written Communication* 21(2): 171–200.

Sowden, Colin. 2005. "Plagiarism and the Culture of Multilingual Students in Higher Education Abroad." *ELT Journal* 59(3): 226–33.

Spigelman, Candace. 2000. *Across Property Lines: Textual Ownership in Writing Groups*. Carbondale: Southern Illinois University Press.

Thompson, Paul, and Chris Tribble. 2001. "Looking at Citations: Using Corpora in English for Academic Purposes." *Language Learning & Technology* 5(3): 91–105.

14

Writing Activities for ESL Writers

Kevin Dvorak

Up to this point, the chapters in this part of the book have offered strategies for tutors to implement during their tutoring sessions. This chapter expands on these ideas and also offers something a little different. It offers ideas for writing activities that can be used during tutoring sessions with English as a second language (ESL) writers as well as ideas for creative writing workshops and how you can facilitate them. These workshops differ from familiar workshops in that they focus primarily on the act of creation rather than requiring students to bring in works they have already written. I offer a rationale for incorporating these workshops for ESL writers in writing centers, provide examples of workshop activities, and show how to get them started.

Writing as the Center Activity

Experiencing the act of writing creatively can allow ESL writers to engage in the many layers of English other than the academic. Providing writing activities and creative writing workshops to ESL writers helps writing centers add to the diversity of experiences ESL writers have with English, to the diversity of experiences tutors have with ESL students, and to the diversity of literacy practices writing centers promote.

I have long wondered how much writing happens in our spaces we call writing centers. Much of the work we do centers on working with writers who have already produced texts rather than producing them with us or while in our company. While we have long prided our centers as being places where communities of writers get together to work, talk, and learn with one another, I still believe many writers, particularly ESL writers, work for long periods of time alone, perhaps in the garrets Lunsford laments,[1] prior to entering a writing center to talk with a tutor. This is not necessarily wrong, and it is not necessarily a bad thing; however, as a writing center director and as someone who teaches and tutors writers, I like to see writers engaged in the act of writing while in our center. I like helping them figure out new ways of dismantling their own writer's block and helping them draft their initial ideas as quickly as possible.

During the course of the last few years, I have found myself implementing more and more writing activities into tutoring sessions and classroom environments with ESL writers. Much of this comes from a notion that writers sometimes need to take a break from the serious work of the academy and incorporate playful activities into their academic work routines.[2] Many of the activities I use during tutoring sessions are helpful for both native English-speaking (NES) and ESL writers, and they can be done with one student or a room full of writers. I have chosen to share the specific activities below because I have used them successfully during sessions with ESL writers and because they can build upon one another. All three are essentially invention and drafting strategies, though they can easily be modified to help writers during the revision process.

The Alphabet Exercise

I sometimes use this activity with ESL students when they visit early in their writing process and have not yet determined what they want to write about. If a student has few solid ideas to work with, I often ask if she would like to play a quick A to Z topic generation game to see if she can develop ideas to include in her essay. This activity has long been a favorite with my students, NES and ESL, because it challenges vocabulary skills, quickly produces a whole list of ideas, and becomes a new invention strategy for students to use with future assignments.

First, we discuss the overall assignment for a few moments, and then I ask the student to write the alphabet down the left side of a sheet of paper. (This activity can be done on a computer as well.) I challenge the student to come up with one or more words or phrases that pertain to their assignment that begin with each letter of the alphabet. During the process, I engage in a conversation with the student, helping out when appropriate. For example, last semester, an ESL student, Daniela, visited the writing center to discuss an assignment for her college writing class in which she had to write about struggles associated with college life. (Her entire class had this assignment; I will discuss other students in her class below.) She wrote the alphabet and began filling in the blanks: *A* became "academics," *E* became "essays," *M* became "money." Daniela struggled, though, with some letters like *J* and *K* (*Q* quickly became "quizzes"), but came up with more than one word or phrase for several others. In about five to seven minutes, she had generated approximately thirty ideas for her assignment. She was excited at the number of ideas she had generated, and I would like to think that this boosted her confidence regarding her vocabulary.

After students complete the activity or as much of it as they can—*X* rarely gets a word—I typically have them do either of two things: (1) Freewrite about one or more of the topics or (2) group similar topics so as to create potential paragraphs with main topics and supporting ideas. Daniela and I narrowed her list down to the three topics she felt were the strongest and then she took some ideas from other letters and placed them underneath her main topics as supporting ideas. She then constructed a basic outline and began drafting paragraphs about each topic. Upon completing this task, she had a list of ideas to write about, demonstrated her vocabulary skills, and was ready to approach the next step in the writing process. I'm also glad to say that she had some fun with writing and the writing center.

Computer-Based White-Write

We often work with writers faced with daunting writing tasks and who are trying to chip away at writer's block. This can be especially strenuous for ESL writers, whose difficulty with the rhetorical situation can often be compounded by the fact that they are still in the process of developing their languages skills and a cultural understanding of the situation. I remember writing essays for one of my advanced Spanish courses, and I never felt comfortable just focusing on the assignment because I was always hyperaware of my deficient—but growing—Spanish writing skills. For this reason, I believe regular freewrites do not always work as well as we hope they will with ESL writers. That is why I have modified the basic concept of the freewrite in a way that makes it more challenging, but in my opinion, a bit easier to get through.

I call this type of freewrite a "white-write." A white-write happens when a writer sitting at a computer station turns the font color to white so it matches the color of the background. They can also turn off all grammar and spell checkers, but this is not required. I have writers do this so they can watch the cursor move on the screen as they type; yet they are not distracted by their concerns about how the language is developing on the screen.[3] This activity can take some getting used to before writers are comfortable with it. Even during their struggles, though, I have watched many ESL writers work through the white-write without going back and revising. Instead, I have seen them focus only on writing what they are thinking.

Like freewrites, white-writes focus on quick text production. White-writes allow writers to rapidly transfer thoughts from their minds onto the computer screen. They also provide a text for writers and tutors to begin discussing. I have found that when using this activity regularly over the course of several weeks, ESL and NES students alike can produce more text in a short amount of time (usually five to seven minutes), and for some, the latter texts are more polished.

Essay Draft: Twenty-Five Minutes, More or Less

This activity is often an extension of the previous two and is something I often do with first-year writers, NES and ESL. It's another invention strategy ESL writers can add to their writer's toolbox, and it also helps many of them conceptualize the structure of a traditional academic essay. For this activity, students can either white-write or freewrite in the traditional way. Here, I discuss how students complete this activity while working at a computer station.

I begin this activity by discussing and drawing the basic concept of what is often called the traditional academic essay. My drawings include the following: (1) an introductory paragraph with a thesis statement toward the end of the paragraph; (2) three separate body paragraphs (a circle, a square, and a triangle), each of which discusses one main topic; and (3) a concluding paragraph that summarizes the work as a whole. Sometimes, I will draw this on the white board in our writing center, especially if I am working with more than one student, but I prefer drawing it quickly on a sheet of paper so the student can take it and refer to it again. (And I look forward to the day when I can convince a student to draw it for me as I explain it.) While some students are already familiar with the traditional essay format, there are others who are not; either way, many find the concept difficult, and I find the visual representation sometimes appeals to their learning styles. After discussing the concept with them and showing them the drawing, I remind them that what we are about to do is produce a draft—not a final product. This activity, I say many times during these sessions, is simply one step in a complex writing process. (See Chapter 3 for additional discussion of using visuals).

Prior to writing, I ask students to think about three separate ideas concerning their overall assignment. For example, two other ESL students from Daniela's class visited our writing center after having been assigned the same assignment on the struggles college students face. I started working with one student, Diego, while Sam, a senior tutor, was working with the other, Manny. We decided to combine our sessions so we could all be a part of this activity. Diego and Manny had already developed some ideas, so we decided to forgo the alphabet game and, instead, focus on drafting an essay. Given their assigned topic, we discussed several struggles they felt were important, and we narrowed the list to three: money, time management, and peer/family pressure. Both students agreed to this list, so we moved on to the next step.

The next step begins the actual drafting. After having explained the concept of an introduction, I asked the students to write one general statement about their topic. After the students wrote their first sentence, I asked them to write a follow-up sentence that was a bit more specific, one that started pointing them toward their potential thesis statement. Sam sat between the two and watched as they wrote; she offered suggestions whenever their typing slowed down. I then reviewed the general concept of a thesis statement and asked them to write a statement that used the three concepts we discussed in the order they planned to discuss them. A thesis statement, I reminded them, establishes the essay's organization. After they drafted potential thesis statements, I confirmed that their main topics were in the exact order and used the exact language we discussed. This all happened in about six minutes.

- *Tip*: To do this effectively, the activity leader has to encourage writers to work much quicker than they normally would and without worrying about completion. The activity leader should reassure the writers that production is the goal of this activity and that they will go back and revise the rough draft later. This is important because it helps writers push beyond their inner editors.

After the introductory paragraph is written, I ask students to hit the enter key twice. I believe the extra white space between paragraphs serves as a reminder that they should return to the paragraphs and continue adding, subtracting, and revising. The extra white space also makes the essay look more like a work-in-progress and less like a completed product.

The next step is writing the body paragraph. I asked them to think about their first main idea—in this case, struggles with money—and write only about that topic for four or five minutes. Then, after the time expired, they again hit enter twice, and I asked them to spend four or five minutes writing about their second topic, time management. The same went for the third body paragraph on pressure. In a span of approximately fifteen minutes, Diego and Manny had drafted three body paragraphs.

Finally, we reached the conclusion. I explained the concept of a concluding paragraph and approached their drafting of this paragraph similarly to the sentence-by-sentence approach I did with the introduction. First, I asked Diego and Manny to write two or three specific statements that reflected the main ideas in the body paragraphs. Then, I asked them to write a general summary statement similar to the one they wrote at the start of this activity. And finally, I asked them to write one final concluding sentence. The drafting process of this activity ended here, after about twenty-five minutes. I then reminded them that this was only one step in the writing process. They both agreed to continue revising their work when they got home and to bring their revised drafts back to the writing center.

Creative Writing Workshops

While it is great to see writers generating writing for their assignments while in the center, it can also be fun to have them generate writing just for themselves, for pure enjoyment and for extra practice. That is why I believe creative writing workshops for ESL writers can be a great way to enhance the learning experiences of ESL writers and writing center tutors.

Creative writing is too often an overlooked and undervalued form of literacy learning in the academy, especially when it pertains to learning English as a second language. Most contexts in which ESL students use English outside of the academy are less formal and more creative than those they use in classrooms; however, academic instructors do not ask these writers to cross the lines between academic composition and informal, creative writing as often as they should.[4]

Creative writing benefits all language users by encouraging writers to express themselves in more creative and colloquial terms, ways nonnative speakers are more likely to hear and speak English when not in classrooms.

As writing center tutors, we can place ourselves in a unique position to affect the literacy development of ESL writers by offering them opportunities to write creatively. Because writing centers are commonly nonauthoritative, cosmopolitan hubs where students come together to interact with each other's ideas and written languages, they are prime locations for ESL writers to develop these types of writing abilities. By offering creative writing workshops to ESL writers, writing centers become gathering spots for various language users as they

- promote writing as a fun activity—fun that is often overlooked when trying to compose pressure-filled, academic, formal prose
- create an environment where nonnative speakers interact with tutors in literacy activities
- encourage ESL writers to take risks while writing—risks they may feel intimidated to take in academic writings.

I believe providing this type of atmosphere is a fantastic opportunity for both ESL writers and tutors to experience diversity development. The risks to be faced, the conversations and readings involved, and the fun that surrounds them all combine to offer ESL students the experiences they usually do not receive in classrooms but can use for personal growth.

Releasing Writers into English

Let me begin by explaining what I mean by *creative writing workshop*. By this phrase, I do not mean a text-centered workshop where students bring in drafts of creative writings they have already written. Instead, I emphasize the middle word in this expression: *writing*. These are creative *writing* workshops, workshops that are centered around the act of writing.[5] In these workshops, ESL writers should produce stories, poetry, short fictional scenes—anything that implies "creativity" beyond common academic writing. In all, these should be interactive social environments where writings are produced and shared in an encouraging community setting.

- *Tip:* The facilitator should make it clear to the participants that these acts of writing are, essentially, acts of freewriting. In fact, it may help to clarify the following three points about freewrites:
  1. They are not revised or refined.
  2. They have not gone through the whole writing process as we usually define it.
  3. They are supposed to sound rough.

There are hundreds of writing activities that can be used in a creative writing workshop. Many writing activities you've experienced can be used outright or modified. One of the best things about these activities is that they can be manipulated so that a group may engage in the same general tasks but in ways that vary enough from one another so that they do not appear the same.[6] First, let's look at some activities you can do in a creative writing workshop, and then we'll see how to set up the workshop itself.

Activity One: Basic Collaborative Fiction Write-Around[7]

This write-around can serve as a creative way for participants to introduce themselves by allowing ESL writers to create fictional scenes, images, and identities about themselves and the worlds around them. Writers begin by writing fictional narratives about their lives. If it helps, writers can be given the following opening line: "I am _____, and I am from _____."
Writers should then write for a few minutes. When time is up, have the writers pass their writings to one side so each writer has another author's writing. Have each writer read her new passage quickly and continue where the previous author stopped. (It may even be fun to allow each writer to read only a few of the just-written lines of her new work before writing.) While writing, writers should be encouraged to add dialogue, scenery, concrete images, even a word written in their native language—anything that will add to their uniqueness.

- *Tip:* Play along. This is a learning experience for everyone. Every participant has a role in the creation of this atmosphere. Everyone is a writer, a reader, and a listener. And always provide specific instructions before starting each activity.

Activity Two: Prompted Quick-Writes

A second activity is freewriting from prompts. Prompts can be found almost anywhere, from books about creative writing to asking someone to call out a prompt and having each writer write from it for a few minutes. Another way is to have each writer write a prompt on a small piece of paper, put them all into a bowl, and then either have each writer pick one prompt from the bowl and write from it or pick single prompts from the bowl and have everyone write from them. These freewrites should be quick. By writing one after another, writers are challenged to shift ways of thinking quickly and to take their thoughts in new directions.

- *Variation:* Instead of quick-writes, students can write poems from the prompts. This encourages ESL writers to use English in nontraditional ways.

Activity Three: Picture This

Another activity is writing from pictures. Bring a variety of pictures to the workshop from magazines, newspapers, catalogs, online stock photos, family photo albums, and so on. Or have writers bring pictures from their own cultures and make this a fun way for everyone to share images and experiences of their home cultures. Pass them around and have the writers construct stories about the photos they receive. By looking at photos of other people's lives and creating scenes around them, writers can situate themselves in comparison to others.

- *Variation*: Either the stories or photos can be passed around at intervals. (See Activity One or Two as a guide.)

Activity Four: A Portrait of the Writer (Guided Self-Portraits)[8]

This activity allows writers to construct storylines about themselves or other characters. To do this, create a number of sentence-level prompts that will build on one another in an effort to develop a paragraph (or more) about someone or something. For example, three consecutive sentence-opening prompts could be: "I was walking . . . "; "And then I found . . . "; "But, before I could. . . ." Or, a facilitator could follow Wendy Bishop's guidelines from *Released into Language*. Bishop asks writers to think of a person they want to write about, choose a title for their piece, begin with an opening sentence, and follow with sentences that focus on using descriptive language such as "Write a sentence with a color in it;" "Write a sentence with a body part in it;" or "Write a sentence with a smell and a color in it."[9]

- *Variation:* This game can be played as another write-around, this time constructing a letter to someone (especially funny if it is to another participant). The first person begins the letter with a greeting ("Dear _____" or "Hey _____!" or "Yo _____!"). Then, fold the paper over to cover the writing and pass it to one side, where the next writer opens the letter. These could be the first three prompts of a progression: "I saw you . . . "; "But you were . . . "; "And now we are. . . . " The last writer should close the letter with a sign off.

Facilitating Creative Writing Workshops for ESL Writers

Now that you know some activities, it is time to organize them into workshops. The following is a quick, three-step process that will take you from organizing a workshop to facilitating one.

Step One: Choose a Facilitator or Facilitators

The first step in facilitating a creative writing workshop for ESL writers is deciding who the facilitator is going to be. At our center this past year, we began the University Writing Center Creative Writers' Utopia (UWC-CWU), an informal creative writing organization run by the UWC staff. The main goal of this organization was to organize and facilitate some form of writing workshops. Two of our tutors, Sam and Alexis, took the lead.

I suggest workshops like these be run by tutors who have interests in both teaching ESL writers and working with creative writing. Facilitators could also include one student interested in ESL pedagogy and another in creative writing pedagogy. In our case, Sam and Alexis had interests in both.

Step Two: Build It and Writers Will Write

Workshop organizers need to determine who is going to be asked to participate. The following are a few key questions that will need to be answered: Will only first-year ESL students be invited? Will upper-level and graduate ESL writers be invited? How will the workshop be advertised? In the previous edition of this collection, I hazarded combining NES with non-NES writers, but now, several years and many workshops later, I do not caution against this. In fact, I greatly endorse combining writers from all levels to participate, especially ESL. I have found that as long as a comfortable atmosphere has been created, these workshops can benefit all writers.

Step Three: Timing the Whole, Timing Activities

Before beginning a workshop, facilitators should set a specific length of time for the whole workshop—usually between forty-five and ninety minutes—and for each activity. Here lies a crucial situation: not letting the whole workshop or any one activity last too long. Keeping activities short keeps writers engaged.

- *Tip:* Use time effectively; downtime, when many are not reading, writing, or listening, can cause writers to lose attentiveness. If writers feel they want more time, encourage them to write more outside of the workshop and bring it to the next workshop to share.

A Final Word

When creative writings have been community-created, as described by the previous activities, they can be fun to write, read, and listen to because they are not sole products of one person but of a community of learners, of writers working together to have fun while engaging in acts of literacy.

All of these activities, whether used during one-to-one sessions or in creative writing workshops, can add to an ESL writer's experience with English. They help writers add new invention and revision strategies to their writer's toolboxes and hopefully help writers relax during the initial stages of the writing process. They also allow writers and tutors to engage in activities beyond the common practice of reviewing an already written text, which can make the writing center an even more exciting, productive experience for both parties.

Notes

1. Lunsford, 110.
2. Miller (2008).
3. I have experimented with other ways of doing this, such as by turning monitors off, but I believe it is vital that the student knows her work is being recorded. I had a class full of students turn their monitors off once, and as several of them wrote, they accidentally hit the "Alt" key, causing the computers to stop recognizing the typing function. We couldn't recover their work, but we learned a valuable lesson.
4. Bishop (1994).
5. Reid (2008).
6. I could describe enough prompts for an entire book; however, I'd rather refer to a few guides: *Madlibs*; Susan Woolridge, *Poem Crazy* (1996); and Wendy Bishop, *Released into Language* (1990).
7. See Bishop (1990), 117, for another version of this activity.
8. Bishop (1990), 98. For this activity, Bishop offers a fifteen-sentence guide to construct a descriptive paragraph.
9. Bishop (1990), 99.

Works Cited

Bishop, Wendy. 1990. *Released into Language: Options for Teaching Creative Writing*. Urbana, IL: National Council of Teachers of English.

———. 1994. "Crossing the Lines: On Creative Composition and Composing Creative Writing." In *Colors of a Different Horse: Rethinking Creative Writing Theory and Pedagogy*, edited by Wendy Bishop and Hans Ostrom, 181–97. Urbana, IL: National Council of Teachers of English.

Lunsford, Andrea. 1995. "Collaboration, Control, and the Idea of the Writing Center." In *Landmark Essays on Writing Centers*, edited by Christina Murphy and Joseph Law, 109–16. Davis, CA: Hermagoras.

Miller, Scott L. 2008. "Everybody Jumped for Joy! (But Joy Didn't Like That, So She Left)." In *Creative Approaches to Writing Center Work*, edited by Kevin Dvorak and Shanti Bruce, 21–47. Cresskill, NJ: Hampton.

Reid, Julie. 2008. "Building Labyrinths in Order to Escape: A Guide to Making Play Work." In *Creative Approaches to Writing Center Work*, edited by Kevin Dvorak and Shanti Bruce, 193–205. Cresskill, NJ: Hampton.

15

The Role of Writing in Higher Education in Germany

Gerd Bräuer

At some point, American tutors may wonder how English as a foreign language (EFL) students are accustomed to working with writing center tutors in their home countries and whether writing instruction abroad is the same as it is in the United States. These questions are important to answer because tutors may gain a greater understanding of the ways that EFL students' writing experiences in their home countries affect their tutoring sessions in American writing centers.

The Situation

Imagine this: A student who grew up in Germany comes to your writing center to get help with his first paper he has to prepare for a class. The paper is already done, and he just wants to drop it off to be edited as soon as possible. After you tell him that tutoring writing doesn't work like this and that he would have to make an appointment to actually work *together with a tutor* on his paper, he gets rather upset and is ready to leave.

The Problems

Even though the educational culture that this student grew up with is probably different from an American educational cultural context, the example shows the following:

- The student has a specific understanding of the role of the tutor as either editor or teacher. With this in mind and now being confronted with a different function of tutoring, he either gets upset and leaves the writing center or (mostly subconsciously) tries to manipulate the tutor to fit his expectations.

- The student envisions text feedback as something done only after he has finished writing and as surface editing mainly in regard to spelling and grammar.
- The student has experienced the role of writing in his classes mostly as a mode of documentation and reproduction of knowledge.

From my own experience with international student writers in Germany, the Czech Republic, the Netherlands, Switzerland, and different universities in the United States over the past two decades, I suspect another similarity among many writers coming from outside the American context of higher education: that of *not coming* to the writing center at all. An international student, who out of despair that she could not finish her bachelor's thesis in time, eventually sought help during her last semester of study from the writing center I started in 2001 at the University of Education in Freiburg, Germany.[1] When I asked her why she didn't come earlier, she wrote this:

> For a long time, I simply didn't know that there is a writing center at the university. Then, when someone pointed it out to me, I kept asking myself what a writing center actually is and does. When I finally had the guts to ask my academic advisor, I heard from him that you discuss your manuscript with a writing tutor. For a long time, I felt too embarrassed to actually do it. I kept telling myself: What would we talk about? I don't have anything interesting to say in my papers. And help with grammar I can get from my . . . friends.

For U.S. tutors, this example helps show the consequence of the three problems mentioned above: Lack of incentive for feedback in the context of instruction, writing seen as a mode of knowing instead of finding out, and feedback seen as related to either instruction or correction—all this together held the student back to explore the learning opportunities of the writing center. To solve these problems in a sustainable way, tutors need to better understand why these problems exist. And to do that, tutors who work in writing centers in the United States and who have not studied abroad for a significant length of time need to know something about the ways in which writing is taught in colleges and universities overseas.

Reason One for the Problems: The Role of Writing in Higher Education

Outside of Anglo-American higher education, the idea of writing centers and peer tutoring that goes beyond fixing language issues is still rather new. In Europe, for example, institutional writing support has started to develop only since the early 1990s. The Academic Writing Center at the University of Copenhagen, Denmark, founded in 1992, and the Writing Lab at the University of Bielefeld, Germany, founded two years later, were among the first ones when Western European universities began to adopt the Anglo-American modular and credit system and to develop extracurricular services complementing bachelor's and master's programs compatible with those in the English-speaking countries.[2]

Since the beginning of the new millennium, the number of university writing centers has grown steadily in many parts of the world, and a variety of different approaches to writing center pedagogy have emerged. European universities developed some interest in tutoring second language writers, which originated from the so-called Bologna Declaration. This agreement, initiated in 1999 between the twenty-nine countries of Europe, established until 2010 a uniform transfer-credit system among themselves in higher education and the mission to internationalize higher education in the European countries. Other new writing centers, such as the Center of Professional Writing at the University of Applied Sciences in Winterthur (Switzerland), focus on writing in the professions—for example, journalism and engineering.[3] These centers often concentrate on writing research and the development of writing curricula and methods of training professional writers. Last, but not least, there are writing centers also emerging as part of teacher-training institutions like the writing center at the University of Education in Freiburg (Germany). Here, attention lies in the conceptualization of school development and faculty development (e.g., setting up high school writing/reading centers) and the initiation, organization, and evaluation of local and regional literacy projects.[4]

There is one aspect currently influencing European writing pedagogy across the educational pyramid, and this is something that American tutors are likely to be familiar with: Portfolios and writing as reflective practice are gaining importance for learning and instruction in primary and secondary education, at the university level, and in professional training including continuing education in the professions.[5] Because the introduction of portfolios is often done as a means of top-down educational policies, writing centers are called upon as change agents providing concepts for portfolio implementation and faculty training, as done by the Academic Writing Center of Radboud University in Nijmegen (the Netherlands), which helped start the implementation of doctorate portfolios across campus.

Nevertheless, despite all these initiatives over the past few years, the traditional role of writing as a note-taking device in large lecture classes and as a mode of reproduction of already existing knowledge in a few fifteen- to twenty-page seminar papers during and one fifty- to seventy-page bachelor's or master's thesis at the end of studies is changing only very slowly toward writing as a mode of discursive instruction and learning. Due to rigid time constraints for finishing thesis work, students tend to avoid feedback and revision, and professors are often overburdened with too many students to help them in their process of writing through written feedback and one-to-one conferences.[6]

One significant change is visible in a growing number of colleges and universities in Western Europe. With the introduction of electronic learning platforms such as Claroline and Blackboard across the curriculum, writing seems to be used, at least in this specific e-learning environment, more often as a tool for collaborative learning. Often by chance and without pedagogical concept, students and instructors practice the different tools provided by e-learning platforms such as chats, blogs, forums, and wikis. This way, different kinds of writing that can be labeled as informal, expressive, reflective, and communicative contribute to the emergence of an approach, writing to learn, that has been proven by process writing research to be a highly important and very powerful first step toward effective texts for a specific audience.[7] In other words, in the near future, American tutors are likely to encounter a growing number of international students from Western European countries who will be visiting U.S. writing centers with an expanded functional understanding about the role of writing on their way to a degree in higher education. In the process of tutoring, American tutors should remind them about their use of online writing in the genres mentioned above when it comes to pointing out the need to apply writing to learn strategies and peer collaboration to the production of academic texts.

Nevertheless, this tendency toward a changing role of writing in European higher education seems to be challenged by a general hesitation among students from countries in Western Europe toward using too much time for working on the computer and the Internet. When asked where this self-limitation originates from, often the answer is that students favor personal, direct contact over what many of them call the impersonal and therefore emotionally detached exchange via the Internet. U.S. writing tutors helping writers from Europe should be aware of this motivational limitation and make sure to stress the specific benefits when they suggest writing and tutoring electronically.

Even though there has been research on process writing (prewriting, drafting, peer feedback, revision, and editing) in Europe for years,[8] institutional consequences on a large scale, drawn out of research and theories about the nature of writing, began to appear only as a result of the curricular reform I mentioned earlier toward bachelor's and master's programs and the urgent search of administrators for study support. Now at almost every university in Germany, workshops provide an introduction to process writing and to the specifics of academic writing. Nevertheless, these workshops are not mandatory and, in many cases, are offered just once each semester. Given the small number of workshops and their voluntary character, my estimate is that only about 5 percent of the student population participates. As a result, coping strategies for specific problems in the various stages of text production are still not mainstream, and if in existence at all, their efficiency will most of the time neither be reflected upon nor evaluated despite the fact that forms of reflective writing like learning logs (as weblogs) and portfolios are starting to appear. Therefore, it is important for American tutors to keep in mind that the consciousness of being (or becoming) a writer who is able to grow if he makes use of the resources of the writer's community is still underdeveloped at least among students at universities in German-speaking countries. From my work with students from other countries during the past twenty years, this also seems to be the case in other educational cultures that rely heavily on the idea of writing as reproducing knowledge, excluding the other functions of writing such as the *reflection*, *transformation*, and *development* of knowledge.

Reason Two for the Problems: Rhetorical Traditions

In the first book about writing centers and writing programs in Europe, Lotte Rienecker and Peter Stray Jörgensen introduce an interesting distinction between what they call the "Anglo-American" and the "Continental" way of writing,[9] with the Anglo-American way being more systematic and "caring" toward the reader, making sure at any point in the text the reader would be able to follow the line of argument by, what I call, *reconstructing* the text. We all know the extreme version of this kind of writing: the five-paragraph essay. In contrast, the Continental way of writing is not systematic in a sense that the reader would be able to predict the development of the argument from the beginning of the text. It is expected that the reader *coproduces*, so to speak, the text by puzzling together the various argumentative aspects that the writer has to offer. Whereas the Anglo-American mode of writing would deliver the major thesis of a text right at the beginning, its Continental counterpart expects the reader, in ever-narrowing hermeneutic circles, to unfold the major thesis of the text itself, getting a chance, in some cases, to compare the writer's intention with one's own findings in the conclusion of the text.

Despite the historical roots,[10] this distinction between rhetorical patterns of writing in the Old and New World is indeed a theoretical one. True, there are Anglo-American writers who write well in the Continental style and Continental writers who write superbly in the Anglo-American style. Nevertheless, the distinction can be important for EFL tutors to understand; there *are* different traditions in the practice of rhetoric, and novice academic writers try to imitate distinct rhetorical patterns from what they read. We writing tutors may not know the details of the tradition that has influenced a certain EFL writer throughout her educational upbringing, but we need to show during the tutoring session that we *acknowledge* and *honor* the existence of those cultural roots. This can easily be done by expressing interest in the way the EFL student is accustomed to writing. We need to make clear that learning how to compose texts in a foreign language does *not* mean having to give up one's native writing traditions. It is sometimes easier, however, for the writer to first make progress in mastering the linguistic aspects of the newly learned language by focusing on a rather simple yet self-explaining or referential style such as the Anglo-American and then try to incorporate aspects of her native style of writing later on when the linguistic concerns are felt to be less cumbersome.

Reason Three for the Problems: The Faculty

In the light of the two problems described above, the role of writing in higher education and the rhetorical traditions in Europe, it doesn't come as a surprise to find a third reason for the second language writing problems of international students: the people who taught the EFL student writers in their home countries.

In Germany and perhaps in a number of other educational cultures, many faculty have little knowledge about writing pedagogy, and they don't consciously reflect on their own writing processes. They take for granted that one learns how to write in grade school, and if they perceive any need for writing support at the university at all, they would expect it to be covered by the first language department. It is widely unknown that the process of learning how to write never really ends in a writer's lifetime, especially when he enters new discursive communities such as in freshman year or declares a major of study and experiences new genres of writing in the discipline and the professional field(s) related to the major.

Unlike American tutors, most faculty are neither familiar with what in the United States we call "writing across the curriculum"—the notion of a shared responsibility of all faculty in a U.S. college for the development of academic writing skills—nor with "writing in the disciplines" in which U.S. students learn about text genres central to a certain discipline and experience the specific demands of writing in their future professions. As a result, outside of the first language departments, little to no attention is paid to the quality of texts, with the possible exception of issues of grammar and spelling. Therefore, most of the time, students don't get concrete comments about why they did poorly on their papers. This, unfortunately, leaves students thinking that the reason for their failure is a lack of knowledge in their discipline. These students seldom realize that they could actually clarify and improve upon their ideas through *developing* them in and through writing. This is no wonder because to use writing as a tool for learning is rarely encouraged or recognized by their faculty. Techniques—such as brainstorming, clustering, freewriting, or mind-mapping—that do promote thinking have just recently found their way into primary and secondary education but less so into colleges and universities. Watching their college instructors, students get the impression that they are *geniuses*, writing articles and books and never having any writing problems.

Most of the faculty at universities in Germany, for example, don't share with students their lives as writers who experience the daily struggle of getting the right words on paper. They don't encourage students to come forward with their writing problems. All in all, everyone ends up believing that whoever struggles with writing doesn't belong at the university. Therefore, when these students go abroad and start writing in another language, many continue to think that composing a text successfully is all about disciplinary knowledge, foreign language problems excluded. If composing a text successfully is all about disciplinary knowledge and if peer tutors don't belong to the same discipline as the tutees, EFL students might question the tutor's ability to make helpful comments on their drafts. For foreign language problems, the student would simply seek someone who could help edit the final draft.

Dealing with the Problems

What can tutors in American writing centers do to make the tutoring of EFL writers more effective? The effort should start long before the actual tutoring session takes place. Writing tutors could support writing center administrators and faculty in the following ways:

- Urge your writing center director to advertise broadly on campus not only the existence but also the kind of work a writing center is doing. Make sure to point out the differences between tutoring writing (the concern is focused on the development of writer *and* text) and editing (the concern is focused only on the text). Look for opportunities to tell EFL students that their previous experience as a first language writer matters greatly as a springboard for successful foreign language writing.

- Contact your university's international office about providing incoming international students with informational sessions about the process of writing and the importance of feedback throughout the development of texts. Show them the specific nature of peer tutoring and what sets this kind of interaction apart from conferences with instructors. Let EFL students know that their cultural expectations about how to deal with their drafts are being considered in the writing center.

- Enlist the support of other tutors and publicize outstanding results of student writing that profited from interaction with the writing center. Don't forget to include EFL texts as well as texts in foreign languages written by students whose first language is English to demonstrate that *everyone* can improve as a writer.

- Discuss with your director the need to hire nonnative-English-speaking tutors and collaborate with them to publicize the potential your writing center has for the shaping of a distinct ESL and EFL writers' community on campus where students will learn how to interact with each other as writers in a constructive and supportive way.

- Provide material about the writing center in an informational packet given to new international students so that they can familiarize themselves with the university writing center before they actually arrive on campus. This will help them direct their expectations about becoming writers in college at an early stage.

- Collaborate closely with the ESL and EFL faculty to ensure that students will be sent to the writing center as part of fulfilling their writing assignments. This will help them remember reflective practice and text feedback as common aspects of their daily writing routine.

To learn more about different cultures of writing and dealing with writers and their texts, go to other countries as writing tutors (see Chapter 16 for a discussion of the value of international exchanges) or collaborate with international writing tutors and share your experience and expertise. A number of new writing centers in Western Europe have emerged in recent years, among them the SchreibCenter at the University of Klagenfurt (Austria), the Schreibzentrum at the Europa-Universität Viadrina in Frankfurt—Oder (Germany), and the Schreibzentrum at the University of Education in Zürich (Switzerland). They are active in a growing online community of the European Writing Centers Association (http://ewca. sabanciuniv.edu/eng/). You can also participate in the international handout wiki initiated by the International Writing Centers Association (http://writingcenters.org/handouts/index.php/Main_Page). In addition to developing handouts in English, consider creating handouts in other languages (see link to "Resources in Languages Other than English" on the IWCA website at http://writingcenters.org/).

You might also consider getting in touch with international writing tutors via email—for example, from the University of Education in Freiburg, Germany, who go through a four-semester certification program before they start working for their writing center. To learn more about your peers in Freiburg, visit their website (www.ph-freiburg.de/schreibzentrum) or contact them (info@schreibzentrum-freiburg.de). I encourage you to write to them about your personal experiences tutoring ESL and EFL writers. Tell them about your successful strategies, ask questions, and express your doubts. Ask them about the tutoring strategies they prefer. Invite them to contact you for advice when they run into problems with American students abroad. I am convinced that there is much to learn from this kind of interaction.

Notes

1. See Foster and Russell (2002) for a more in-depth analysis of academic writing in higher education in Germany and other countries.
2. Foster and Russell (2002).
3. See Kruse, Berger, and Ulmi (2006) for an overview of approaches and projects in writing in secondary, higher, and professional training.
4. For more information about the development of the Freiburg Writing Center and the training of peer tutors in both college and high school, see Bräuer (2002) and Bräuer (2006).
5. See Bräuer (2007) for a concept of portfolio work in teacher education.
6. See Kruse (2006) for an overview of the development of academic writing in Germany.
7. See Tynjälä, Mason, and Lonka (2001) for an integration of theory and practice in writing-to-learn approaches in Europe and Van Waes, Leijten, and Neuwirth (2006) for research findings on writing and digital media.
8. See Olive and Levy (2002) for contemporary process writing research methodology.
9. Rienecker and Jörgensen, 102–03.
10. See Kruse (2006) for a description of the historical roots of the so-called Continental style of writing.

Works Cited

Björk, Lennart A., Gerd Bräuer, Lotte Rienecker, and Peter Stray Jörgensen, eds. 2003. *Teaching Academic Writing in European Higher Education.* Amsterdam: Kluwer Academic Publishers.

Bräuer, Gerd. 2002. "Drawing Connections Across Education: The Freiburg Writing Center Model." *Language and Learning Across the Disciplines,* 5(3): 61–80.

———. 2006. "The U.S. Writing Center Model for High Schools Goes to Germany: And What is Coming Back?" In *The Clearing House: A Journal of Educational Strategies, Issues and Ideas (Special Issue: The Writing Center and Beyond),* edited by Pamela B. Childers, 80(2): 95–100.

———. 2007. "Portfolios in der Lehrerausbildung als Grundlage für eine neue Lernkultur in der Schule." In *Lernprozesse dokumentieren, reflektieren und beurteilen. Lerntagebuch und Portfolio in Bildungsforschung und Bildungspraxis,* edited by Michaela Gläser-Zikuda, 45–62, Bad Heilbrunn: Klinkhardt.

Foster, David, and David Russell. 2002. *Writing and Learning in Cross-National Perspective: Transitions from Secondary to Higher Education.* Urbana, IL: National Council of Teachers of English.

Kruse, Otto. 2006. "The Origins of Writing in the Disciplines. Traditions of Seminar Writing and the Humboldtian Ideal of the Research University." *Written Communication* 23(3): 331–52.

Kruse, Otto, Katja Berger, and Marianne Ulmi, eds. 2006. Prozessorientierte Schreibdidaktik. Schreibtraining für Schule, Studium und Beruf. Bern, Stuttgart, Wien: Haupt.

Olive, Thierry, and Michael C. Levy, eds. 2002. *Contemporary Tools and Techniques for Studying Writing.* Dordrecht, Boston, London: Kluwer Academic.

Rienecker, Lotte, and Peter Stray Jörgensen. 2003. "The (Im)possibilities in Teaching University Writing in the Anglo-American Tradition When Dealing with Continental Student Writers." In *Teaching Academic Writing in European Higher Education,* edited by Lennart Bjork, Gerd Bräuer, Lotte Rienecker, and Peter Strau Jörgensen, 101–12. Amsterdam: Kluwer Academic.

Tynjälä, Päivi, Lucia Mason, and Kirsti Lonka, eds. 2001. *Writing as a Learning Tool: Integrating Theory and Practice.* Dordrecht, Boston, London: Kluwer Academic.

Waes, Luuk Van, Marielle Leijten, and Christine M. Neuwirth, eds. 2006. *Writing and Digital Media.* Amsterdam: Elsevier.

16

Being a Linguistic Foreigner

Learning from International Tutoring

Linda S. Bergmann, Gerd Bräuer, Robert Cedillo,
Chloe de los Reyes, Magnus Gustafsson,
Carol Peterson Haviland, and Brady Spangenberg

During the spring of 2007, the writing center at California State University, San Bernardino (CSUSB), arranged for two writing tutors, who were also students in the MA in English Composition program, to be tutors at European writing centers. Chloe de los Reyes became a guest tutor in Freiburg, Germany, at the University of Education's Schreibzentrum [writing center] tutor training program directed by Gerd Bräuer. Robert Cedillo became a guest tutor in Göteborg, Sweden, at the Chalmers University Centre for Language and Communication directed by Magnus Gustafsson. Chloe and Robert were mentored by Carol Peterson Haviland, professor of English and writing center director, CSUSB. Arranged independently in an adjacent site, but subsequently linked with the project by both geography and interest, Brady Spangenberg, a graduate exchange student from Purdue University, spent the academic year at the English Seminar, Albert-Ludwigs-Universität Freiburg (ALUF in Freiburg, Germany). Linda Bergmann, associate professor of English and writing center director, Purdue University, was the consultant for the projects.

Over the past decade, discussions and exchanges among international writing center directors have yielded valuable insights about cultural and linguistic issues in tutoring and teaching writing. However, very few tutors have participated in these exchanges, and thus the insights they might offer to tutors who work with English as a second language (ESL) students have been missing. In this chapter, we share our experiences piloting such tutor exchanges, reflecting on what we've learned about tutoring and international exchanges and how we were all changed by the experience in one way or another. We conclude with some lessons learned about being a linguistic foreigner that we feel are important for all tutors and especially for those who would like to participate in an exchange program. "Being foreign" creates opportunities and challenges for tutors, and it provides a window into the experiences of the ESL students we encounter in our writing centers and into ourselves as tutors.

Rushing In?

All three students were aware that their roles would differ from their roles as tutors in the United States. Indeed, they would be foreigners in many aspects. However, they hoped that this foreignness might allow them to see things that they might have missed as insiders, which would allow them to contribute in useful ways to both their guest and home institutions. Chloe's assignment at Freiburg's University of Education was to help the Schreibzentrum connect more fully with writing faculty and classes in the English Department as well as to increase the center's visibility within the university generally. She also planned to do thesis research on Freiburg's students' language acquisition practices as well as to learn more about European writing centers in general. In Göteborg, Robert was to be part of a writing-across-the-curriculum/writing-in-the-disciplines program that was preparing to set up a writing center. Robert also expected to study Swedish students' ways of learning English, specifically academic English. Brady was asked to spend his year developing and maintaining a writing center where one did not yet exist.

The most important gain for all participants was a new appreciation for what "being foreign" means, both as opportunity and as challenge. For example, Chloe and Robert arrived in Germany and Sweden, respectively, speaking no German or Swedish and knowing only a little about how European writing centers and writing programs operated. As Chloe says,

> Tutors often explain the particularities of English through rules because ESL students know grammar rules, but something always is "lost in translation." There are things in the language that rules cannot explain. I "knew" that hearing me explain English usage was difficult for the students I worked with in California, but I didn't really "feel" it. When I was in Germany trying to learn German, I experienced what it was like to be on the receiving end. I felt helpless: someone was trying very hard to help me understand, but I just didn't get it.

This is a great reminder for all tutors who work with ESL writers. Learning another language can be a very difficult process; although you may be working hard to explain "the rules" and students may be working hard to understand what you are trying to share with them, you may not be successful during the first or even second or third sessions. But, take a deep breath and remember Chloe. And consider this: No matter how frustrating it is for you as the tutor, it is probably more frustrating for the student who needs to understand what you are saying in order to complete an assignment and succeed in a class. Patience and the right attitude will get you through these times, and with any luck, the students will return. In one of those sessions, you will make that connection, share that example, or point to that resource that will finally make sense. And when that happens, we are encouraged and reminded of why we keep working so hard to make the writing center that unique space where students can ask the same questions and bring the same writing challenges in over and over until they "get it."

Although Robert interacted more with faculty members than with students, he too found his inability to speak Swedish frustrating:

> The Chalmers faculty were really impressive in their ability to move seamlessly from Swedish to English and even to third and fourth languages, and they were very considerate about speaking English when I was present, but still I felt my foreignness acutely, and this was humbling. I couldn't use "their" language, and for the first time I really understood what nonnative speakers experience in the United States. Not only did I miss nuances, but also I was always aware they were having to adjust to my presence, to speak more slowly, to translate technical terms, to make sure idioms made sense to me.

Robert reminds us that even though we may not mind making adjustments in the ways that we normally interact with writers and each other when ESL students are present, ESL students might be sensitive to our adjustments and feel as if they are imposing on us. This is why it is important to spend those few extra minutes interacting with students in a friendly way and helping them feel welcome in the center. See Chapter 3 for further discussion about welcoming students and putting them at ease before a session. See Chapter 18 for some ESL students' perspectives on interacting with tutors and navigating the American writing center.

In contrast, Brady arrived in Freiburg with a near-native command of German, so his linguistic foreignness was less visible. Although he conducted most of his tutorials in English, all departmental meetings were held in German, as were many of his conversations with colleagues and staff members. Thus, even though knowing the host language allowed him to participate more fully in the department's discussions and was particularly useful when dealing with bureaucratic matters such as procuring an office space or doing publicity work, his "Americanized" understanding of university culture still set him apart. In some cases, his expectations created even greater disjunctions because people assumed that he understood localisms and nuances that he did not. Although Brady's German fluency made his life somewhat easier than Chloe's or Robert's, he too returned to his home campus with some new insights about writing center work.

For example, he quickly learned that proficiency in one area does not mean proficiency in all areas. Thus, although Brady could speak German well, but because of his lack of experience in Germany, he missed much of the nuance and culture that was present when the language was spoken by native speakers in their native country.

Likewise, in Chapter 18, we meet Sami, a native of Saudi Arabia. He is a fluent English speaker, but his expertise in speaking does not translate to writing. His skills in that area are limited. Tutors should never assume that students who speak well will necessarily write well or vice versa. Finally, no matter how fully ESL writers' skills are developed in both areas, keep in mind that the nuances and culture of your writing center may still be very foreign.

What's In a Name?

Even when all participants prepared for these international assignments using a "common language"—in this case, English—they made missteps. For example, all five of the original planners (Carol, Gerd, Magnus, Chloe, and Robert) spoke English fluently and had participated in public presentations and private conversations in a variety of multilingual/multicultural settings. Rather than smoothing the way, however, these commonalities led to some inaccurate assumptions about "shared" language. In particular, the terms *tutor*, *expert*, and *writing center* became sites of miscommunication, which opened important discussions:

1. They needed to ask what tutoring might mean, how roles and expertise might shape those meanings, and how far those meanings could stretch without dissipating entirely.

2. They needed to consider how, in different institutional settings, writers could collaborate yet maintain authorial integrity.

3. They needed to rethink the overriding question of what roles writing centers can or should play in creating these meanings and putting them into practice effectively.

The terms *tutor*, *expert*, and *writing center* often reflect institutional culture as well as departmental or individual expectations. For example, in the United States, tutoring sessions are commonly viewed as conversations between peers rather than top-down instruction because the tutors are often students themselves. However, these peer tutors are also seen as "experts" who have useful knowledge about writing and are taken seriously by both faculty and students. In contrast, at many European educational institutions, tutors are most commonly faculty members, and the *peer* label has an "equal to students" connotation, which connotes a more general lack of experience or expertise; thus, peer tutors' stature and work are viewed quite differently. These differences lead to very conflicting definitions of expertise and very contrasting expectations about writing center practices.

For example, Robert was uneasy during his first weeks at Chalmers because he felt he was being looked at as an expert. In some ways, of course, he was. He is a native speaker of English with training in writing instruction, and he was definitely more experienced than the rest of the Chalmers faculty in one-to-one tutoring. On the other hand, he couldn't speak Swedish, he didn't have teaching experience, and he wasn't able to do the kind of tutoring he was used to and successful at. However, the more important aspect of his foreign- ness was his resistance to being construed as an expert because his tutorial pedagogy was American: creating a peer writer-to-writer relationship rather than an expert-to-novice relationship. So what looked like terminological con- fusion hid a much deeper shift in pedagogical emphasis. As Robert observes,

> I could not assume the kind of peer relationship I had with my students in San Bernardino—an experienced, interested, intelligent reader who could help writers reflect on the writing they were producing. Rather, the Swedish students saw me as expert because I was a native speaker of English. What I discovered was that I could not interact with them as a peer without their consent, because relationships cannot be dictated—they are negotiated. With each student I was tutoring, I had to rethink how we understood the term *expert* before we could establish a writer-to-writer relationship that was dif- ferent from what either of us had previously known. And this is tricky. To be true to the writing theories that inform my practice, I had to help my Swedish students (and the Chalmers faculty) see me as a different kind of expert, but I had to make this kind of expertise make sense to them.

Chloe, working in Germany, recalls a similar need to negotiate roles:

> What I found is that students expected me to tell them what to write or how to turn their German sentences into English sentences. My habit, however, was to ask them what they wanted to say and then help them find and organize the words. Also, they seemed frustrated when I suggested that we look up a rule or idiom together instead of simply giving them the answer. In San Bernar- dino, I helped the writers I worked with learn about language; I showed them how to find what they wanted to say and how to consult sources. In Freiburg, I had to learn to do this without leaving the students with the impression that I just didn't know much myself. In other words, I wasn't the kind of expert they expected.

Like the students Robert and Chloe met, many ESL students studying in the United States regard writing center tutors as experts and look to them for "the answers." Negotiating traditional American tutor training and international student expectations can be tricky. If this seems to be an issue during a ses- sion, it may be helpful to take a few minutes to stop and explain how the tutoring process works at your center and what the student can expect from this and subsequent visits. Engaging students in a conversation may help them understand and make the transition to feeling comfortable with your center's tutoring approach. Again, though, remember that not all students will make this transition easily. For some, it may take time, and for others, it may never become a fully comfortable situation.

Gerd, who hoped Chloe's visit would help establish closer ties between the writing center and the English Department, noticed similar expectations among the English faculty. "My colleagues were looking for Chloe to validate their way of instruction, which is heavily grammar based and narrowly focused on a few texts. They were under the impression Chloe would continue their way of teaching not only in writing workshops but also during tutorial sessions."

The misunderstanding surrounding the terms *tutor* and *expert* extended to a third term, *writing center*, a difference their names only begin to suggest: Schreibzentrum, University Centre for Language and Communication, and English Seminar. Coming from CSUSB, where all tutors are peer tutors and where they themselves were students in a variety of graduate and undergraduate programs, Chloe and Robert were accustomed to frequent and informal interactions between tutors, students, and faculty. A hallmark of CSUSB's center is ongoing conversations about tutoring practices—it's a noisy place, full of conversations about writing. Tutors are taught that they don't need to have all of the answers but rather need to know how to pose good questions and discover answers, both with the students they tutor and with other tutors. It's not uncommon for a tutor to say, "Can you tell me more about that; I'm not sure how that works in a biology lab report," or to ask another tutor to suggest a better way to explain *ethos*, recommend a good website dealing with intellectual property, or venture a theory about why native English speakers get *on* airplanes but *in* cars.

These scenes contrasted sharply with Chloe's initial impressions of the Screibzentrum. Even though the building's glass walls invited people in, students remained passers-by, making use of the writing center most often in emergencies, and they almost never dropped in to chat about their writing. Likewise, tutors did not talk much with one another other than at weekly team meetings where, under the guidance and supervision of their instructors, they reflected on the past week's tutorials, discussed the strategies they used, and looked for alternatives—but always in a very formal tone. Also, the Schreibzentrum was not a part of the English Department or its writing program, both of which focus on short writing assignments and grammar and thus dominate students' experience of language learning, whereas Gerd encourages tutors to focus on writing as a process. Gerd, who had been a faculty member at Atlanta's Emory University for nine years, tried very hard to establish the more collegial tone of U.S. writing centers when he started the Schreibzentrum, but institutional divisions and instructional formality persisted. Even as a native German, he could not succeed:

> After three semesters of desperately trying to interact with the writing tutors throughout the day so we could continuously learn from one another, I decided to conduct my daily routine from my faculty office. Students felt weird seeing me at the writing center, often asking me what was wrong. Since I was a member of the faculty, they expected me to be their boss; this meant I would not be spending so much time in the writing center unless "something was wrong." So I began coming to the writing center only if there was "busi-

ness" to take care of, and part of this business was the weekly "supervision meeting" when students expected me to know the ultimate answer to all the tutoring challenges they had recently faced.

Upon his arrival at the ALUF English Seminar, Brady experienced a similar situation. The ALUF was attempting to overhaul its curriculum at both an institutional and a departmental level, partly in response to a European Union initiative to create so-called elite universities and partly because faculty members realized that many students were and still are arriving at the university with underdeveloped composition skills. Creating a writing center was conceived as a way to provide a broad range of students with immediate, individualized help without drastically altering the current curriculum or program of study.

Therefore, the department was looking for someone who could both build an American-style writing center and function as its expert and tutor, but misunderstandings arose about what kind of "help" the writing center should offer. Some instructors believed that the writing center should provide only linguistic (i.e. grammatical) help to students, serving as a type of writing clinic or "fix-it" shop. This led many students to focus almost exclusively on crafting perfect sentences even though they had concerns about the content, organization, and argumentation of their texts and wanted help developing their arguments or finding support for their ideas.

This emphasis on formality and correctness not only dominated departmental writing expectations but also shaped much of the interaction between faculty and students. Doors were rarely open, even during office hours. In contrast, the open-door policy of Brady's writing center was viewed as "typical American." As a result, Brady had to negotiate a space that met professional academic standards yet remained inviting and helpful to students.

Robert had an experience of being foreign at Chalmers as well. He was part of the technical and professional faculty, and most of the writing tutoring he was expected to do was situated in these fields rather than with writers from all university disciplines. Also, although the original plan had been for him to work chiefly with concerns such as rhetorical aims and composing processes, he found that students expected him to police their grammar and usage and were disappointed when he tried to create a greater balance with some of these larger textual issues.

These disjunctions have made us realize how much our ideas about tutors and experts shape the way writing centers operate, and we are now more likely to challenge our assumptions. Robert says,

> Going to Chalmers, I quickly discovered that my tutoring repertoire, though useful to the staff, was inadequate for my own thinking and practice in a setting where, suddenly, I had lost the core of my identity (that of student-tutor). This loss of balance left me playing catch-up for the remainder of my time there; at the same time, it compelled me to expand my own understanding of *tutor* as it pertained to my own practices.

Just as students are challenged to negotiate the tutor–tutee dynamic, so too are tutors. When you encounter these challenges, take time to reflect on them. Share them with other tutors on your staff and discuss them with your director. We can learn a lot from each other when we share our experiences. Chances are, you're not the first—and you won't be the last—person to face this particular challenge.

How Is International Tutoring Changing Us?

The new ears that Chloe and Robert developed have changed the ways they were able to hear when they returned to the CSUSB writing center. Chloe says, "I began to understand language struggles more fully, especially the inadequacy of rules. My experience in Germany has made me much more aware of the signs that students are not understanding what I am saying." And Robert adds, "I returned to CSUSB much more aware of how easily being a linguistic foreigner makes you an outsider on many levels. It doesn't feel good! When I work with nonnative speakers of English now, I can put myself in their shoes much more easily." In addition, he observes,

> Since my return, my thoughts about writing center work have become more complex, and my tutoring has changed for the better. Not only do I better understand how to approach a particular student, but also I can better appreciate the difficulties of adjusting to significantly different systems of learning and instruction. I feel more confident about adapting to individual students' needs, and I have new ways of articulating not only nonnative speakers' frustrations with English but also the frustrations of students learning new academic or disciplinary discourses. This offers an interesting parallel with the experiences of new tutors: though prospective tutors may read and internalize writing center theory, it isn't until their first tutoring sessions, which add a raw physicality to their thinking (for example, their stomachs may leap—in excitement or terror), that tutors really come to *know themselves.*

Robert's self-examination occurred both in Sweden and on his return to the United States. In Sweden, it took considerable reflection for him to realize that he could still function effectively but that he would have to stretch himself hard and function quite differently than he had been accustomed to. On his return to the United States, he notes that again it took more time than expected to reflect on and make sense of what he had experienced: "It was only after Carol pushed me to articulate my learning that I had a clear understanding of what I *had* learned. This gaze inward was necessary in order to attempt to explain something that was as much a feeling as it was a practical learning experience."

This stretching and reflection has improved not only Chloe's and Robert's hearing but also other tutors' ability to hear the needs and frustrations of students in the CSUSB center. Their mentor, Carol Haviland, notes that she and the tutors in the CSUSB Writing Center now hear themselves through Chloe's and Robert's ears. For example, at a recent meeting, a tutor said that he was mystified why a native Russian speaker kept missing the point about plagiarism that he kept so carefully explaining. When he began to re-create his explanation, Chloe and Robert jumped in almost in unison, showing how his discussion of textual originality, collaboration, and citation practices were so American based that it could not possibly make sense to someone from a different linguistic and textual culture.

Similarly, on his return to Purdue, Brady has become an eloquent advocate for hearing and responding to the needs students express in tutorials, particularly when they request direction in issues of genre and sentence construction (i.e., grammar). This has helped Linda shape the practicum for new graduate tutors and has led to the creation of a "grammar group" where students and staff alike can stop in and discuss language questions directly but informally.

Not only did these tutors' experiences reshape them and their home institutions, they also had an effect on the European writing centers in which they worked. Gerd notes that the Schreibzentrum is not the same as it was before Chloe's internship. First, the workshop Chloe started for English as a foreign language (EFL) writers continues, more and more students participate, and the English Department now supports the workshop financially and logistically. Likewise, the informal conversation group Chloe suggested in hopes of drawing EFL students to the writing center has continued, and most students in the conversation group now use writing center tutors to help them with their written work as well.

In a more general sense, the informal gatherings of EFL writers have made the atmosphere of the writing center more appealing, a place not just for work and supervision but also for sharing personal views about college and life. Overall the number of students using the Freiburg writing center has grown since Chloe's internship. Clearly, her foreignness had a positive influence, Gerd says, "for it is becoming easier for me to come into the writing center when I don't have 'business' and not have terror wash over all of the tutors' faces!"

Activities and perspectives have changed at the Chalmers site as well. Magnus says,

> Robert's presence has helped our conversations about writing strategies in our various courses to become more informed through enhanced understanding of tutoring and writing strategies. As a group, we now use more nontraditional curricular approaches and assign peer tutors more often, even to students who are writing theses in Swedish. In short, our first-hand encounter with Robert's peer tutor philosophy has increased our confidence about sharing some of our tutoring responsibilities with students, and this influence continues to spark new insights for new situations in our developing activities.

Reciprocity? Transfer? Give and Take?

Reflecting on what we have learned raises some important questions about transferring knowledge and practices from one site to another. For example, in continuing international projects, what can or should tutors take from their home writing centers to centers in other countries? Conversely, which practices might they bring back with them to influence writing center practices in the United States? The term *transfer* as used here should be distinguished from the more measurable concept of linguistic transfer. Rather, we use it to describe the way learning in one course or domain can be transferred to another. The experiences of the participants in these exchanges—as lived and as discussed among the writers of this chapter—give rise to the following conclusions about intercultural give and take. First, concepts transfer more successfully than methods. Second, understanding the theories on which those concepts are based and the practices they lead to is essential in fitting new concepts into unfamiliar cultural and organizational settings.

During and after the pilot exchanges, we discussed the very basic notion of peer tutors and what peer tutoring implies in different organizations. This was important on at least two levels. First, context matters, even when all participants have a similar understanding of the relationships between language and knowledge and even when they share beliefs about how writers shape and are shaped by texts. Understanding new contexts is essential in deciding who should change or adapt and why. To what extent, for example, should Chloe, Robert, and Brady adapt to the ways that German and Swedish students and their professors expected them to deal with grammatical issues? And how many of these adaptations should they take back with them to CSUSB and Purdue University? What role should the different expectations that Germans, Swedes, and Americans have for university education play in making these determinations, and how might they extend and change the understanding of what writing centers can and should do? These questions have pushed all participants to think hard about their assumptions, a time-consuming, mind-stretching, and sometimes even stressful activity but an essential one.

This question of transfer is equally important at an institutional level. For example, during Carol's initial inquiries, she learned that almost all of her international colleagues worried that introducing peer tutoring would affect the academic status of faculty or staff working in writing centers or providing writing instruction. Thus, it became important to think seriously about the ways that peer tutors might affect the already tenuous working conditions of existing staff. Brady encountered another set of fears while in Freiburg. Although some instructors worried that he would provide students with all the answers, others viewed the writing center as a remedial and therefore less respectable place.

These are issues that U.S. writing centers have been dealing with for some thirty years, but they can have a different impact when raised in the context of newly created writing centers in other countries. The answers and approaches that U.S. writing centers have developed cannot be simply imported and imposed elsewhere. The crucial differences in institutional structures and missions that these exchanges showed tutors, hosts, and directors back home affect the ways writing centers are conceived and, more important, the methods they use, and should consider using. We need to tread carefully when considering who, in short, might be appropriating whose culture and to what effect.

Prepare and Prepare Some More

Other than having taken part in brief meetings during international conferences, the writing program/center directors involved in the project knew each other only though limited conference or email interactions. As the project progressed, they realized that they had glossed over the assumptions and practices of their respective institutions. We now recognize that a working partnership between the institutions is essential to the success of these exchanges and that only by formulating and explicitly communicating these details will expectations be realistic. In addition, hosts, mentors, and sponsors need to support the tutors they send into new sites, helping them anticipate new and confusing scenes; tutors who are considering an exchange program should inquire about this support before they commit themselves to the project. Everyone needs to discuss how, for example, tutor/expert roles may be very different, how to talk openly with home and host mentors about what appear to be incongruities with home practices and expectations, and how to admit that they just don't understand what is going on. Further, we have come to see that these projects should be reciprocal, not one sided, in order to engage the partners more equally and to better understand issues of transfer and reciprocal change.

Finally, the participants need to address language preparation directly. On the one hand, because Robert knew no Swedish and Chloe knew no German, they were able to appreciate more fully the experiences of international students who study in the United States. On the other hand, everyday activities, such as eating or grocery shopping, often turned into hour long challenges. More complex language-based activities, such as opening a local bank account or registering for a residency permit, posed even greater problems. Although most Germans speak English, Chloe found that many important bureaucratic transactions, particularly when it came to dealing with her stipend, were extremely difficult to manage, partly because without German she couldn't handle these transactions herself. She comments, "Not only did I always have to wait for someone to translate for me or take me somewhere, I had to sign paperwork without really knowing what was going on or what I was signing."

In addition, both Chloe and Robert felt their language limitations negatively impacted their workplace interactions—they often felt left out and unable to contribute their expertise. Even though the staff at both host institutions spoke English fluently and were very considerate about using English at staff meetings and other gatherings, Chloe and Robert still missed nuances whenever someone slipped into the local language.

And in a simple but important way, the inability to speak the local language sometimes triggered homesickness and self-doubt. As Chloe remembers, "When it took me two hours to figure out how to use the washing machine or when everyone was trying really hard to include me but still my ears ached for Southern California–accented English, I felt generally incompetent and wondered whether I was of any use to anyone. I just wished I could have my two dogs curl up beside me, hear my colleague Al's stupid jokes, and order dinner from Del Taco."

All in all, being better prepared for feeling "foreign" could have smoothed some of the rough edges that Robert and Chloe experienced. CSUSB might also have placed greater emphasis on their acquiring basic Swedish or German before leaving the United States and/or studying the language intensively in addition to their writing center work. Yet this solution is not without costs: Ensuring that tutors have at least some host-country language fluency will markedly limit the number and range of possible exchanges. At any rate, we now know this issue needs to be considered in advance, for clearly Brady's German fluency eased at least some of his linguistic foreignness.

And, preparing for foreignness isn't one-sided either. Gerd and Magnus also had moments of frustration that found them longing for a Friday afternoon beer after a week of being middlemen between the faculty and the foreigners who needed everything explained. They knew that their centers were the richer for the foreigners' presence, but it wasn't cost free.

One thing seems universal: Getting a university faculty to understand what writing center people do is a struggle everywhere. And whether in the United States, Germany, or Sweden, faculty members all express the fervent hope that somehow, somewhere, someone other than they will fix their students' writing and that maybe that place is the writing center.

We'd Do It Again

Given all the above experiences, we nevertheless wholeheartedly endorse international tutor placements. Even with our struggles, we all consider our investments richly rewarded. For others interested in setting up international tutor exchanges, we have the following suggestions:

1. Make the exchange of ideas the goal, not the one-time placement of a single tutor.

2. Initiate and debrief pilot projects at conferences and on websites.

3. Have everyone involved negotiate expectations; formalize agreements in writing.

4. Become familiar with both institutions' administrative and financial structures. Be sure that the necessary arrangements and permits for residing and working in a foreign country are in place.

5. Integrate visiting tutors into the host writing center teams in ways that help them carry out their responsibilities autonomously.

6. Create both official and unofficial channels for working out problems. Having a peer mentor at the host institution can be of great help to exchange tutors as they struggle to understand a new institutional terrain; here a student's point of view may be much more useful than a faculty member's. These peer mentors can also help with the inevitable culture shock.

7. Plan regular one-on-one meetings in which the host director and the exchange tutor discuss how things are going; at least some of the time, the sponsoring institution's director should join these meetings by teleconference or video feed. Also set up a regular method of communication (such as Skype) between the home director and the exchange tutor.

8. Halfway through the project, hold a reflective meeting with the writing center team, the tutor, and a representative from the sponsoring institution (via teleconference or video feed) and adjust the project goals accordingly.

9. Think of a tutor exchange as not only a teaching project but also a research project that has both an investigative and an ethical framework. Establish transparent criteria for success and methods of observation and evaluation by tutors, their supervisors, and students (if not faculty) at host institutions. (These opportunities for generative assessment should focus on identifying necessary adjustments, not assessing the foreign tutor's success.)

Tutor exchanges are valuable if sometimes stressful learning experiences for tutors and their sponsors and mentors, and additional research will no doubt result in better practices for both host and home institutions. To reach credible, usable, and replicable understandings of how exchanges work, we need to use early accounts of projects like this one to discover how to incorporate assessment practices that solicit information from all stakeholders and help us make good choices about structuring and sustaining future exchanges.

These caveats do not, however, diminish our enthusiasm about continuing these exchanges or sharing what we have learned about being linguistic foreigners. Each of us has come to see writing and language acquisition practices as well as global language issues in more complex ways; this experience and the conversations at subsequent international conferences have highlighted the unexplored assumptions and imprecision in our discussions of tutoring English, such as just what English is this, who decides, and with what implications? Clearly, our three centers are the richer because of this pilot project, and we hope our experiences will spur others' interest in initiating and participating in tutor exchanges.

17

English for Those Who (Think They) Already Know It

Ben Rafoth

By some estimates, English is used by roughly one in six people on earth, either as a mother tongue or a second language. It is the *lingua franca* for much of the world's trade, media, and e-commerce.[1] In India and some African countries, it is the mother tongue for many people as well as their nation's official language, as in Nigeria and Zimbabwe. Even in countries where English is not the national or predominant language, it is often woven into existing languages, giving us, for example, Deutschlish in Germany, Franglais in France, Singlish in Singapore, and Chinglish in China.

With so many varieties, English means different things to different people, and it thrives in an array of forms with hybrid vocabularies, styles, and accents. Students who visit the United States to study in colleges and universities often have a good deal of exposure to English in their own countries, though not necessarily to any variety of the language most Americans would recognize. They may bring with them a mixture of varieties of English gathered from multilingual teachers, Hollywood movies, and Hong Kong shopping trips. And when they land in the United States, they will find that English in the States is as diverse as the population itself, from the border towns of Texas to the hills of Appalachia. Writing center tutors who are nonnative speakers of English are probably well aware of this. By contrast, for many teachers and tutors in the United States, there are not multiple Englishes but only one English: Standard American English (SAE). Native-born Americans do not know what it is like to learn English in a non-English country from multiple sources. Most Americans learned English in the relatively closed environments of families and neighborhoods. As children, they skated through all of its irregular verbs, collocations, and crazy compounds. American-born native English-speaking (NES) tutors would do well to revisit aspects of learning English that they probably take for granted. Despite what some American tutors believe, English is not all that logical for new learners and "just thinking about it" doesn't often help.

In this chapter, I would like to reflect on some of the grammar-based reasons why learning English seems easy for its native speakers and challenging for those who are learning it as a second or third language. Along the way, I hope to point out a few facts about the language we ought to keep in mind when we help English as a second language (ESL) students. NES tutors who make an effort to understand English from a linguistic perspective and bring this understanding to the writing conference will be better tutors than those who do not make this effort.

A Flimsy Jacket Versus a Jacket That Is Flimsy

Because they did not have to learn English by studying it in school, NES tutors can have difficulty explaining why it is correct to say something one way and not another. This can be frustrating when an international student is trying to correct an error and asks you to explain it. For example, in English why can't adjectives follow nouns as they do in Spanish and many other languages (e.g., *casa grande*). Sometimes the answer seems easy. We know, for example, that adjectives pitch their tents before nouns or after linking verbs, as in "the flimsy jacket" or "the jacket is flimsy," but English does not allow them to follow nouns, as in "jacket flimsy." A tutor could probably explain this to an ESL student by pointing to the nouns, verbs, and adjectives in a sentence and then stating a general rule based on these examples. For example: Adjectives can go either before nouns or after linking verbs like *is* or *seems*.

But as often happens, just when you think you have this rule figured out, you discover that some adjectives don't cooperate—they refuse to follow verbs. This is why we can say "the previous class" but not "the class is previous." And so there is a conundrum: *Previous* and *flimsy* are both adjectives but only one of them can follow verbs. Why can we say "the jacket is flimsy" but not "the class is previous"? If an ESL student were to ask this question, most American tutors would probably answer, "That's just the way we say it." Perhaps *previous* is a fluke. But things get even flukier: A few adjectives behave the opposite of *previous*, and they refuse to associate with nouns: A deck can be awash but it cannot be an awash deck. Soldiers can stand abreast but they cannot be abreast soldiers. So, something as outwardly simple as putting adjectives together with nouns masks an inner complexity that can be befuddling to nonnative speakers, and isn't much clearer to the rest of us. Although tutors know how to use words like *flimsy, previous, awash,* and *abreast*, explaining the rules that govern these words can be maddening. This example helps make one of the points of this chapter—whether we are an NES or a nonnative English-speaking tutor, we can all benefit from thinking about some of the things that make English challenging to learn as a second language.

Not a Particularly Difficult Language to Learn

One thing we can rule out right off the bat is any notion that English is a harder language to learn than others. This may come as disappointing news to those who think English is supposed to be difficult. For some loyalists, English is uniquely inscrutable, imbued with conceptual richness not shared by other languages. Like people everywhere, many English speakers regard their language with deep pride and believe it brings them strength and power—an admirable sentiment. The truth is that every language is unique and loathes to give up its secrets to anyone but its native speakers. Children the world over learn their native languages at about the same rate, and by six or seven years of age, they have mastered its basic grammatical structure. Then once we reach puberty and the magical moment is over, our brains start to close the gate, and to get in, *you have to pay.*

The degree to which learning any language—English, Korean, Athabaskan, or some other—is more difficult than learning another is a question linguists have pondered. The consensus is that no language is more difficult than another in an absolute sense. But in a relative sense, yes. If English is your native language then it is easier to learn Dutch, German, or other Germanic languages than to learn, say, a Turkic language like Kazakh or Tatar, or a Bantu language like Zulu or Xhosa.[2] Similarly, it is easier for a Swede to learn Norwegian than Polish, and easier for a Czech to learn Polish than Norwegian. "The major reason for this," explains one linguist, "is that the vocabularies have so many similarities in both form and content in the related languages."[3] This assumes that all other things are equal, and they rarely are. If you have traveled extensively in another country, spent time with relatives who speak the language, or enjoy some other advantage, the task can be significantly easier for you. On the other hand, if you are stuck in a strange and faraway country, feel homesick, and dread the food, you may not be terribly motivated to pick up the new language and may even resist it until you can resolve these feelings. The ease or difficulty of learning any language, then, is always more about the learners than the language.

With more than five hundred thousand words in the most comprehensive dictionaries, English does have an exceptionally large lexicon. One could argue that this fact alone makes English harder to learn than languages with fewer words. But consider this question: Is it easier to express one's thoughts in a language with a large lexicon or a small one? With lots of words to choose from, it may be easier to choose from a large lexicon when trying to express a thought or to rephrase an expression for someone who does not understand. At the same time, a language with fewer words is not necessarily any easier. There is a verb in Nootka, an American Indian language, that means "I have been accustomed to eat twenty round objects while engaged in. . . ." The structure of Nootka verbs is so complex that the language's relatively small vocabulary does not make up for the difficulty of learning its verbs. Or consider the fact that the average American high school graduate has a vocabulary not of five hundred thousand words but forty-five thousand to sixty thousand words.[4] Similarly, carpenters, airplane mechanics, and chefs may not always have the most advanced university degrees, but they have extensive technical vocabularies. In other words, the number of words in the dictionary is not nearly as important as knowing the ones you need to know to get along in the culture, to work there, or to pass your college's proficiency test.

A Gift from Foreigners

English's large vocabulary is in fact a point of pride, but the reason for this is largely historical, and foreigners are responsible for much of it. Roman merchants and Christian missionaries brought many Latin words into Old English during the first millennium. Then in 1066, the invader William the Conqueror and his armies catapulted hundreds of words into English from the Norman dialect of French. Before 1066, for example, the Anglo-Saxons had only the word *king* to express ideas about anything that was kingly. But after the Norman invasion, English gained the synonyms *royal*, *regal*, and *sovereign*. It may be said that the House of English was a mere hut before the foreign-born words took up residence but a castle afterward, as Robert McCrum, William Cran, and Robert MacNeil exemplify in clusters like *rise-mount-ascend*, *ask-question-interrogate*, or *time-age-epoch*.[5] Today, a thousand years later, English is still adding wings onto the castle, thanks to the constant influx of new words from cultures around the world that have enriched the language beyond measure: *bizarre* (Basque), *nirvana* (Sanskrit), *amok* (Malay), *mojo* (Kongo), *taffeta* (Farsi), and *amen* (Hebrew). The worldwide music and entertainment industries transmit words from a variety of cultures into songs and movie scripts heard around the world. The English lexicon grows with words even from alien life forms (*tribble*, *muggles*, *borg*, and *hobbit*).

If foreigners have given English thousands of new words, they have not made us spell them the way we do. We have inflicted that pain entirely on ourselves. No discussion of the challenges of learning English would be complete without mentioning the enigma of the English spelling system. It's so bad, George Bernard Shaw pointed out, that he could spell *fish* as *ghoti*: *gh* from tough, *o* from women, and *ti* from nation. English spelling evolved over centuries and settled down into fixed forms somewhat haphazardly around the time of the printing press and thereafter. Noah Webster tried to regularize spelling, and we owe him for helping with at least some of our more commonsense spellings. He regularized *tyre* to *tire* and *fibre* to *fiber*, among others. But the number of words in print even during Webster's time was enormous, and he could only do so much. He left untouched, for example, the thirteen different ways of spelling the *sh* sound: *shoe*, *sugar*, *issue*, *mansion*, *mission*, *nation*, *suspicion*, *ocean*, *conscious*, *chaperon*, *schist*, *fuchsia*, and *pshaw*.[6] If there is any consolation in the chaos of English spelling, it is that the way they are pronounced and the way they are spelled can never be matched up for very long. Pronunciation is forever the wanderer, while spellings are homebound. Pronunciation is restless and shuns commitment; spelling is sedentary and dedicated. We could change tomorrow all the spellings to fit the way we talk. In a few hundred years, maybe less, we would all look back and wonder why we ever wasted our time trying to reform a relationship that was meant to be on the rocks. Meanwhile, for ESL learners as for the rest of us, there is Spell Check.

There are other aspects of English that make it both a curse and a blessing for new learners. Although there are only about 180 irregular verbs, many of them occur often. They don't follow much of a pattern (it's why we call them irregular), and they have to be memorized, words like *went, shut, heard,* and *flew.* Some languages have far more irregular forms, and although nonnative English speakers may make errors with verb forms, when it comes to writing, they are like many native speakers of the language who also have trouble with verb endings, prepositions, and agreement. One reason for this is that these features often convey little meaning. English could lose many of its verb endings and hardly miss them, not to mention agreement between pronouns and their antecedents and between subjects and verbs. On the other hand, prepositions are essential to English but they're fickle. Does it matter whether we ride in a boat or on it? Walk in the door or through it? No, and yet English insists that we lie *in* bed but *on* the couch.[7] So when nonnative English speakers struggle with prepositions, there is some consolation in remembering that they are not always all that important in the first place. In fact, we could all embrace the learner dialects of ESL writers and simply agree that, so long as the meaning is clear, it is okay to overlook prepositions and articles used in nonstandard ways (see Chapter 9 for an in-depth look at articles). This would have the added benefit of taking many NES students off the hook, too. (Or is it *off of the hook*?)

English is quite flexible in its ability to convert verbs to nouns to adjectives, as in *fly-flight-flighty.* One might imagine ESL learners would welcome such fluidity because the words are so closely related in form and meaning. Or are they? English can be both amusing and treacherous. If you know the meaning of *corn,* does that help when you encounter the word *corny*? How about *horn* and *horny*? *Hip* and *hippie*? *Flighty* does not describe someone who flies on an airplane. *Weighty* does not describe something that is weighed. But that's the point. This is the kind of embarrassment that ESL learners fear when they open their mouths and try to use words they have just learned. Learning a new word in English or in any language for that matter can make you soar or drop you in quicksand.

Writing Centers as Language Centers

Ironically, conundrums like the difference between *flight* and *flighty* or *weight* and *weighty* are one reason why ESL students visit writing centers in the first place. They hope to find a place where they can interact with native speakers and discuss aspects of the language that puzzle them. Tutors are usually happy to have the interaction but not very fluent when it comes to discussing linguistic puzzles: "That's just the way we say it." Heavy sigh. Why is it so hard to explain the English language to ESL students in ways that make sense?

Some tutors may believe that English is made up of random rules and no real explanation is possible or that grammar is logical and you just have to "think about it." Or maybe they are not familiar enough with linguistic concepts to be able to answer ESL students' questions. Either way, the truth is that most of what might appear to be random in language can be explained, though not always simply. Like all languages, English is a product of complex rules, intricate patterns, diverse cultures, and a lot of history. This means that the grammar rules learned in school don't even begin to tell the story of how English is really put together. Tutors who can begin to understand the reasons why English works the way it does will begin to appreciate the labyrinthine set of do's and don'ts their ESL writers have to navigate every day, and they will make some fascinating discoveries about the patterns that lie deep beneath the labyrinth, as linguists do.

Let's return for a moment to the puzzle at the beginning of this chapter over the way that certain adjectives seem to have special requirements for where they can be used. We saw that unlike most adjectives, some (like the word *previous*) work only with nouns and never with verbs; they are nonpredicable adjectives. Others are just the opposite (like *awash*) and prefer the company of verbs over nouns; they are predicable adjectives. Let's assume that we could explain this to our ESL students when the need arises. So far, so good. But there is more, and this is an example of why it is beneficial for tutors to learn more than the minimum about the structures of English. The difference between predicable and nonpredicable adjectives is that they make sense only when they are paired with certain nouns and not others. Some adjectives work in both positions (recall "flimsy jacket" and "the jacket is flimsy"). But take the adjective *nuclear*, for instance. A *nuclear bomb* is a bomb that is nuclear, but a *nuclear scientist* is not a scientist that is nuclear. Similarly, *a nervous writer* is a writer who is nervous, but *a nervous habit* is not a habit that is nervous. Sometimes an adjective–noun combination results in ambiguity so that one interpretation is as plausible as the other: Does *dramatic criticism* refer to criticism of drama or to criticism that is dramatic?[8] This can be a frustrating thing for nonnative speakers to deal with, and tutors need to be patient when students struggle with it. There is no fairy dust to sprinkle on these adjective–noun combinations that will unlock the logic behind them, but there are ways to test whether an adjective is predicable or nonpredicable, and this can help nonnative speakers make some sense of the situation. You can read about the tests in many linguistics texts, such as George Miller's *The Science of Words* (see Works Cited at the end of the chapter). Until then, here is a hint: Nonpredicable adjectives are not pure adjectives, like *flimsy*, but are variations of nouns: *previous*, *nuclear*, *nervous*, and *dramatic* are takeoffs on the nouns *preview*, *nucleus*, *nerve*, and *drama*. So, nonpredicable adjectives usually make sense only when they appear before nouns. This is why we say "the previous class" instead of "the class is previous" and "the nuclear scientist" instead of "the scientist is nuclear."

Sometimes we tend to overlook the mistakes native speakers make and exaggerate the errors of nonnative speakers. It's good to remember that English lays down enough challenges for everyone. One of the most interesting is the plural form of words called headless compounds. They are puzzling because they make us stop and think why we treat them the way we do. Words like *Walkman*, *low-life*, and *flatfoot* form their plurals by adding *s* (Walkman*s*, low-life*s*, and flatfoot*s*), and this is contrary to the way we would pluralize them if they were simply *man*, *life*, and *foot*. In other words, why not *Walkmen*, *low-lives*, and *flatfeet*? What's going on here, and how do we explain it? It's a fascinating puzzle, and one that no one explains better than linguist Steven Pinker.[9] Could it be that *Walkmans*, *low-lifes*, and *flatfoots* are just exceptions? The short answer is that our brains do not think of *Walkmans*, *low-lifes*, and *flatfoots* as types of men, lives, and feet. If they did, we would treat them like the irregular nouns they are and pluralize them as Walkmen, low-lives, and flatfeet. Instead, our brains store these words according to what they refer to— electronic devices, undesirable people, and detectives. When we ask our brain to pluralize these words, it tells us to follow the main rule for making plurals and just add *s*. In other words, our linguistic brains won't be fooled by mixing up these look-alikes with the real thing. So, the brain regularizes them, and it will continue to do the same with any other screwball compound that fiction writers create in the future. Interested in buying a new pair of shoeloafs? They'd look good with your derby-dices. Alas, English shows it can be regular and predictable when you least expect it.

English from a Linguistic Perspective

Admittedly, figuring out how English works is something you cannot just squeeze in between tutoring sessions. So what is a tutor to do when he finds himself speechless over some aspect of English that cries out for explanation? Acknowledge the truth and admit you don't know. Then, make it a point to find the answer and become a student of the language. Until we try to understand the patterns that shape the way our language works, we know the language in only a very narrow and limited way. There is no easy strategy to overcome these limitations when they arise in tutoring sessions. The only way to overcome them is to study English by observing, reading, asking questions, and pursuing answers wherever you can find them. Doing so not only makes for some fascinating discoveries but also brings about more interesting and helpful interactions with the students we tutor.

Native speakers of English sometimes wonder why it is important to learn, say, the linguistic theory that lies behind a language they learned as children. Indeed, even many composition teachers in the United States downplay the importance of learning grammar. They believe that all of the grammatical knowledge students need for writing will emerge naturally. If this is true, tutors may wonder, then what is the point of tutors learning about the structure of English? The answer is that it clarifies why you know what you know about English. It also makes you a more informed and helpful tutor for people who don't know English but want to learn it. To appreciate these facts, consider the discoveries of the most important linguist of our time, Noam Chomsky, who proved that grammatical knowledge is bestowed upon every human being as a birthright.[10] He observed that native speakers possess insights into their language that even the most advanced linguistic theories strain to describe. For example, native speakers recognize that a sentence like "They are eating apples" can have two entirely different meanings because they know intuitively that *eating* functions as a verb in one interpretation and as a modifier of the noun *apples* in the other. Native English speakers know this even though they may never have studied grammar or learned the terms *verb*, *modifier*, or *noun*. How long does it take you to recognize the two different meanings in each of the following sentences?

Billy grew a foot last year.

Visiting relatives can be a nuisance.

They loaded the cart in the parking lot.

I love her dancing.

And an old favorite of linguists (cover your ears)—

It takes two mice to screw in a light bulb.

We can be amused by sentences like these because each one is perfectly grammatical and yet conveys two distinctly different meanings. They are well formed, and one can imagine contexts where they would make sense—for example, "With the help of advanced cloning techniques, Billy grew a foot last year, reversing a birth defect." We recognize the two meanings because we possess knowledge about parts of speech, word meanings, and how words go together; this knowledge enables us to decode the dual meanings almost effortlessly. Computers can decode them too, of course, but not before they are programmed with a library full of dictionaries and linguistic algorithms. Native speakers know instantly when a phrase or sentence written by a nonnative speaker does not sound right to them.

The point of these examples is to show that even though native speakers possess an instinct for using the language, they don't usually have much insight into the framework of this knowledge, and they definitely don't have the vocabulary to talk about the knowledge until they begin to study it—by taking some linguistics classes, reading books that delve into it,[11] and becoming more observant of the cultural context in which language functions. Once they do, they will find that discovering this knowledge and learning how to discuss it can be rewarding for everyone.

Notes

1. Three useful books on English as a global phenomenon are Kachru, Kachru, and Nelson (2006); Kachru, Strevens, and Ayers (1992); and Crystal (1998).

2. Andersson, 50.

3. Andersson, 50–51.

4. Miller, 135.

5. McCrum, Cran, and MacNeil (1992).

6. McCrum, Cran, and MacNeil, 29.

7. There are many good, free websites to help ESL students with prepositions, articles, and other troublesome parts of English. One is http://cctc 2.commnet.edu/grammar/prepositions.

8. Miller, 195.

9. Pinker (1994), 141–45.

10. Pinker (1994).

11. Tutors who are interested in the science and psychology of language, including the ideas of Noam Chomsky, will find these books accessible and interesting: Pinker (1994, 2007), Bialystok and Hakuta (1994), and Jackendoff (1994).

Works Cited

Andersson, Lars-Gunnar. 1998. "Some Languages Are Harder Than Others." In *Language Myths*, edited by Laurie Lauer and Peter Trudgill, 50–57. New York: Penguin.

Bialystok, Ellen, and Kenji Hakuta. 1994. *In Other Words: The Science and Psychology of Second Language Acquisition.* New York: Basic Books.

Crystal, David. 1998. *English as a Global Language*. New York: Cambridge University Press.

Jackendoff, Ray. 1994. *Patterns in the Mind.* New York: Basic Books.

Kachru, Barj, Yamuna Kachru, and Cecil L. Nelson, eds. 2006, *The Handbook of World Englishes*. Malden, MA: Blackwell.

Kachru, Braj, Peter Strevens, and Lauren K. Ayers, eds. 1992. *The Other Tongue.* Urbana: University of Illinois Press.

McCrum, Robert, William Cran, and Robert MacNeil. 1992. *The Story of English*. Rev. ed. New York: Penguin.

Miller, George A. 1996. *The Science of Words*. New York: Freeman.

Pinker, Steven. 1994. *The Language Instinct*. New York: Morrow.

———. 2007. *The Stuff of Thought*. New York: Viking.

18

Listening to and Learning from ESL Writers

Shanti Bruce

This chapter is intended to return the focus of the collection from theories of culture and linguistic concerns to the individual student because, after all, that is what our work and this publication are ultimately about. Toward that end, this chapter is devoted to sharing excerpts from several conversations I had with second language writers attending universities across the northeastern United States. Before writing this chapter, I asked each of them to spend some time talking with me about their experiences learning to write in English and using the writing center. With their permission, I recorded our conversations and preserved much of their speech patterns in the transcription process. Adding their perspective reminds us that each English as a second language (ESL) student we encounter is an individual. In this chapter, we go beyond just hearing their voices and their personal experiences to reflecting on what we can learn from each one: how they impact our understanding of culture and how tutors may conduct themselves more effectively during writing conferences. We explore times when tutor feedback sheets may not tell the whole story, when privacy becomes an issue, when a student's cultural background causes tutors to be judged on age instead of skill, what happens when students don't understand the mission of the writing center, and more.

The topics emerged directly from the conversations and relate to the specific information and suggestions offered in previous chapters. For example, we will meet Sami, Jung-jun, and Helene, who all express their insecurities about visiting the writing center for fear of being seen as weak students. Jung-jun also questions tutors' capabilities if they do not meet her culturally based criteria for writing instructors: They must have extensive experience and be older than she is. These issues of privacy and elder-as-teacher are culturally based and influence the tutoring session, frequently without the tutor's knowledge. Jung-jun's comments about how important her first impression of a tutor is to the success of the session directly relates to suggestions in Chapter 3 about making a good start. And when Zahara expresses how helpful it is to have her paper read aloud by a tutor, we can look to Paul Kei Matsuda and Michelle Cox's advice in Chapter 4 about how to pick the right approach to reading a student's paper.

I encourage directors and tutors to experience their writing center environments through the eyes of their second language students. For me, talking with ESL students directly about their needs and experiences made my own study of abstract theories and pedagogical practices come alive. The students you will meet could have easily sat in any one of our centers asking for help, and getting to know them will reveal what we are and are not accomplishing during conferences. I hope that this chapter will prompt even more discussions among tutors about the experiences of second language writers when working with native English-speaking tutors in the writing center.

Sami

I waited for Sami near the coffee bar in the library. It was a warm Saturday afternoon, and I looked forward to meeting him since our only correspondence had been through email. I came early and sat at a table facing the entrance. We spotted each other at the same time. I stood and smiled as Sami walked toward me. He was a major presence—tall with a full beard, and as we shook hands, he offered a kind smile.

At the beginning of our conversation, Sami told me that he was a student from Saudi Arabia and that he had started at the university in a bridge program designed to help students prepare for credit-bearing classes. He also said that I should know before we began that he didn't use the writing center. I was stunned. I knew I had clearly explained the topic of the project through our correspondence, and he had never let on that he wasn't a candidate. Unsure of where to go from there, I asked him why he had agreed to meet with me. He said that he didn't want to say "no" when I asked for his participation. I was stunned again at his desire to help me with this project despite the fact that he didn't think he had much to contribute.

As it turned out, my meeting with Sami added a great deal. He mentioned that he had in fact been to the writing center a couple of times but that he quit going. I asked him to tell me about that, and he explained the reasons he stopped going. He said that the tutors were not capable and that he had not received the kind of help he needed. I wasn't completely convinced by his reasons for not using the writing center because he was the only Middle Eastern male student on campus to agree to meet with me. I had asked several, and while they were all friendly, they consistently said that they had no experience with the writing center. Eventually, Sami revealed the real reason he avoided the writing center, and it had nothing to do with the tutors' skills. His was an issue of privacy and of being seen as weak by others.

By examining the cultural issues of privacy and pride, we learn firsthand how cultural influences are sometimes responsible for students' dissatisfaction with writing center experiences. This also proves to be an example of a time when tutor feedback sheets might not have told the whole story. Sami would most likely have written down the same reasons for his dissatisfaction that he initially shared with me. It took him a long time to become comfortable enough to share the truth during our conversation, and I believe those feelings would never have made it onto a session feedback form.

He began:

> Whenever I start a writing assignment, I have this difficulty of arranging my ideas, putting my main topic, supporting what I wanted to say. Really, I didn't have that ability to write a good writing, so I went to the writing center asking some people who work there to help me. I made it once or twice, but I didn't find it helpful because what they were doing is just looking for the grammar stuff and the grammatical mistakes and things on the surface. While I didn't want that, what I wanted was somebody who tells me about the ideas, how to explore my ideas, how to put my ideas, how to write the theme of the topic or the piece of writing that I wanted to write and how should I support my theme or my main topic.

Sami articulated his dissatisfaction with the writing center staff's ability to help him with global writing concerns. Many writing center response forms make it easy to mark these types of concerns, and he would have likely been comfortable mentioning them to a professor or writing center director. He went on to call into question the competency of the tutors based on their age and experience.

> Many of these people who work at the writing center do not know how to work with the ESL students, so I thought that they were not able to help me the way I want. I did not ask them directly to go in-depth, but from the one or the two times that I went, I felt that they just looked at the surface things, so I decided not to go there anymore and try to look for someone who is in a higher-education level. I'm assuming that he or she will be interested in working with ESL students.

Sami insisted that the writing center was to blame for his decision to stop going, but because I found Middle Eastern male students' avoidance of the writing center so noticeably different from the African and Asian student populations, I asked one more question to try to get to the bottom of this apparent cultural difference. I asked Sami if he would go back to the writing center if a graduate student who had experience working with ESL students met with him and addressed all of his global writing issues in the ways that he had described to me. Forty minutes into our conversation, Sami finally revealed the truth.

> OK, I didn't want to go to that place where everybody can see me sitting and talking about the papers. I wanted to stay in private with the person whom I feel comfortable with and have the discussion and the working privately. That is the reason I preferred not to continue going to the writing center. Maybe

from the cultural perspective, I don't want so many people to see me as the one that is in this program and whose ability in writing is weak. From the couple of classes I went to, I found myself not qualified enough to write the way that the professors want me to write. For a simple reason is that I haven't been taught in a way that I should be writing because back home they do not focus attention to enhancing the writing ability of us as ESL learners. They focus on the speaking, the listening to some extent, the reading, but I believe my weakness is in writing. The moment I noticed that, I said, "OK, I need to work on this weakness, but I want to make it as private as possible. I don't want the others to know about my weakness."

Sami looked away from me while he admitted these things, and I thanked him for his honesty. Clearly, he would never have written these comments on a feedback sheet. I could not have predicted that Sami would have such extensive writing problems. He had an impressive vocabulary and spoke clearly and confidently, but as Matsuda and Cox explain in Chapter 4, quoting Alister Cumming, "the relationship between language proficiency and writing proficiency is not simple; the ability to speak English does not necessarily correspond directly with the quality of texts [ESL students] produce." As we were leaving the library, he continued to tell me that Middle Eastern men generally do not want to be seen as needing help, and he reminded me to make sure to use his pseudonym.

Sami's story illustrates a writing center dilemma common among native and nonnative English-speaking students. They need the help the writing center offers, but they are embarrassed to admit it.

In this case, cultural issues, not the competency of the tutors, were responsible for keeping a certain student population away from the writing center. In Chapter 15, Gerd Bräuer names "not coming to the writing center at all" as one of the common problems among ESL writers. Sami's background made it impossible for him to feel comfortable getting help in a public area such as the writing center. For Sami, the writing center setting compromised his need for privacy when getting help and created the opportunity for shame should he be perceived as weak by others. Uncomfortable with the idea of needing help in the first place, Sami did not want to be seen publicly accepting it. Privacy issues such as these can be addressed by providing meeting spaces that are private or semiprivate, but if resources don't permit, at least directors and tutors will know that sometimes there are reasons, beyond what is written on the feedback sheet, why some students are not happy with their writing center experiences.

Jung-jun

When I heard that Jung-jun used the writing center regularly, I approached her about this project, and she agreed to meet with me on a Friday afternoon. We chatted casually about the weather and her program of study as we climbed the stairs to the library study room I had reserved. I learned that she had spent her summer auditing classes and that she took her studies very seriously.

I began by asking Jung-jun how she had heard about the writing center, and she carried the conversation by recounting experience after experience and offering many strong opinions. She was particularly adamant about the qualities she expected from writing tutors. She insisted that a qualified tutor would be older than she was, have extensive writing and tutoring experience, and be a native speaker of English. While Jung-jun began talking with bold confidence, it wasn't long before she softened and shared more personal experiences and feelings. She admitted to some of the same insecurities Sami had expressed, including the fear of being seen as incapable or unprepared for instruction in a U.S. university, and she described experiences that had left her confused and uneasy. Many topics emerged while talking with Jung-jun, and from these we learn about cultural expectations, insecurities, and communication challenges.

Jung-jun began:

> I came here as a second language learner from Korea. My teacher recommended, "You can go to writing center," but I had no idea what is that. Maybe probably they help in writing, but yeah, wow, there is a writing center! In my country, no writing center.

In Chapter 15, Bräuer points out that many second language students do not know about or understand the writing center. He urges writing center directors to "advertise broadly on campus not only the existence but also the kind of work a writing center is doing." For example, ESL students often don't realize that writing centers generally aim to go beyond surface issues to talking about the content of a paper at any stage during the writing process.

Jung-jun had a lot to say about the age, experience, and nationality of the tutors.

> Sometimes I feel tutor is pretty young. When they are younger than me, I don't trust them. Teacher has to be older; then I can trust them. I would rather not an undergraduate student help me. I would like for graduate student and an American, so I feel that he knows something. I wonder if they had to be tested before becoming a tutor. I doubt them, but maybe they are good students, right? Probably good writers, right? I want to see what is their experience. What, do they publish writing? Is usually a tutor from English department? Sometimes I am not sure they are really qualified. I've never had an international student as my tutor. I saw an international student tutor, but I didn't get help from her because I wonder how well she really writes. I doubt she writes well.

From these statements, we learn that some students have very specific beliefs about who they think is capable of being a good tutor. Though it may seem unfair that Jung-jun was unwilling to give an international student tutor a chance and would have clearly been unhappy if she had to meet with a younger, undergraduate tutor, her beliefs are strong and come from years of cultural influences. Nancy Hayward explains that "some ESL students may distrust younger tutors, feeling they do not have the experience and authority of older, more experienced tutors."[1] Bräuer (Chapter 15) names this "specific understanding of the role of the tutor as . . . teacher" among the common problems ESL writers have with the writing center. He says that these students often try "to manipulate the tutor to fit [their] expectations." Students like Jung-jun usually do not enter each new tutoring situation with an open mind but with long-standing culturally specific expectations. Hayward explains how "the culture from which we come has much to do with our assumptions of the way things 'ought to be.'"[2] While making the tutors' qualifications public might alleviate some students' concerns, we should learn from this that students might not always be judging their tutors solely on their professionalism and ability to communicate and aid in the writing process.

Similar to Sami, Jung-jun expressed her insecurities about being perceived as needing help when she told me about a time when her writing center tutor turned out to be one of her classmates.

> One day, tutor was my classmate, so I don't want to show my paper to him. It was kind of like, awkward. It was weird. This was an older, American student, but still I don't feel comfortable. I don't feel confident because I need help. He doesn't have to come to writing center because he can do his without help. So I feel . . . I shrink. I know he was capable of helping, but I don't want because maybe he look at me and think, "You're here in the [United States], and you still need a writing helper?"

I saw the embarrassment on her face as she told me about this experience. She drew clenched fists tightly into her chest and her voice got low when she said, "I shrink." Students like Jung-jun may feel more comfortable if they have a better understanding of who uses the writing center. Most writing centers are no longer considered primarily places of remediation. In fact, successful students visit the writing center every day because they know the value of having a second reader. They understand how a fresh pair of eyes can spot a misstep in a paper and how talking about ideas with another person can clarify meanings. Graduate students and tutors alike recognize the advantage of exchanging papers and receiving feedback, but not all students, especially international, realize the true mission of the writing center and who actually frequents it. Why ESL students may not understand the U.S. conception of a writing center is discussed further in Chapter 15.

Jung-jun continued our conversation by telling me about a recent experience that left her feeling troubled.

> Two weeks ago, I met a woman tutor, and she said, "Okay, what do you want me to do?" And I said, "Check grammar," but she said, "You know what? Sometimes people abuse tutors." She said that! I was surprised! She said, "People just bring a draft in and then ask a tutor to make the paper into final

version, but it takes a lot of time." She thought that's abuse! I know what she
said, but I try as much as I can.

Jung-jun got very animated as she told me about this encounter. She was especially concerned about the tutor's use of the word "abuse," which she considered inappropriate and harsh. According to Jung-jun, the tutor was accusing
her of attempting to abuse both her and the situation. Jung-jun was caught off
guard and became defensive and confused by the tutor's remarks.

   If this situation happened as Jung-jun recounted it, would she have been
justified in lodging a complaint with the director? In most writing centers,
yes, because the tutor would have been considered at fault for assuming the
worst and taking out her frustrations on a tutee. If the tutor felt that this was
becoming a serious problem, perhaps she should have taken the time to explain to Jung-jun that the writing center's policy is not to edit student papers
but to talk about global concerns, including content, organization, and clarification of meanings. First and second language writers often don't know how
to ask for help with anything besides grammar, so this explanation would
provide Jung-jun with more options. Then, if Jung-jun insisted she needed
help with grammar, the tutor could have agreed to focus on one or two items
during the session. Afterward, the tutor could have taken her concerns to the
director. The director and tutor could then decide how to deal with situations
like this in the future.

   But what if Jung-jun misinterpreted the situation and the tutor's intentions?
Cultural backgrounds could be at the root of this awkward situation, and the tutor
might be very surprised to hear Jung-jun's rendering of the encounter. Hayward
explains that "the United States is a country where directness, *telling it like it is*
or *laying it all out on the table*, is valued. Other cultures find this approach blunt
and offensive. . . . When tutors work with international students . . . they should
understand that one culture's openness is another's rudeness."[3] Perhaps Jung-jun
mistook this tutor's culturally ingrained openness for rudeness.

   This led Jung-jun to comment on tutor personalities and professionalism.

   It is really important, my first impression. If in the beginning I feel comfortable, then I can talk more. If the tutor doesn't smile or is not kind, then it's
   like *oooh*. I'm really affected by the tutor's personality or attitude. There was
   a tutor—he doesn't even focus on my writing. I wasn't really happy with him
   because he's watching people going back and forth, and getting the phone,
   and he say to me, "Okay, I'll be right back in five minute." He kept leaving
   and coming back.

Jung-jun's desire to work with a kind person is not unique to ESL writers.
Personalities and attitudes invariably set the tone for all sessions and affect
productivity. It is certainly not too much to ask of a tutor, or a tutee, to make
an effort to be pleasant and focus on the work at hand. (See Chapter 3 for more
on opening a session.) While Jung-jun describes this situation as one in which

she felt the tutor did not make an effort to devote his complete attention to her needs during the conference, I wonder if the same tutor might be admired by a native speaker for his ability to multitask, a skill valued by employers in the United States. What if the center became busy and he was the only tutor there at that hour? Who would answer the phone or the questions of the other students passing by? In most situations, an effort should always be made to minimize distractions during a writing conference, but should a tutor find herself in this situation, talking about the circumstances could prevent the feelings of neglect that Jung-jun experienced.

Zahara

Zahara showed up at the local coffee shop in a khaki suit with exquisite jewelry and purple lipstick. I noticed right away how striking she was. She told me that she was a professional woman as well as a wife and mother of two. She looked at her watch a couple of times indicating that she was eager to get down to business, so I began our conversation by asking her to tell me a little bit about herself.

> I am originally from Uganda, West Africa. My husband is now a professor here in the [United States], so I'm taking some courses on and off. My mother language is like Ugandan, but when you start school, you have to learn English because all of the textbooks are in English. Uganda is a British colony, so English is official language. Still though, I find it hard because American English is different from British English.

I then asked her how she learned about the writing center and how she felt about its services. Her responses were positive for many writing center practices. First, she praised the campus for having a place where students could get help with their writing. Then, she talked about how helpful it is to discuss her writing with another person and how she benefited from having her paper read aloud by a tutor. Without knowing the technical term, Zahara commented on the facilitative approach the tutors employed and how she grew more competent as a writer by learning to find the answers for herself. Her statements reflected writing center theory being put into practice, and she showed that these practices work for her and are appreciated.

> When I was taking English 101, our professor said, "You can go to writing lab if you feel like you need help when we're writing papers." I don't know about other people, but for me, I want a chance for someone to read my paper before I hand it to the professor. I mean sometime you may write a paper and don't have anyone to help you, so it was good that the writing lab was there and they can help you where your weakness is. So I used it, and it was helpful.

Zahara continued by talking about the way the tutors read her text out loud and how beneficial she found this practice.

I had good experiences with them. Sometimes I'll write the paper and everything sounds good, but when they read it, they'll catch some things like organization and grammar that I didn't catch. When you read your paper, sometimes you don't see the mistakes, and the tutor does. It was very helpful. I took each assignment there two times. I prefer for the tutor to read it out loud, so you can just listen and catch your own mistakes. When you hear someone else reading it, you find the mistake and you correct it. It's like it is their paper.

For Zahara, this provides an opportunity to see her paper through someone else's eyes. In Chapter 4, Matsuda and Cox explain that while it often helps native speakers to read their drafts aloud, "It may be more helpful for the ESL writer to hear the tutor read the paper out loud—to note when the reader stumbles, pauses, fills in missing articles and modifiers, or reads smoothly." In fact, "for many ESL writers, reading their paper out loud may shift their attention to the pronunciation of the English language—an aspect of language proficiency separate from writing in English."

Next, Zahara commented specifically on the facilitative techniques the tutors used to help her learn to correct her own mistakes.

When I went there, they would help with grammar, organization. And sometimes I'm not so good with spelling. They would say, "Here, maybe you misspelled this." You write on your paper because they like for you to be handling it. You sit next to each other and do it together. I would put a note on it with a red pen, so when I go home I can use a dictionary, and that helps me to learn more because I am correcting my own mistakes and seeing what I did wrong. I always remembered what to change because when they were teaching me, I made sure to write everything I needed to correct.

Here Zahara identifies her need for error correction, something writing centers typically shy away from. In Chapter 10, Cynthia Linville says that sometimes, attending to errors is just what the student needs. In fact, recent writing center research suggests "lifting the ban against proofreading." Linville explains that "When a student can learn what her most frequent errors are and learn to recognize and correct her own mistakes, then she will be a proficient self-editor." Luckily for Zahara, she met with tutors who were willing to work with her on error correction in a way that would ultimately help her to help herself.

Zahara also mentions that she "always remembered what to change because . . . [she] made sure to write everything" down as they went along. This is a good strategy for tutees to use during conferences; however, some ESL writers may not have the writing proficiency needed to take notes during conferences. In Chapter 7, Jennifer Staben and Kathryn Dempsey Nordhaus suggest that "one of the simplest things you can do for students is to serve as a scribe." Assisting students in recording the topics covered and suggestions made during the conference will go a long way toward the success of the meeting and the goal of helping writers to become proficient self-editors.

Zahara ended our conversation with even more praise for the center and the role it played in her success as a student.

> They have a comment sheet there where you grade the tutor and write how it went. Everybody got high grades from me. I got an A in my class, and I think that if I didn't go there I wouldn't have gotten an A. I recommend it to other people because I always felt comfortable there. They have different tutors there, but everybody I met, male/female, they all knew what they were doing. I never asked if they were graduate or undergraduate students. It didn't matter because they gave me what I wanted.

Every tutor hopes tutees will leave their conferences feeling as satisfied as Zahara was. While results so consistent are impossible, it is inspiring to hear positive accounts from pleased students. Besides sharing stories like this with tutors during staff meetings, Bräuer encourages centers to "publicize outstanding results of student writing that profited from the interaction with the writing center . . . to demonstrate that *everyone* can improve as a writer" (Chapter 15).

Jane and Yoshi

An ESL professor introduced me to Hui Ping, a Taiwanese student, and Yoshi, a Japanese student, between classes one day. Hui Ping immediately asked me to call her Jane because that was the "American name" her teacher in Taiwan had given her. I asked her if she liked being called Jane. She paused for a moment, and then looked up at me and said, "No, we didn't like the names, but she just gave them to us. But you call me Jane." I could see that she was used to a rigid educational system but that she had definite opinions of her own. I agreed to call her Jane and thought briefly about how accustomed she was to not questioning authority and how that might affect the tutor–tutee relationship.

I followed Jane and Yoshi into an empty classroom and began to talk with them about how they learned about the writing center. Jane told me that one of her professors had told her class about it, and Yoshi said,

> I heard about the writing center from my friend. He was from Japan too and told me that there is a kind of place where native tutors are kindly helping students with their writing assignments. We can go there as much as we want for free, so I go there almost all the time I have writing assignments, plus whenever I need to make error-free English sentences.

Yoshi mentioned visiting the center anytime he "need[s] to make error-free English sentences," which includes filling out school forms and job applications, writing résumés, letters, emails, and anything else requiring clear writing in English. Yoshi likes using the campus writing center to fulfill all of these needs, but whether these services are really the job of the writing center is debatable. Paula Gillespie explored this conundrum, remarking that "this is a question we ask often in writing center work, but international students are by no means the only ones who make us wonder about the boundaries of our tutoring jobs."[4] She discusses many questionable uses of the writing center and concludes by saying that these decisions will have to be made by directors on an individual basis and will "surely depend on how busy your center is, on the demand for writing help."[5]

After discussing these issues with Yoshi, the conversation turned to Jane. She agreed that writing center conferences were helpful but said she often felt frustrated when she tried to go back and actually make the changes in her paper after the conference.

> Sometimes when I went back and tried to correct what the tutor helped me with, I find that I am confused. Did she say to write like this or that? Sometimes, we don't go back to check it again, so it will be mixed up. If we can do things like that, go over it the first time and the second time we read it the correct way, it will be more organized, more helpful. I know that they don't have so much time to go over the second time, but I get confused when we don't.

Unlike Zahara, Jane did not take efficient notes during the conference and ended up forgetting much of what was discussed. Staben and Nordhaus (Chapter 7) remind us that "the spoken word can be extremely powerful, but when placed on a page, writers tend to think of it as permanent." Jane is one student who would benefit from having a tutor serve as scribe. "Harness[ing] the power of paper to work for the student's benefit" is explained in detail in Chapter 7.

The Japanese tendency is to give vocal indications they are listening much more than Americans, so Yoshi stayed very much in the conversation by nodding and agreeing while Jane was talking. When I tried to turn the conversation back to him, he didn't give me any real specifics about his experiences. He simply stated that he didn't have any complaints and that "the tutors are always very hard working and willing to help." I hope that this is true, but I wonder if Yoshi held back a little because of his desire to be polite. Did Yoshi see me as an advocate of the writing center? Did he not want to offend me by showing any dissatisfaction with his experiences? Was I second-guessing too much?

Jane offered to say more about her experiences. She commented on her struggles mastering U.S. forms of language. She talked about trying to translate her ideas from Chinese into English and her fear of losing meaning in translation due to incorrect forms and phrasing.

> I go there because I want to make sure that my writing is correct. When I write a paper, I translate my idea from my language to English. My first language is Chinese, so for example, "Tomorrow I'm going to the supermarket." I think it in Chinese, and I try to translate the idea into English, but you know with translation there will be something happen, like maybe the American people don't say the sentence like this, but actually the grammar is correct, but people don't say things like this. So, I want to make sure.

Even if the ESL writer you are working with has had a great deal of experience writing in English, she may still worry that her form gets in the way of communication. In Chapter 7, Staben and Nordhaus encourage tutors to ask questions and interact with a tutee's text so that the writer will see how a reader views his work. This is what Jane is looking for when she visits the writing center.

Jane's translation conflict between Chinese and English demonstrates the difficulty of translating an idea from one language to another. Her strategy of thinking in Chinese and translating into English is having limited success because there are concepts, even words, that defy one-to-one translations. By showing her writing to a tutor, Jane can make sure that translation has not skewed her intended meanings. (See Chapter 8 for a discussion of helping writers clarify intended meanings.)

Helene

Because of distance, I had to settle for email correspondence with Helene. As with everyone else, I asked her to tell me about her experiences working with tutors at the writing center. Eager to share her stories with me, Helene responded to my inquiry promptly, commenting on the skills she needed to improve and her insecurities about visiting the writing center.

> My English writing skills were rather poor. My thoughts were disorganized and unconnected. My grammar was at times unbearable, as I switched tenses and wrote according to a German grammar scheme. In addition, I used many Genglish (German/English) words that aren't usually used or not in the particular content that I was using them. I went to the writing center with the determination to improve upon those weaknesses.

Helene found herself following the rhetorical strategies of her first language, German, while writing in English, and knew that it was interfering with the meanings she was trying to convey. Like Jane, Helene needed the eyes and ears of tutors to help her learn to control the form of her writing. Hayward explains contrastive rhetoric as "the ways that cultures differ in their expectations about rhetorical patterns or logical organization of a text."[6] (Staben and Nordhaus also cover ESL students' insecurities about form in Chapter 7.)

Similar to Sami and Jung-jun, Helene also expressed insecurities about going to the writing center. At first, she thought it would mark her as a weak student and felt self-conscious about admitting her problems with writing.

> At first, I was a little bit embarrassed to go to the center, since I viewed it as being there for especially weak students, and I definitely wasn't going to count myself among those. However, I started to feel more comfortable accepting their services when I realized that writing is like any other subject and that not being able to express one's views clearly through writing is nothing to be ashamed of. It's not a disease. It takes work to learn to write, and that is what the writing center is there for.

Because of the writing center, both Helene's writing and her self-esteem improved. She learned that problems with writing are simply problems with writing. They are not an indication of intelligence or a determiner of potential.

Sami, Jung-jun, Zahara, Jane, Yoshi, and Helene provided us with first-hand accounts of their writing center experiences. What we learn from them is now up to us. Take these stories and talk about them. Interact with them, learn from them, and build on them. Whether we are faced with the challenge of calming feelings of insecurity, recognizing and understanding cultural divides, or simply editing line by line, our jobs are at once arduous and rewarding. But the incentive to keep working and to keep learning lies in the possibility that each new day will bring one more student closer to understanding and enjoying the process of accomplishing the goal of learning to write in English.

Notes

1. Hayward, 13.
2. Hayward, 3.
3. Hayward, 12.
4. Gillespie, 117.
5. Gillespie, 118.
6. Hayward, 7.

Works Cited

Gillespie, Paula. 2004. "Is This My Job?" In *ESL Writers: A Guide for Writing Center Tutors*, edited by Shanti Bruce and Ben Rafoth, 117–26. Portsmouth, NH: Boynton/Cook.

Hayward, Nancy. 2004. "Insights into Cultural Divides." In *ESL Writers: A Guide for Writing Center Tutors*, edited by Shanti Bruce and Ben Rafoth, 1–15. Portsmouth, NH: Boynton/Cook.

Glossary

appropriate   To take away a writer's own words or expressions by naturalizing them to sound more nativelike.

behaviorism   As applied to language, behaviorism is the theoretical view that language learning occurs through habit formation. Learners mimic the language they hear, and when they receive positive feedback, that language becomes a habit. Critics believe it does not explain how a child can acquire something as complex as a language with so little input and feedback. *Compare* **innatism**.

bilingual   The ability to speak two languages almost equally well.

collocations   Words that tend to be associated with each other. Some words that collocate well with *wedding*, for example, are *white*, *cake*, *ring*, *shotgun*, and *vows*. Collocations are important in **ESL** because they help explain why a learner's language can be grammatically correct and have clear meaning, yet the utterance seems strange. For example, in North America, "I am going to clean my teeth" is grammatically correct and comprehensible, but *teeth* collocates so well with *brush* that it seems awkward. Collocations often interfere in nativelike production as learners substitute the collocations from their own language into English grammar. Korean **ESL** learners, for example, may say, "I am going to go *eye-shopping*" in place of *window-shopping*.

contrastive rhetoric   An area of research based on differences across cultures and used to help **ESL** learners understand English rhetorics by comparing them with the rhetorics of other cultures.

EFL   English as a foreign language; refers to English taught and learned in a country where it is not the primary language, for example, Japan.

ELL   English language learner; a more general term that avoids distinguishing between English as a second or foreign language.

English   A dominant or official language in more than sixty countries, with numerous **varieties**. English is the primary language in the United States, United Kingdom, Ireland, Canada, Australia, and New Zealand, with the United States having the greatest number of native speakers. Many people also learn English as their native tongue in multilingual countries such as India, Liberia, and Jamaica.

error   An incorrect usage that occurs when learners don't know the correct form; errors relate to a failure in competence, having the wrong knowledge or lack of knowledge. *Compare* **mistake**.

ESL   English as a second language; ESL is used when English is a speaker's second, third, or fourth (etc.) language, within a country where English is the primary language.

fluent   The ability to speak or write easily and smoothly.

fossilization   Occurs when an **error** becomes a habit of speech and the learner's language becomes automatic before it is nativelike.

Generation 1.5   Refers to students between first-generation immigrants (foreign-born and foreign-educated) and second-generation immigrants (children of immigrants who are U.S.-born and -educated and whose dominant language is English). These students come to the United States as children or adolescents. They possess some characteristics of their parents' culture and some of U.S. culture.

higher-order concern   Writers are usually encouraged to focus on their ideas and organization (higher-order concerns) before attending to grammar and mechanics (lower-order concerns). The two levels often overlap, however, and must be considered together.

idiom   A figurative word or expression like "a sign of the times"; idioms are often difficult to translate into another language and are usually learned gradually through experience.

immigrant student   A student from another country who has settled in the United States, often with relatives, and usually speaks English as a second language. *Compare* **international student**.

innatism   As applied to language, this is the theoretical view that children are born with knowledge of the structures of language. It is because of this innate knowledge that children can learn a complex language with relatively little input. Innatism can be contrasted with interactionism, a theory positing that meaningful interaction along with innate knowledge combine to make language acquisition possible. *Compare* **behaviorism**.

interlanguage   A stage in which language learners acquire forms of language that are in-between their first language and their target language. For example, they incorrectly apply rules of their native language to their target language, or they have not completely learned the extent or limitations of a rule, and so they misapply it systematically or **overgeneralize**. It may seem correct in the mind of the language learner, and it may be a part of a natural learning process in which rules become more refined as more input is received.

international student   A student from another country studying abroad with the permission of his or her government who plans to return home after graduation. Increasingly used instead of "foreign student." *Compare* **immigrant student**.

L1   An abbreviation for first language, native language, and mother tongue.

L2   An abbreviation for second language, **target language**, and any language learned after the first language is acquired.

language acquisition   The process by which children learn their native language, usually in the home; they can achieve full competence in speaking without any formal instruction.

language learning   The process by which we learn a language through formal instruction. Adults taking English classes are *learning* the language, not *acquiring* it. The distinction sometimes becomes blurred as in the case of children learning a second language at school or an adult picking up a language by living in the country but not taking language classes.

lower-order concern   *See* **higher order concern**.

mistake   An incorrect usage that occurs when language learners know the correct form but, for whatever reason, don't use it; mistakes relate to a failure in performance, for example, a slip of the tongue or typos. *Compare* **error**.

native language   The language a person learns growing up, usually at home. *Compare* **L1**.

NES   Native English speaker; anyone for whom English is their first language, usually learned in the home.

NNES   Nonnative English speaker; anyone for whom English is a second, third, or fourth (etc.) language.

NNS   Nonnative speaker.

NS   Native speaker.

overgeneralization   Application of a language rule beyond its range. For example, students learn that superlative forms of adjectives can be made with *-est*, such as *nicest*, *quickest*, and so on. If they start to produce incorrect superlatives like *goodest*, *comfortablest*, and *expensivest*, they are overgeneralizing.

primary language   The first, native, or dominant language spoken by an individual.

proficiency   The level of skill in using another language as determined by context; for example, a speaker's proficiency may be beginning, low, intermediate, or advanced.

prosody   The rhythmic and intonational aspect of language.

reformulation   A process in language learning that involves the revision by a tutor of an incorrect statement by the learner. For example, changing "green*room* effect" to "green*house* effect."

register   A variety of language used for a particular purpose or in a particular setting. Individuals can switch between various registers, depending on context.

SLA   Second language acquisition; a term for the field of study that has to do with learning a second, third, and fourth (etc.) language.

target language   The language one is trying to learn or use (besides the **L1**).

TEFL   Teaching English as a foreign language. *See* **EFL**.

TESL   Teaching English as a second language. *See* **ESL**.

TESOL   Teaching English to Speakers of Other Languages; refers to both the field of study and the professional organization.

transfer error   An error caused by interference from the learner's first language. Unlike other types of errors, transfer errors are difficult for **L2** learners to detect on their own, and so it is helpful when tutors point them out.

variety   A term used by linguists instead of *dialect*, *accent*, *argot*, *jargon*, *slang*, and so on. For example, in the United States, Southern dialect, Black English Vernacular, and Standard American English are all *varieties* of English.

Contributors

Linda S. Bergmann, associate professor of English at Purdue University and director of the Purdue Writing Lab, has started several WAC programs and directed writing centers at three universities. Her teaching experience includes undergraduate courses in composition, literature, pedagogy, and literacy and graduate seminars in writing program administration. She has published more than fifteen articles and chapters and coedited *Composition and/or Literature: The End(s) of Education* (National Council of Teachers of English 2006). She is currently completing a textbook on undergraduate research writing for Longman.

Kurt Bouman works in the writing center at Madison Area Technical College in Madison, Wisconsin. He notes that nonnative English speakers make up about 20 percent of the writers who visit the center and that these students speak more than 115 different languages, almost seventy of which are different first languages. His current research explores how writing tutors and teachers can use ideas from contrastive rhetoric and genre analysis to help writers better understand the particular nature of writing in English for an American academic audience.

Gerd Bräuer is director of training and projects at the Freiburg Writing Center hosted at the University of Education, Freiburg, Germany. In 2006 to 2008 he was head of the European Writing Centers Association (EWCA). After more than ten years of teaching at U.S. universities and promotion to associate professor at Emory University, in 2001 he founded the Freiburg Writing Center as the first of its kind in European teacher education. His research interests include the development of curricular and institutional structures needed for teaching and learning in the field of international literacies. His publication list of ten books includes *New Visions in Foreign and Second Language Education* (coed.), LARC Press, 2004.

Lee-Ann Kastman Breuch is an associate professor in the Department of Writing Studies at the University of Minnesota where she teaches courses in first-year writing, technical communication, computer and online pedagogy, and usability testing of online interfaces. Her research addresses writing theory and pedagogy in technical disciplines, composition, and online environments.

Shanti Bruce is an assistant professor of English, chair of the Master's in Writing Program, and coordinator of the Undergraduate Writing Program at Nova Southeastern University in Fort Lauderdale, Florida. She is coeditor, with Kevin Dvorak, of *Creative Approaches to Writing Center Work* (Hampton Press).

Robert Cedillo is a doctoral student in Composition and Rhetoric at the University of Nevada, Reno, where he also works as a writing center tutor. He has worked in the writing center at California State University, San Bernardino, and the Centre for

Language and Communication at Chalmers University of Technology in Göteborg, Sweden. His research interests include writing across the curriculum, second language learning, and intersections of English Studies and the writing center.

Linda S. Clemens is a graduate writing consultant, Center for Writing, and doctoral candidate, Rhetoric and Scientific and Technical Communication, in the Department of Writing Studies, University of Minnesota. In the Center for Writing, she is a member of the SWS.online team and consults both online and face-to-face. She studies the relationships between writing pedagogy and interactive technologies and students' perspectives on online tutoring and other online learning opportunities.

Michelle Cox is an assistant professor of English at Bridgewater State College in Massachusetts where she teaches first-year writing for ESL students and a variety of undergraduate and graduate writing and composition theory and pedagogy courses. She directs Writing Across the Curriculums and serves on the ESL Advisory Board. She is currently the chair of the Northeast Writing Centers Association. Her research interests include second language writing, workplace writing, and rhetorical genre theory.

Sharon K. Deckert is an assistant professor in the Composition and TESOL program at Indiana University of Pennsylvania. Her research interests include questions of how individuals, such as second language speakers/writers, construct identities in relation to social institutions.

Chloe de los Reyes is a master's student in English Composition and writing center tutor at California State University, San Bernardino. During the spring of 2007, she was an international exchange tutor, working with Gerd Bräuer at the University of Education, Freiburg, Germany. Her research interests include writing centers, second language writing, and writing and learning in international contexts.

Kevin Dvorak is an assistant professor of English and director of the University Writing Center at St. Thomas University in Miami Gardens, Florida. He is an executive board member of the Southeastern Writing Centers Association and is coeditor, with Shanti Bruce, of *Creative Approaches to Writing Center Work* (Hampton Press).

Magnus Gustafsson directs the Center for Language and Communication at Chalmers University of Technology, Sweden. He works to facilitate integration and progression of technical communication in Swedish and English in the engineering programs and courses at the university. The center's faculty work closely with course and program managers in teams, thus promoting educational development and a better understanding of language and communication in engineering and learning environments. This work in technical communication also involves academic and professional writing and various forms of writing-to-learn interventions to enhance communication and education.

Carol Peterson Haviland is a professor of English, writing center director, and WAC coordinator at California State University, San Bernardino. She teaches undergraduate and graduate courses in writing, composition theory, writing center pedagogy, and literacy studies and is particularly interested in intellectual property issues, writing pedagogies and politics, defining Englishes, and international tutor exchanges. Coeditor of *Who Owns This Text? Plagiarism, Authorship, and Disciplinary Cultures; Teaching/ Writing in the Late Age of Print;* and *Weaving Knowledge Together: Writing Centers and Collaboration*, she has published a number of journal articles and book chapters.

Ilona Leki is a professor of English and director of ESL at the University of Tennessee, author of books and articles on second language writing, and coeditor of the *Journal of Second Language Writing*. Her research interests include academic literacy development among bilingual students and the literacy experiences of English learners.

Cynthia Linville, who conducted her graduate research in a university writing center, teaches both mainstream and ESL composition courses at California State University, Sacramento. Her research interests include intercultural communication and civic involvement, and her poetry has recently appeared in The Sacramento Poetry Center's *Poetry Now*.

Paul Kei Matsuda is an associate professor of English at Arizona State University where he works closely with doctoral students in rhetoric/composition and linguistics, master's students in TESOL and linguistics, and undergraduate students in linguistics. Founding chair of the Symposium on Second Language Writing, Paul has published widely on second language writing in journals and edited collections in both composition studies and applied linguistics. He has edited several books and special journal issues. His website address is http://matsuda.jslw.org/.

Amy Jo Minett is a doctoral candidate in Composition and TESOL at Indiana University of Pennsylvania and an English instructor at Madison Area Technical College where she also codirects a Title VIA International Studies and Foreign Language grant. She worked throughout Eastern Europe for nine years before starting the doctoral program at Indiana University of Pennsylvania. Her dissertation research explores the relationship between English Language Teaching and the building of open societies.

Kathryn Dempsey Nordhaus is a writing and speech instructor at Gateway Technical College in Kenosha, Wisconsin. She has worked in writing centers at DePaul University and at the College of Lake County in Illinois. Her research interests include second language acquisition, second language writing, business communication, and creative nonfiction.

Ben Rafoth is a professor of English and director of the graduate program in composition and TESOL at Indiana University of Pennsylvania. He directed the Writing Center at IUP for twenty years. He is the author of *A Tutor's Guide: Helping Writers One to One*, Second Edition. He was an executive officer for the International Writing Centers Association and is a recipient of the Ron Maxwell Award from the National Conference on Peer Tutoring in Writing.

Jennifer J. Ritter teaches writing and linguistics at Salt Lake Community College where she also tutors in the Student Writing Center. Her interests include teaching and tutoring second language writers, in particular, immigrant and Generation 1.5 writers. Previously, she coordinated the Writing Center at the University of Alaska Anchorage, where on occasion moose would appear right outside the windows.

Trygve Sandvik teaches written and spoken English at Chizhou College in Anhui Province, China. He received his master's degree in English rhetoric at the University of Alaska Anchorage in 2007; his thesis focused on composition students' responses to online tutoring. Still very much tied to his home region in northwest Alaska, Trygve plans to return to his hometown and develop a writing center network to serve students in his and the surrounding Inupiaq villages.

Carol Severino is an associate professor of rhetoric and director of the Writing Center and the Writing Fellows Program at the University of Iowa. She researches and teaches about how culture and language background influence writing and writing pedagogy and serves on the editorial boards of the *Journal of Second Language Writing, College Composition and Communication, Writing Center Journal,* and *Learning Assistance Review.*

Brady Spangenberg is a second-year doctoral student in comparative literature at Purdue University. He has worked in Purdue's Writing Lab for two years and, prior to that, worked to develop and maintain a writing center at the Albert-Ludwigs-Universität in Freiburg, Germany. His research interests include English Renaissance literature, German literature, classical Latin, grammar, and second language acquisition.

Jennifer E. Staben is a professor of English and the faculty coordinator of the Writing Center at the College of Lake County in Illinois. She had her first tutoring experiences as a graduate student at the University of Iowa and has since worked in writing centers in Minnesota, Pennsylvania, and Illinois. Her research interests include writing centers, literacy, and second language writers.

Theresa Jiinling Tseng is an assistant professor of English at Tunghai University in Taiwan, where she teaches undergraduate and graduate courses in writing, theory and practice of teaching writing, and applied linguistics. Prior to teaching EFL college students in Taiwan, she taught both native English-speaking and ESL college students in the United States. Her research interests include second language writing and second language acquisition. She has coauthored three writing textbooks for high school and college EFL writers.

Author Index

Subject Index

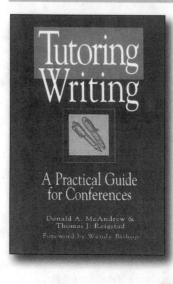